SHE RUNS WITH WOLVES

She Runs with Wolves: Book 1 in the Pogrom War

Cover Design by Melissa Williams Design

Interior Formatting by Melissa Williams Design

www.kimberlythennessy.com

SHE RUNS WITH WOLVES

BOOK 1 IN THE POGROM WAR

KIMBERLY T. HENNESSY

The ancient book of T'ra wrote 'the dead inherit the living.'

(Circa pre-Pogrom War)

— BOOK 1 —

The Sacred Cup

After the Pogrom War, humanity's new position in the food chain pushed them to the brink of extinction. To survive earth's collapse and the AI dominion, pockets of Homo Sapiens fled underground.

The same nano technology used to create their enemy, they used on themselves, and a new race emerged, the Sidhe.

The centuries came and went, and this superhuman breed adapted to life's harsh realities, but some better than others. A select few inherited special abilities and became known as the Grimnìr. Chosen by the Gods, these anointed priests and priestesses led their people back to the desolate surface. After a millennium, however, nothing but relics and a single prophecy had survived a forgotten age.

It foretold a barren woman would birth a child with the ability to open and close the gates of heaven, and lead the Sidhe to salvation, but like most prophecies, what should have been remembered was lost.

Where there's a cub the mother never strays far. She is judge, and her wrath will scorch the earth.

CHAPTER 1

Hunger

Have faith, Eira thought, rocking back and forth. After all these years you can trust Dwr. Eira reminisced the first time they had connected. The memory was still so vivid and soothed her aching mind.

She had staggered inside the roundhouse in the middle of the night. A thread of smoke filtered the air, but the winter draught snatched the elusive blanket and blew it out the door. The prisoners grumbled as they huddled against one another on the floor near the fire pit. Its bright embers cast an orange glow on their angry faces, somehow making the wilderness outside more welcoming.

Minutes later their breathing slowed and filled the quiet room. Eira's moist breath had lingered in the chill air, which she preferred to the inmates' muggy breath, not to mention how much more the heat aggravated her wounds.

There was no reason King Lorcan had beaten her this time, but he didn't need one. No one denied the living embodiment of Khaõs, the creator and destroyer of worlds. Unifier of the North and South Clanns, and everything in between ranging up the Eastern Coast, with her windy Cape to the Western Himarta Valley and beyond her mountains. King Lorcan was the High King of New Ysberg, and heir to the Gods.

He had purged the land of the Grimnìr religion, and spared no one. No one, that is, except her. Eira wasn't like the other prisoners, that much was clear as she watched the guards secure the ropes binding her wrists to the post near the entrance.

As far back as she remembered they had tied her to this stake. King Lorcan always said she was special, but she never understood why he had saved her from those faceless daemons, the treacherous worshipers of old, and though her childhood memories were shapeless, and hard to piece together, she never forgot those wild eyes and bloody teeth trying to kill her. They still paralysed her with fear like a vile aftertaste coating the inside her mouth. "The dead inherit the living. The dead inherit the living," they said over and over.

Eira owed King Lorcan, but all she needed to know, he had said, was that he was her saviour, and a day would come when Eira would repay her debt to him. Every full moon, from the time she was captured, he had cut her flesh and mixed their blood. He prayed to the other Gods, and drank it during the ritual, but she didn't understand why.

Why her? It made Eira wonder whether she had abandoned the Gods after accepting her fate, or if the Gods had abandoned her because she'd surrendered to this monster in the first place.

After the guards had left, Eira crouched to her knees on the modest fur pelt she used as a bed. She wished to curl into a ball and forget the night all together, but the lacerations across her back had spiked with pain. She eased onto her bum, draped her head across her knees, and scanned for Dwr's presence, but the cramped room was too dim to see beyond the fire's dull radius.

Eyes closed, Eira quieted her breath when a hand caressed her neck. The sensation was nice. Tilly, her caretaker, had never been so gentle, and Eira let her shoulders droop when the side door to the servant quarters grated against the dirt floor.

Another servant? Strange. Tilly let no one interfere between them, not that any prisoner volunteered to help, but the caretaker preferred it that way. Habit was the enemy of surprise, she'd say, and Eira agreed. She could have done without tonight's surprise. After tasting her blood, the King had flown into a rage.

"What are you doing?" Tilly had snapped.

Eira wasn't sure what to think. If Tilly was over by the door, then someone else was petting her hair. Startled straight, pain exploded across Eira's back.

"Poor girl." Tilly had flung to the ground, and wrung out the cloth from her water basin, and wiped Eira's brow. "There, there, I'm here."

The throbbing in Eira's back pulsed, making the room spin.

"I'm sorry," Dwr choked.

Eira froze. It's him?

"You didn't look well, and I . . ."

Eira had craned her neck to meet his gaze. It wasn't their first soulful encounter, but this proximity differed from his furtive glances across a dark room. Dwr knew the rules – no one, except Tilly, spoke to Eira.

"Thank you." Tilly was curt. "I'm here now."

Dwr had gotten up to leave, but without thinking Eira touched his hand. "Do you want me to stay?" he asked.

The answer had caught in Eira's throat. She turned to Tilly for approval, but the woman's lips pinched into a hard line, and fear struck Eira's heart. It flip-flopped inside her chest, and she muttered a frantic 'yes' before he left, or Tilly objected.

The corners of his mouth peaked into a crooked grin. "Are you sure?"

Eira had looked away, afraid to speak.

"I'll stay, Mn'keur."

Too shy to ask what he'd just called her, in some ancient dialect, Eira had lifted her bloody tunic from her shoulders. Tilly hastened to cover her nakedness, and for once Eira was grateful to the tired woman.

Dwr eased Eira on her side, and the gentle sting of water prickled her lesions, but it was the intimacy that had soothed her that night. An intimacy that has grown these past years, she thought, her mind rushing into the present. You've shared so many wonderful nights since then.

"Tell him," she hissed under her breath. "Trust him." Fear swelled in Eira's chest. The plan's too dangerous, we'll get caught, and the King will kill him. "Stop," she muttered, grabbing her hair.

Eira was going mad. Talking to herself, nit-picking every single detail drained her mentally, but she couldn't help it. Her mind ran non-stop day and night since her decision to escape three moons ago. Time was pressing.

Tonight, when King Lorcan summoned her, she'd steal the last piece she needed, a blade, and then she'd tell Dwr, but the more she thought about it, the faster she rocked. Eira glanced the door. The guards were coming . . . I can't do it. It's too soon . . .

The knots in her stomach wrung their nightly churn. Forget the outside, she needed protection from the evils within the village, but then Eira remembered the fur cape and leather hides stashed under the woodpile.

Forgotten garbs left over in the King's hut by his mistresses. Eira had stolen the garments one piece at a time beneath her linen shirt. If she could do that, despite watchful eyes, then tonight's plan was no different, but she'd have to be careful. The proof was the scars on her wrists from being tied to a post for so long, or her healed cuts on her hands, arms, and thighs. She winced at the memory of how they were inflicted, and the mental image riled Eira.

They'll be here soon . . . Her belly twisted tighter, and Eira forced the ropes up her arms and she rubbed her lips against her brown, bumpy flesh rocking back and forth. He's calling for me . . . She cramped into a tight ball, and a large woolly rat poked its head from behind the post.

"You shouldn't be here," she said to her rodent friend. "They'll catch and eat you."

The rat sniffed her filthy toes when something grabbed Eira's arm. They're here, but she changed her mind. The King wouldn't take her. She growled and bore her teeth like those animals that wandered into the village before an arrow split open their head.

"Quick, grab it," Eira heard someone say.

The squeals and squeaks echoed, and Eira lashed out to the King's guards, clawing the air in front of her, hoping to scratch their eyes out.

"Shh, Shh, it's okay," the voice said, "it's me."

"Tilly?" Eira croaked. It took a moment for her to gain her bearings. The whole room came into sharp focus with the stout woman staring down her nose. Tilly held the poor rat fighting to free itself inside a giant handcrafted net, which she handed to her helper, Kit.

They'd captured it, but they'd get her too, she wanted to say to the poor creature.

The glum roundhouse reeked of dirt and urine. Its pointed ceiling crushed Eira, and she cowered at the sight of the dead animals spread across the walls. Ancient wolves with their jowls open, waiting to sink their teeth into her.

Sinister shadows crept towards the firelight and revealed a dozen downtrodden faces. The prisoners stared at her wide-eyed, and her mouth turned dry.

Eira read disgust in their glare, or was it pity? A sour taste crept up her throat and spilled into her mouth. Whatever it was, she looked away. She didn't belong with these prisoners. They didn't want her. Nobody did. Except for him, the King . . . No, no, not the High King.

Eira swatted the air to rid the unwanted thought. Dwr wanted her, didn't he? His sombre gaze, and skin as black as night blended with the shadows. She couldn't see him, but they were in this together, and he'd help her. Where was he?

"Eira? Look at me. It's Tilly." The woman had dark circles puffing the amber skin under her eyes. Tilly pointed to Eira's bowl. "Why haven't you touched your food?"

Eira ignored her caretaker and scoured the darkness beyond the fire. "Where is he?"

"You need to eat." Tilly's harsh tone pulled Eira's attention from the room. "No food, you die. Everything dies." The caretaker's fixed gaze penetrated deep into Eira's secret garden. It was the one part of her still unsoiled by the King's shackles. She imagined little trees tucked away behind her heart guarding her most private thoughts, her darkest secrets.

Did Tilly know? It took Eira back, and her pulse quickened. Maybe she'd rattled her secret out loud? "Stupid. So stupid," she said, hitting her face.

"Stop that" —Tilly grabbed Eira's arms— "Here, have another bite." Eira wasn't hungry, but she always did as she was told out of fear and swallowed the spoonful of gristly meat and fat. The ball of food grated her throat.

What if Tilly told the High King before she could escape? What if he already knew? "No, no, no, this isn't happening." Eira shook the cobwebs that snared her brain and took a deep breath. "I can do this. It won't be like those other times. It won't," she whispered.

What was the worst that might happen? Eira pictured the pit of frozen bodies, their limbs twisted at odd angles, and a chill rippled her creamy skin into gooseflesh. Her spindly fingers scratched the gnats from the puff of black hair that sat on her scalp.

"Eira!" Tilly forced her back into the unwelcome space. "One more bite."

She pushed the servant woman's arm aside. Fool! She wasn't hungry.

Tilly's jaw dropped "Eira!"

Eira flinched with panic, but Dwr popped out from behind the caretaker. "Let me do it," he said.

The prisoners gasped with surprise, and Eira blinked with disbelief. "You . . ."

Except for a few wrinkles around the eyes, Dwr's skin was taut and young. Grey strands peppered near his temple, and on his chin stubble, which showed his true age. "Are you really here?" —Eira touched him— "Where do you go? You disappear."

Dwr didn't answer and pulled the wooden bowl from Tilly's hands, but the caretaker tugged it from his commanding grip. "Let me handle this," she said.

"You're responsible for her," Dwr said, kneeling in front of Eira. "She's trembling."

"Mind your mouth," Tilly snapped, "I've been caring for her far longer than you've taken an interest."

Eira ignored their quarrel and leaned into his warm hand cupping her cheek.

"That's my girl. I'm never far. You'll get through tonight. You always do," he said, and inched closer.

Get through it? "What do you mean?" Eira slapped Dwr's hand away and jumped to her feet, ready to pounce.

"Mn'keur, it's me," Dwr said, "I'll loosen your restraints before the guards get here."

Eira hissed. "Don't touch me." Loosen her restraints? She wanted his help to escape.

"Leave her alone" —Tilly pushed Dwr out of the way— "you're upsetting her."

"Yes, you upset me." Eira shouted, and her head swarmed with sensory overload. The wolves, the heat, the food, the eyes, they weighed her down. "Where do you go? Where do you hide?" she said, rocking back and forth. The prisoners transformed into the daemons of her past. Their hideous, noseless faces rushed towards her, and she fell back.

"Eira?" One of them tried to touch her.

"Go away," she said, and shrunk behind the pole restraining her.

"What's wrong with her? She's getting worse." The thing spoke.

Eira covered her ears to block their guttural cries, and repeated the words that had haunted her all these years. "The dead inherit the living. The dead inherit the living."

"That's enough!" The daemon barked and grabbed her wrist. "It's me, Dwr."

Startled, Eira focused on the scary face, and it morphed into Dwr. She sniffed his fingers, not unlike the twitchy rat that had sniffed her toes. She was hunting for something foul when she saw a ropy scar jutting out from under Dwr's sleeve shirt, and she knew from watching him undress every night they covered his body. Dark lashings spread across his back and torso, reminding her of venomous Arctic snakes. Scars that mirrored her own inside and out.

"I'm here to help, Mn'keur," Dwr said, releasing his grip.

"Mn'keur," she mumbled. The pet name rolled off her tongue. It meant 'my heart' in the old-world dialect no longer used today. Only a few words still lingered in some clanns, mostly spoken by the elders. It made her feel special.

Eira settled back into a tight ball. "I search for you, Dwr, but you're never there when I need you. You hide where the daemons lurk," she said to him.

The prisoners whispered to each other, unable to hide their shock. They were usually more discreet, but she didn't care. It was time to escape, and she wanted him by her side. Dwr had said the world threw them together because they were meant to help one another.

Dwr's tone hushed. "I'm sorry."

Eira caught the spectre that haunted his thoughts, and her heart ached. No, she was sorry. She shifted her weight forward and spoke so nobody could hear, not even Tilly. "I've something to tell you. It's a secret."

Tilly skirted between them. "That's enough."

"Oh, no!" The caretaker was too close, and Eira withdrew from Dwr.

"Stay with me Eira." Dwr lifted his hand to prevent Tilly from coming any closer.

Eira focused on him. He was her pillar.

"That's my girl. Brave to the bone, Mn'keur." Dwr extended his arm, palm open, and waited for Eira to reach out.

Their fingertips grazed, and her hand sprung to life just as the door swung open. An unforgiving icy wind seized Eira's body. The guards were here, and with the blink of an eye Eira's anchor disappeared in a wisp of smoke. Dwr retreated with the rest of the ogling prisoners while Tilly scampered through the side door into the servant quarters.

Eira's insides dropped with a thud like a rock hitting ice. She was alone with her secret, and she'd always be. Why would that ever change?

Her body went limp, her muscles relaxed, and the knots in her stomach vanished. The two guards jerked her flaccid arms and freed her from the post. They kept her hands and feet tied with the nylon rope to prevent her from running off or fighting back. They'd learned their lesson over the years, but she would not give them trouble. Tonight, Eira had one mission. Find a weapon.

The guards pulled Eira's restraints, and her bare feet dragged into the ground. The stuffy roundhouse was not big enough to contain her anymore, and she needed the open air. As if she had shed a thousand pounds of fat in seconds.

Eira glared at every single prisoner. It was their turn to look away, shifting from leg to leg trying to avoid her reproachful stare, or was it their guilt? At that moment she hated the lot of them with their sad little pup-faces and chin-up smiles. Eira wanted to stab them in the eyes. She didn't want their pity, she needed their help. But it never came.

Dwr slipped behind everyone, but Eira sought his gaze before he skulked into the darkness. Her chest tightened. Never again would she rely on him, or anyone.

CHAPTER 2

Hollow

The guards shoved Eira outside, her mind and body disconnected. A distance grew between her and the people around her as if she wasn't part of the world anymore. She didn't care about them, and they didn't care about her.

Eira shuffled up the icy path on tiptoe, varying the time spent on each foot, but the ground singed the soles of her feet as if she walked on fire.

She busied her mind with the layout of the village. The endless walk through the main artery abutted a series of longhouses, roundhouses, and pit houses scattered at odd angles to their left and right to keep the north winds at bay. The old battered ramparts did nothing to squelch the glacial northern winds and were sore reminders of a once-great village. A century-old thriving market, Tilly had said, overrun by a festering sickness.

The caretaker had probably meant overrun by religious heretics. King Lorcan was keen to remind his people that only he, the true heir to the Gods, the voice of Khaõs, had the power to create a new religion free from the tyrannical Grimnìr priests and their Sidhe daemons. To deny him was to deny the Gods.

A rare glimpse of the moon struck Eira's core. Something about the round disc made her weary, and yet the allure was hard to resist.

It stood out like a shining jewel in the Goddess Ny's black hair. Fear and awe seized Eira as the soft glow cast a pale light on her sullied skin, and the surrounding snow. Suddenly, she saw her scars as a testament to her strength and survival.

To her right, the edges of the tattered meat caches shone bright as they swayed up on top of the totem poles, each bearing a series of carved emblems dedicated to Khaõs the God. It comforted Eira to watch the wood yield to the whims of Tempest, the Goddess of wind.

The empty shells whistled their lament instead of pulling apart, holding together through sheer stubbornness.

In the distance, through the derelict ramparts, she caught sight of wolves running in the forest, and she envied them. Their lean, muscular frames ploughed through the snow, and filled her with vigour.

Wolves were rare beasts in these parts. Their presence was a sign. Eira wouldn't be defeated, but they vanished as the moon disappeared behind the permanent clouds stretching across the sky. The cold had touched her brain, and her eyes were playing tricks.

She swung her attention west towards the lofty watchtower. The lookout post atop the lolling hill looked quiet. She squinted, but couldn't tell if there was a guard keeping watch.

They passed an ancient earthwork dug deep into the snow, an old Grimnìr shrine with strange markings she couldn't read engraved in the stone. The King had disposed of such things after the purge, and now it stored wood. Near it, stood two large rectangular vessels with deep hollow bellies. Usually, fossils such as these were rusted through and through but these prize possessions had been recovered from the ice in good condition and the King converted them into meat smokers. They offered the villagers a luxury many surrounding clanns could not afford.

They reached the crest of the hill, and the path opened to a huge bonfire in the middle of a square. Smoke wafted around her, and she clenched her jaw, breathing through the mouth. Large open flames had always set her teeth on edge, but she focused on King Lorcan's hut gleaming behind the blaze.

His warriors muddled around, egging each other into battle, but their resolve waned as soon as they lay eyes on Eira. "Well, well, our village cluck comes to rut," one warrior grunted, and pretended to dry hump her. The man's buddies laughed and made rude slurping noises, trying to outdo one another, but the more Eira tried to avoid them the more they teased. Fresh meat was hard to ignore.

Another man came from behind to grind against her, but Eira elbowed the warrior. "Aw, Pretty little thing," he said mocking her. "You know you want to suck it." He grabbed his crotch, and the warriors laughed.

'Pretty little thing.' That was King Lorcan's pet name for her, and to hear them say it sickened her. She struggled to keep her wits. Soon she'd vanish like those wolves in one of those caves Tilly talked about, nestled in the mountains. Lost in thought, the guards pulled her to the right, towards the Hall.

Whatever plan she'd been percolating came to a shuddering halt. Eira knew where in the hut the High King stashed his weapons—a secret hatch near his bed. But the Hall was a different story. This was the house of the damned.

Eira should have sensed the storm brewing. The King had been on a binge these past weeks. He was restless, and his flaring temper hovered in the air like a bad smell. A flicker of fear stirred in her, and Eira wished to cling to the sensation, but it was like the moon's pale reflection with nothing to grab.

A gust of biting wind pushed her back, and the powdery snow pulverised her skin until the gale blew straight through Eira. She felt empty. She'd become those battered meat shacks, a hollow vessel humming a flat tune.

Eira's instinct was to shield herself with her arms, but she let the dry glacial air needle her flesh because the pain reassured her. There was a battle raging inside Eira fighting between protected and unprotected, alive and frozen, whole and shattered.

Snow snaked across the ice and disappeared with a swirl in front of the cavernous hall's bloodstained door. The red pigment was a reminder of the King's absolute dominion over anyone who entered, but crossing the bloody threshold meant something different tonight.

To survive, Eira had to let go of her precious garden that kept the monsters at bay and invite them to play.

CHAPTER 3

Cracked

The warmth of the Hall wrapped around Eira's body, but the rank odour of sex and firewater filled her nostrils, and made her gag. A collective hush descended. Force of habit whenever she showed her face anywhere.

At the far end of the room, the King sat on his throne of skulls. Hunched over massive shoulders, perched atop his thick neck, the old warrior's head bobbed in every direction. He was drunk and reminded Eira of a drawing Dwr had shown her of a west-valley muskox, a migratory animal he'd hunted long ago. Now the resemblance was the only thing she saw.

King Lorcan was a far cry from the human war machine of his youth, but the twirl of madness hadn't disappeared. The lunacy shimmered in the yellow of his sunken eyes.

His bloodlust had won him many battles, but his viciousness had turned to paranoia, and Eira felt his gnarled fingers, like tree roots, suffocating everything that threatened his power.

Even in his advanced years, the heir to the Gods was larger and stronger than most warriors. His descent was through and through, down to his short white hair cut at odd angles, revealing an old battle wound, a thick gash where the hair stopped growing. Fading tattoos ran the length of his body across his wilting skin, and for the first time Eira noticed how old and weary he looked.

Next to him was his right-hand man, Éarlrick the Dependable. Faithful to his post, the sly tongue leaned in and muttered in the King's ear. A sneer stretched across Éarlrick's face. There was a quality to the shape and colour of his crystal eyes that spellbound Eira, but it straddled something evil.

On any other night, Eira might have recoiled upon seeing his toothy grin, but fearlessness unfurled as she held his gaze. A stillness comparable to a soothing exhale passed between them.

For years Eira suffered in silence as she let these men control her through fear, but with nothing left to lose and everything to gain, her determination to break free grew. She caught her dark reflection in the myriad of black flat screens across the walls. The King enjoyed having these mysterious devices from the past mirroring the room, but mostly he enjoyed scavenging the precious metals each thin rectangle contained.

A shift took place when Eira saw her likeness. The woman staring back looked like someone else like it wasn't really her anymore.

Eira pictured the animal hides covering the walls of the prison quarters, and the wild wolves running through the forest. They awakened her courage, and she drew strength from them.

She stole a glance across the room and counted two dozen warriors flanked on either side of the fire. A mish-mash of men and women sprawled naked on the floor, drunk, and fornicating. The High King's great military fleet at its finest. The most savage beasts nature offered.

More ice treasures littered the floor and covered the walls, the King's stolen wealth, and a testament to the man's immorality and value. Pristine plastic jugs salvaged from the sacred landfills passed from hand to hand. The containers overflowed with water, firewater, and food. Wild winterberries, loads of various smoked meats and fish, and sweet tree sap turned to a rich and dark amber colour.

Ancient decorative rifles, sculptures made out of bizarre metal clubs hung on the wall, and peculiar black boxes with extendable arms that left Eira troubled every time she saw them. Precious spearheads, metal arcs, swords, and battle-axes adorned the walls, and from the ceiling, thin rectangles of different sizes and colour, faded green discs, plugs, and coils hung as ornaments that served no purpose other than technology long forgotten by people that didn't exist anymore, or so the stories went.

Eira had heard of this bygone society defeated during the Pogrom war. Supposedly the Grimnìr priests had crushed them with their powers, and they were never seen again, but those tales didn't impress her in the least. What they left was a barren planet, and remnants of ruinous cities. Her only concern was a weapon. That spearhead mounted on the wall had her name on it, but she'd never get close enough. Her best bet was to find a discreet knife.

The energy in the room shifted, and Eira picked apart the High King's subtle moves. The man's eyes drooped, and he smacked his lips. He was thirsty, but not for drink. It was in the way he licked his lips that she knew the King was ready for her, and he waved her over with a flick of his finger.

Éarlrick amplified the gesture, and the guards released her.

Eira kept her head low and waddled past the snorts and snickers as she made her way to the High King. Some had stopped their carnal pleasure mid-thrust, but their scrutiny glazed with a cruel indifference as she passed them. Her presence was a mere vapour of their drunken stupor. She mattered to no one.

There was enough rope between her feet for Eira to lift one foot at a time and climb the elevated platform. "My Pretty leettle thing," the High King slurred, reaching out his hand. Eira brushed past Éarlrick to get to the King. "Sit on me, wife, I've missed you." His bloodshot eyes swivelled to the back of his head as his fingers vacillated in the air for her to hasten.

Eira did not reach out, but once the King locked her wrists, he lurched her onto his lap, his free hand landing on her breast.

The King moaned, and his hand prowled its way to her belly and groped her crotch. "You've gotten plump." He pulled her up in the same way a child might toss a rag doll. "What has that woman been feeding you? I like it." He was rough and hurt Eira more than normal. "You'll grovel for me tonight. Won't you?"

King Lorcan wasn't asking. Eira had to play with him, make the heir to the Gods believe he was desirable, but his little game was as treacherous as walking a cliff's edge. His mood was impulsive.

His right hand cupped her head, and he cradled it towards his white pasty face. The muskox pressed his lips against hers and forced his tongue inside Eira's mouth. The folds in his oily skin stunk with firewater and clung to her like animal grease. She couldn't bear one more night of his rotting teeth and bit his tongue.

A drop of blood pooled on his bottom lip, and his tattoos twitched along his neck. "V . . . v–ile woman." The King's fingers tightened around Eira's skull. His stammer was a sign of her imminent danger. He flung Eira to the ground and wrapped his hands around her neck. "Ungrateful little wench!"

She choked for breath and clawed at his fingers. Unfettered violence rolled off the King's skin.

"Haven't I been good? I of . . . offered my home, my love. I raised you above all others with our matrimony, and yet you continue to deny me? Why?" For the first time she saw him as he truly was, a petulant child sulking for his prize.

Eira mustered all her strength and spat in his face. If death was her fate, then the bastard would know how she felt. Her hatred for him fuelled her rage, and her desire for freedom.

The King tightened his grip. "You're a filthy trull. Nothing but a plain, worthless Sidhe I should've burned with all the others."

King Lorcan loosened his grip, and Eira sprawled to the ground, gasping, and clutching her throat.

"You're not the chosen one. You're nofing," he slurred. The King rose from his chair of skulls and wobbled. He almost pitched forward, but Éarlrick caught him before the plunge. The old warrior fussed and grabbed Eira by the hair, pulling her down the platform.

She fell flat on her belly, and a swoosh of warmth coalesced inside her stomach. The sensation felt like a spider web holding her innards together. She scrambled to pick herself back up with her elbows, but the Shite dragged her across the room. A bark and growl twitched in Eira's mind. She pictured those wolves, and they titillated her brain. No other thought other than ripping this Shite to pieces existed.

No one breathed or moved except for their sleight of hands scouring the floor. The warriors were grabbing their weapons ready for battle, while the women rushed to get dressed following the madman and his prisoner wife. There would be a different ritual tonight.

Outside, Eira's skin grated against the cold snow as people lumped around her, screaming: "Burn the prisoner-wife, burn the prisoner-wife."

Eira's senses heightened, and the village decompressed with a sigh as she broke the flow of elements faster than she could understand what was happening.

The people's wind-scarred faces were grittier, their gravelly voices irritated her ears, and the heat from the bonfire burned brighter than ever before, a bitter contrast against the chafing cold.

She anticipated each action and reaction, but a mounting pressure inside her brain reached its tipping point.

King Lorcan lifted Eira to her feet. Her insides howled, though no sound came out of her mouth.

His blank gaze mirrored the beast coming alive inside Eira, empowering her, and she shuddered. Stuck between a tug and pull of fear and awe, she lashed out, growling like an animal.

It was like watching from the outside, her mind possessed by something feral. Then a wave of nausea hit and brought Eira back into her skin. Her knees wobbled, and within a split second the King, the people, the snow, the village, vanished.

All of a sudden, it was daytime, and buildings as high as the eye could see surrounded her. This was not her home. This was a time and place she didn't recognize.

Large machines on wheels, she couldn't explain, blocked the road as people ran screaming down the street. Bewildered, Eira turned to watch what they were running from, and saw a swarm of black birds flock towards her, flying away from a wall of water about to swallow her up. Every instinct told her to run, but the rope between her feet stopped her, and she fell. Unable to escape, Eira cowered into a ball covering her head with her arms, waiting to die.

"I'll kill you," the High King screamed.

Eira looked up at the King, and she was back inside the village. What had happened?

"I'll melt the skin from your bones and turn you to ash like your heretic mother."

His words struck a chord in Eira's heart. Her mother? She had no memory of the past, nothing except Sidhe daemons.

"What do you want from me?" Eira pleaded through gritted teeth. "What am I to you?

The King crouched down and pinched her cheeks between his fingers and scrutinised Eira's face. His disappointment was plain to see. "You're nofing! Throw her in the fire," he bellowed.

"Stop!" someone shouted at the back of the crowd.

It was Tilly, making her way to them. A young warrior pushed the gatherers aside to let the caretaker through. Eira had noticed the young man. He was one of the guards, and his eyes bore holes deep inside her like he knew her secrets.

"What do you want, Woman?" the defiant King asked.

"You can't kill her, my Lord," she said out of breath. "Eira's with child."

"What?" The King's wolfish grin turned sullen. He staggered back as if Tilly had struck him with his fist. His mouth opened and closed a few times before he spoke. "That's not possible . . . Eira? Is th . . . th–is true?" His manic tone turned soft.

The ground beneath Eira's feet gave way as everyone stretched out into the distance.

From the darkness Eira woke up cradled in the madman's arms. "Eira?" King Lorcan whispered. "My p . . . p–oor thing."

Distress spread through Eira's body, and her insides shook. Tilly had revealed her secret and ruined any chance of escape. She would've preferred death at the stake than this sick attention.

Standing behind the King, Tilly spoke. "I'll take her with me and tend to her in my quarters."

"No," the King shouted. "Éarlrick, take Eira to my—"

"She needs rest, my Lord," Tilly insisted.

"Yes, yes she will get her rest, and a warm bed."

The corners of Tilly's mouth flit downwards in dismay, but she nodded. "Allow me to check her vitals, then?"

Eira wanted nothing to do with the woman who betrayed her, but Tilly took the King's place and checked her forehead with her palm. "She's burning up."

"Will she be all right?" The High King asked.

"Let me take her, so I can make sure—"

"No," the King shouted. "From this moment until she gives birth, Eira is under guard in my quarters. I'll fetch you when you're needed."

Tilly's lips pinched into a hard line. She placed her ear against Eira's chest. "Your heart rate is high. You need to relax, Eira, everything will be fine, I promise." The caretaker wrapped Eira in her arms.

What was she doing? Eira tried to push her away, but Tilly gripped tighter and whispered in Eira's ear. "Get ready, they're coming for you. Soon you'll be safe."

What? Who was coming? Eira wanted to know more, but the woman broke free. "I'll be in the servant quarters," she said to the King.

"No, go to the Hall, this isn't over, Caretaker," he replied. "As for you Éarlrick, take Eira back to my hut and make sure she's comfortable. Do not leave her side until my arrival. There will be no ritual tonight."

The sly tongue helped Eira to her feet. The crowd dispersed as the two circled the bonfire towards the High King's hut, but away from prying eyes Éarlrick's gentle manners changed, and he yanked on her restraints. "Don't think this makes you special. It doesn't." He clacked his teeth together as though he wanted to take a bite out of her, and Eira jerked away. His eyes lit up, and he laughed. "I'll make damn sure you're ripe for the Mad King."

Too much was happening too fast, and Eira needed to think, but the next thing she knew Éarlrick had pulled her inside the hut and slammed the door. "All's I want is a little taste." Bile soured the inside of her cheeks, and Eira looked down. There, resting on his hip belt, was his hunting knife.

"There's my obedient girl," he said, unfastening the rope around both her wrists.

Time had sped up or stopped, Eira couldn't tell, but a gradual awareness parted the fog in her head. That was a mistake, she thought. One wrist must always stay secured to the rope tied to her feet.

A green-eyed wolf flickered to life near Eira, and an inexplicable trust blossomed between them. Éarlrick pulled the tunic over her head, and a predatory instinct to protect her baby filled Eira.

She slipped her arms out of the sleeves, and in those few precious seconds, trapped within the confines of her dress, Eira visualised the weapon hanging off Éarlrick's hip.

A rush of blood banged against Eira's skull to the point her teeth pulsed with pain. Growls and barks sloshed inside her ears, and sweat poured from her nape down her back.

As before, a tug and pull between awe and fear owned Eira. She saw the flow of motion she needed to execute, and as the tunic came off she closed her eyes, glided her hand through the side-slit of her dress, and snatched the weapon. Éarlrick hadn't finished bundling up the dress in his hands when she'd sliced his gut.

Blood spurt everywhere, and Eira quivered with relief as her green-eyed beast retreated into the darkness, but something felt wrong. A sharp pain pierced the back of her eyes. She blinked once or twice, and the room disappeared.

It was nighttime, and Eira stood outside in the middle of a hellish village, face to face with an old man pleading for mercy. His chin trembled with distress, jolting Eira to help him, but out of nowhere a sword swept through the air and slashed the man's head clean off his shoulders like a hot knife through snow.

A Sidhe daemon with leathery skin and deep angry creases around his eyebrows and mouth wielded the long metal blade. His beady black eyes swam inside deep eye sockets. The noseless trickster's lips stretched into a blood-smeared snarl. It cackled, and fear gripped the pit of Eira's stomach.

The daemons were coming to get her. Mama had warned her to hide, but where? Dozens of faceless creatures stormed the village beheading people.

The pit house! They'd never find her in there, but the headless man crashed in to her and they toppled back. Eira slammed her head against something hard, and the whole village spun out of control. Infernal flames spit wildly as men, women, and children screamed for their lives.

Trapped under the corpse's weight, Eira's brain jerked back to the present inside the High King's roundhouse. Éarlrick's carcass pinned her against the door in a puddle of his warm blood. Panicked, Eira kicked and squirmed from underneath the lifeless body.

What had she done? She had to hide, no, defend herself. Where was the knife she'd used? Whatever feelings she'd felt before, they were gone, and Eira was back to her old self again.

On her hands and knees, she pawed the black goop for the weapon when the door rattled. She stopped moving and watched with bated breath, but visions of daemons skewered her brain.

"Éarlrick?" The High King said his voice strained. The door plied with added pressure, but Éarlrick's corpse blocked it. Eira's heart hammered against her ribcage.

"Open the door, I said." Seconds passed, and a loud thud broke against the wood panels, curving the door.

Eira shrunk with fear, her brain twitching with every blow. She got up and backed away, but the rope tying her ankles made her trip and fall.

"W . . . w–hat's going on in there?" the High King yelled as he beat the door. "I'll claw my way in and kill you both."

"Run . . ." she hissed. Eira threw herself on the floor, scraping the congealed blood until the sting of a metal blade cut her finger. The pain helped her focus, and she started to cut through the nylon fibres restraining her.

Halfway through her task something flew at the door, and the house shook under the assault.

An axe splintered the wood, and the door jarred as the King fought to wriggle the sharp cleaver out from its tight squeeze.

"Faster," she cried, and willed herself to slice through the rope with one hard flick. Free at last, Eira pried her bloody dress from Éarlrick's stiff grip while King Lorcan pummelled the door like a rabid animal. With few seconds to spare, Eira unlocked the hatch to the weapons stash, curled into a ball, and hid.

"E . . . E–ira?" The King's mad pitch sent shivers up her spine as she heard him nudge Éarlrick's corpse with the door to get inside the house. "Eira!" he shouted again. Her absence sparked his anger, and she heard him toss everything in the room. Blood dripped from the latch down her cheek and neck.

"Guards!" he bellowed with all his might.

When, at last, it turned quiet, Eira cautiously opened the latch. Confident the room was empty, she bolted out the hole and grabbed the fur covering the bed before disappearing through the back.

CHAPTER 4

Broken Glass

Eira gripped her weapon and wrapped herself with the heavy hide she'd taken from the bed. It wasn't ideal, but she couldn't risk going back for her stashed furs. She'd have to lie low, and the forest was the best place to hide till things settled down, or at least until her head stopped pounding as if a herd of drift bulls had trampled it.

However, the collapsed fence around the village was still too high to climb, and her only escape route was the empty watchtower, or so she hoped.

"She's gone! G . . . g–et her," the High King barked. His voice carried in the wind, and fear stoked Eira's heart. She glanced past the hut and stared straight into the bonfire. Warriors scurried past in disarray.

"You can do this," Eira thought to herself. "You don't have far to go. It's a few feet from here to the next longhouse." She bolted before losing her nerve, and tears streamed from the corners of her eyes. There were only a few feet left to go when Eira's brain flicked again and threw her back inside the same village as before, dashing over headless bodies and darting inside the pit house. Mama will come for me.

The den was a good ten feet below the surface and filled with vast quantities of curious artifacts. Eira felt she'd been there before, but somehow seeing it with a fresh pair of eyes made the experience surreal.

Fine gold jewellery draped the walls, next to small round caps made of metal with jagged edges turned into earings. Silver utensils like the wooden spoons Eira used hung from the ceiling alongside prongs, and knives half-eaten with rust, but mostly the room brimmed with works of art weaved from waste by the village elders. The land was rife with transparent bottles made from age-old material, and people used them for clothing, insulation, blankets, and art. Most amusing to Eira were the mini-brushes. They were too little to comb hair, which she found peculiar.

Eira recognised metal instruments comparable to various tools still used in the village, but some substances on display in shallow bowls like the bits of black, dry goop crumbling between her fingers were a mystery.

She liked the plastic dolls with bald heads, missing limbs and blank faces, but not as much as the minuscule blocks stacked one on top of the other. Eira wished she could have played with the toys, but Mama wouldn't approve. They cherished these relics passed down to them by their ancestors.

In the corner a pile of tattered, brittle clothing lay next to odd shoes with abnormal spikes jutting out of the heel, but the most impressive was the fresco of scintillating mirrors.

Upon closer inspection Eira realised the fresco was a patchwork of hundreds of colourful rectangles strewn together, similar to the flatscreens in the Hall, but smaller and shiner, and once again her reflection mesmerised Eira.

The cracked glass reflected her likeness, but a strange wolf-like face hovered over hers into a seamless person. Fear coursed through her blood as Eira inched closer and bumped her foot against something on the floor beneath the glass wall.

It was a modest stone slab, a shelf with little importance, until she saw the warped, misshapen skulls. Lit from the inside, their deformed orbs and mouths spewed bright gold rays. The treasure trove was a shrine!

Grimnìr masks materialised on the wall. Cerberus, Ylva, Drakaina and KerRidwen looked down at her. "The dead inherit the living," she uttered. Frightened, Eira stepped back and toppled a shelf of candles. Flames licked the wall, and within seconds fire rained. Eira screamed for her Mama, but a faceless daemon shouted her name and it echoed inside her skull.

"I'm c . . . c–oming for you, Eira." The High King bellowed.

Eira swung her head towards the voice, and she was back outside, curled up against the longhouse, the burst of orange flames gone. "Mama," she uttered under her breath. Her earliest memory was here in this village with the High King. Why was this coming out now? Eira rubbed her eyes, hoping to wipe away the fitful visions clouding her judgment. These delusions came from a life that didn't belong to her, and she willed them to stay silent.

At this rate Eira wouldn't make it. The west exit was still far, but relief struck as she peered along the length of the fence and found a wide gap in the dilapidated fortification.

Eira made a break for it, flying past the longhouses and huts. The dry air scorched the back of her throat, but the mind-numbing cold caused worse damage to her leg muscles, and slowed her to a crawl. Eira couldn't afford to stop, or she'd never get going again, when at last tall haunting trees came into view.

Eira climbed over the fractured wood stumps, and snagged the fur off her shoulders, but there was no time to pick it up, so she left it behind. She ploughed in between the trees, through the dense blanket of ice crystals, and scraped her legs raw.

Her plan to disappear into the mountains was foiled. She had to backtrack and fetch the stashed furs from underneath the woodpile, or she'd freeze to death, but heading south back into the village dampened Eira's spirit. Soon a fleet of warriors would muddle through the forest and find her tracks.

The village ramparts opened at the bottom and Eira saw the beginnings of the teetering woodpile in the distance. She stayed low, hugging the trees for support, but her chapped feet had lost any feeling and she tumbled down the hill at an uneven pace until it was too late to fight the downward pull. Her legs gave out from the strain, and Eira plummeted head-first, snowballing the rest of the slope.

Snow packed inside her mouth and nostrils as she grasped any little thing protruding from the ground, but nothing slowed her momentum until she reached the bottom.

Eira choked her first breath and clutched her mangled body. Thankfully, she had no broken bones.

On high alert, she scanned for warriors. She saw her knife sticking out of the snow a few meters up and crawled to grab the weapon between her twisted fingers. There wasn't much further to go, and she gave one last push until finally she reached the woodpile. Her blistered skin and muscles were mush as Eira leaned against the stack of wood to rest. She massaged her limbs to generate heat, but her hands were frightful claws. Only one thing could get the blood flowing—her stashed furs.

From where she sat she had a clear view of the bobbing torches rallying up at the top. There was still time to find her clothes. The knife slipped from her hands, but Eira chipped away at the ice and freed the garments.

The frost had burned Eira's skin into raw, bloody patches, and she couldn't enjoy the softness of the fur-lined pants and boots as she put them on, but the thought of it felt good.

Eira covered up with a fur hat and poncho, which was stiff from being left outside. The last pieces of clothing she took were fur-laden mittens and a long fur cape, which she swung over her head across her shoulders.

After a few minutes Eira felt the furs working their magic, and she heaved her body upright. She pulled her winter garbs into a tight fit by lashing a leather belt around her waist over her cape, and tucked her trusty knife beneath it.

"How hard is it to catch that crazy bird?" a woman said.

Eira flattened against the timber and listened. Gretchen?

"Enough! I don't want to listen to this anymore."

Eira brought her hand to her mouth in shock. What was Dwr doing here?

"I see what you're doing," the woman said, "but it's wrong. Eira's not a wild animal you can tame. Can't you see her mind is beyond saving? She's been here too long. That woman's as cracked as the Mad King, or haven't you noticed?"

Eira strained to hear and made the snow crunch under her feet.

"Listen," Dwr said.

Eira froze.

"Come on, she's not here, Dwr. I'm sure they found her. She did this all the time back when we first arrived, don't you remember? She never got far."

"Tonight feels different, she wanted to tell me something. She wasn't the same. I don't know why . . . Gods, what are they doing up there?" Dwr said. "They're useless."

Eira assumed he meant the warriors and looked up the hill. He was right, they looked disorganised. This was her chance to escape before it was too late.

"They're not even looking for her," Dwr continued.

"You blame them? The woman is trouble. If we were smart we'd leave too, while there's still time . . . You know what, now that I catch myself saying it, why not? You and me, we could make it," the woman said. "Leave all this behind."

"Think," Dwr barked, "they'd track us in a matter of days and kill us. The King controls every single clann, inland to the coast, there's nowhere to hide. Eira knows this."

"Hmph, fine, let's take our wood and get out of here before the guards catch us," Gretchen finished.

This was her chance. Eira tiptoed toward the end of the cord. The shooting pain in her legs was a good sign. It meant her limbs were warming up, but she feared it might hinder her escape.

The distance between her and the forest was short, but Eira took her time to peek around the corner just in case, and as she feared, she came face to face with Dwr. Surprised, she stepped back.

"Why don't you go after her, it's obvious that's what you want to do" —Gretchen popped out from behind the stockpile, and dropped the kindling from her arms— "by the Gods, I was right, didn't I tell you? I knew she didn't look right. I saw it in her twitchy green eyes."

Dwr raised his hand. "Gretchen, be quiet."

Eira watched them.

"Oh my Gods, Dwr . . ." Gretchen pointed to Eira.

"Yes," he said his voice steady. "Now be quiet."

Eira followed their eyes, and they were staring at the knife in her hands. She wasn't sure when she'd grabbed the weapon.

"Is that blood on her face?" Gretchen said, before hollering to warn the guards. "She's here! She's here!"

Eira stumbled and caught herself against the woodpile.

"Shite Gretchen, shut your mouth!" Dwr snapped.

The guards hadn't moved. Eira circled around Dwr, and gave him a wide berth as she sank deeper into the forest, but she noticed him tightening the gap between them.

"Let her go," Gretchen said, "let her get killed. She's not our problem."

"Stop it!" he snapped.

"No, I won't let you!"

Dwr pushed Gretchen away, but fixed his eyes on Eira. "Mn'keur, you're better than this." His tone was gentle, as if he was coaxing a wild animal. A frightened animal he wanted to tame. "Mn'keur, trust me when I say you won't make it. Look at you. Your hands are trembling. You'll never survive out there in the wild. Let me help you."

Eira must have let her guard drop because the next thing she knew Gretchen stood beside her while Dwr tried to grab the weapon out of her hand. It happened so fast, but Eira swung with all her might in every direction. They'd never tame her! She untangled herself from their clutches and withdrew further into the forest.

She must've wounded Dwr because blood covered his hands, but then out of the corner of her eye, she saw Gretchen falter to her knees, clutching her belly. Blood dripped from her gut.

Dwr rushed to her side and held her in his arms. "By the Gods, what have you done?" he said to Eira. "Get help!"

Eira's tongue thickened and her mouth turned dry, but she held her knife with an iron grip.

"Please Mn'keur, don't do this. I'm begging you," Dwr said. "The King will kill us one by one until he finds you."

Dwr didn't understand. No one did. The people suffered the King's wrath, but his twisted love, his rituals, his desires, his cravings were far worse, and now she had a child to protect. Her baby was all that mattered.

"Let me help you," Dwr said, and he reached out to her, but Eira was wiser to his deceit and cold to his charms.

For too long Eira had kept boxes inside her mind, neat little boxes on how to act, how to please, how to play, but no more. They'd unleashed her tether to this world and cleared the path, and for the first time she wasn't afraid of what lay ahead, only what held her back.

"Mn'keur," Dwr begged.

Eira shook her head and fled into the forest. She hadn't made it far when Dwr cried for help. The King's warriors would be here shortly, but her feet had two huge boulders attached to them and a wave of pain flushed down her thighs and up her back.

Eira lurched forward as her stomach cramped into a hard ball.

Out of every hidden corner, shadows rushed through the trees. Eira could've sworn she saw wolves pushing her to keep going.

By the time her spasm subsided, a stream of warriors had trickled down the hill bearing torches, and Eira had forged a trail straight to her. The only hope was the open ice path bordering the steep slope.

Eira furrowed towards the passage and saw the King standing at the crest of the hill. Goosebumps raised the hairs on the back of her neck, and a desire to rip his throat out burst through her. She could smell and taste his meat, and she groaned, almost growled. One day she'd get her revenge, but for now she savoured the space between them.

The wind picked up and the veil of snow diffused the warriors' torches into floating mystical orbs. Other than the sharp slope to her right, there was nowhere to hide.

A warrior hollered, and in the spur of the moment Eira leapt up the embankment hoping to find better coverage. The powdered snow dragged her down, but Eira fought each step to the top, and dry-heaved the bear meat she ate hours before.

She wiped her mouth and ignored the heaviness weighing her. Shelter was Eira's priority, but the sight of endless ice desert alarmed her. Dreaded curls of fierce wind and snow whipped across the plains underneath black rolling clouds.

This was far worse than she had imagined.

Behind, below the tree line, the warriors' glowing orbs bobbed towards her. It was either back to them, or face the wasteland ahead.

In the distance, a dark outline emerged. Those were the mountains. Freedom called.

BOOK 2

The Book of Hunters

CHAPTER 5

Asylum

Watching Eira slip away reminded Dwr that he'd failed again, and anger swelled in his chest. EKöh, the God of death, had taken everything . . . As if losing his wife and son wasn't the ultimate sacrifice for his sins. Guilt coiled around Dwr's ribs.

His sins . . . They had picked his brains these past ten years till he was nothing more than a husk of self-loathing doubt, but he deserved nothing better. Dwr had vowed to carry his burden with a lifetime of penance and imprisonment, and he did, but EKöh was taking too much.

Gretchen's wound gushed between his fingers. Dwr wailed, and the lament in his voice humiliated him. How could Eira hurt Gretchen? Why did she abandon him? "No," he said shaking his head. This wasn't his fault. What more could he have done?

Warriors hollered.

"We're here, behind the woodpile" —Dwr turned to Gretchen— "Help's coming," he said, holding her close.

One by one, the troops herded around him and Gretchen. "Where's the prisoner?" Pietr the giant warrior screamed.

"This woman's dying," Dwr said. "She needs help."

"Where's the High King's prisoner?" the soldier shouted again.

King Lorcan pushed through his men. "My w . . . w–ife. Where is she?"

It surprised Dwr to see the High King himself instead of Éarlrick. The sly tongue usually took care of Eira, which confirmed Dwr's worst fear. If the High King's involved personally, that meant something serious had happened, and he'd stop at nothing to get Eira back. "We tried stopping her—"

The King placed his sword inches above Dwr's Adam's apple and punctured the skin. Dwr couldn't protect Eira anymore. He had to think of Gretchen and lifted his arm towards the woods.

The King's eyes grew large. "Get her!" the madman snapped.

A horn touted, and fifty warriors rushed into the forest.

Tilly rounded the corner and flung a fur garment across King Lorcan's shoulders. A look of concern flushed her cheeks red after seeing Dwr and Gretchen. "Come, my Lord. Let your men find Eira. You can do no more."

The King ignored the servant and narrowed his gaze on Dwr. "You helped Eira escape! This is your f . . . f–ault."

The metal blade dug into Dwr's throat. "I tried to stop her," he replied in a gruff voice. At that moment a part of him wished they'd find Eira just so he might punish her himself.

A warrior shouted in the distance, and King Lorcan raised his head. His brow softened.

"Stay," Tilly urged, "they'll bring her to you."

The mad King didn't listen, and the caretaker looked stricken, desperate even, as he fled into the forest.

"Help her," Dwr said to Tilly. "Gretchen's dying."

"Yes," Tilly muttered, but she looked miles away.

"You can save her, can't you?" he asked.

The woman peered toward the forest one last time before turning to Dwr. "Bring her to the servant quarters."

He lifted Gretchen from the ground. They didn't have far to go to reach the servant quarters. Tilly's two helpers, Kit and Neve, greeted them. "Put her there," Tilly said, and removed her heavy furs.

The pit house smelled of pine needles and cedar. Dwr lowered Gretchen into a leather cot and watched Tilly scan dozens of shelves around the room. Each one overflowed with containers, cups, beakers and leather pouches filled with coloured jellies, dried leaves, dirt, and vibrant pink rocks. One beaker might have contained minuscule eyeballs, but he wasn't certain. Snow-white rats, hares, and crows bundled up with herbs hung in every corner.

"There," Tilly said, making her way near the hearth and grabbing a flask similar to all the other flasks on the shelf. She emptied the cloudy liquid into a small terracotta pot. "Kit, get the ash."

The scraggly young man grabbed a pouch off another shelf. Tilly dumped the coarse grey powder into the pot and handed the concoction back to Kit. "Grind it."

"Excuse me." The third helper scurried past Dwr with a bowl of white wool. "Here," she said, and handed Tilly the bowl.

"Neve, don't forget the steriliser."

"Steriliser?" Dwr didn't know what that meant.

"Right." The young lady ran near the inside door which Dwr reasoned was the prisoner's adjoining quarters and hauled a jug filled with liquid.

"A knife," Tilly said, "there's one behind you hanging by the door." She pointed behind Dwr, and he slipped the weapon out of its sheath.

Tilly shook her head. "Your friend has lost too much blood."

"Here," Neve said, and poured the steriliser over Tilly's hands.

"What are you doing?" Dwr waited to hand her the knife.

"I'm cleaning my hands. Stand back." Tilly pushed him out of the way, and Dwr tripped over an empty cot behind him as she rubbed her hands together under the stream, which had a strong odour of firewater.

She shook off the excess liquid, plucked the knife out of Dwr's hands, and cleaned it. After she wiped it dry, she cut away Gretchen's clothes with a seasoned hand. It was impressive to watch.

Bent over Gretchen's belly, Tilly wiped the wound, but still more blood oozed. It was a small slit, and Dwr found it hard to imagine something so small could inflict so much damage, but the stout woman didn't hesitate, and dug her stubby forefinger and middle finger inside the flesh.

Dwr recoiled as Gretchen groaned. He hadn't seen such a procedure since the days of the Seiðrs, travelling healers of the past, before the King had purged their hoary ways. His wife had insisted they find one for the delivery of their child, but Grimnìr were rare, even back in those days.

Surely there was no way Tilly could have been a disciple of the Grimnìr faith and still practice the old ways right under the High King's nose? Could she? It's one thing to survive, but to hide in plain sight for so long . . . It wasn't impossible either.

She looked fifteen, if not twenty years older than him, which meant the caretaker might've been a pupil of the Grimnìr priests before their annihilation. She even talked like a Seiðr, he thought. Steriliser . . . who says that, and how had he never noticed before? He shrugged his shoulders. Apparently, there were many things he chose not see before tonight. Guilt's firm squeeze crushed his ribs tighter. Whoever this woman was pretending to be, she was more than a devoted servant to the High King.

"She's fortunate," Tilly said, digging deeper into the wound. "Nothing major has ruptured, but it's difficult for me to tell. She's lost a lot of blood. If she survives, her recovery will take many moons." Tilly pulled out her blood-soaked fingers. "Quickly," she said, and stretched out her hand.

Kit placed a fine bone needle and silky-smooth thread in her palm. It was a beautiful piece of craftsmanship, and Seiðr medicine at its best.

The stitching took longer, but Tilly didn't miss a beat. Her focus was beyond reproach considering Eira had escaped. Once she finished, Kit rubbed the medicinal paste against the suture just as Neve handed her the wool.

Tilly ordered Dwr to lift Gretchen as she dressed the wound, but the wool stank, and he turned away. "What is it?"

"Wool from the wild sheep of the Daïs Mountain. It's very rare, and you're lucky I have some."

"I get that it's wool, but why does it smell?"

"Oh!" Tilly exclaimed. "It's nothing, just a special ointment to help wounds fight infec . . . to help her fight against festering."

Dwr didn't insist and breathed through his mouth till she finished.

"Done, and not a second too soon." Tilly exhaled. The skin around her jawline sagged, and in one instant she looked as if she had aged ten years. Dwr found her fragile as she cleaned her brittle hands and dabbed the back of her neck with her wet fingers, but the stout warrior's respite was brief.

The woman straightened the wild strands of greyish hair into her frizzy brown bob and marched towards the hearth to ladle a steaming bowl of liquid out of her cast-iron kettle.

Dwr had only ever seen one in his entire life, and it looked the same as the one that had belonged to his wife—a family heirloom passed down from her mother and Gods-know how many generations. Forged from precious metal catapulted to earth by the Gods. To own something so special was rare. Then again, perhaps the King had looted the kettle when they'd attacked his clann and given it to Tilly.

Dwr bit the inside of his cheek raw and pushed the memory away as Tilly returned with the bowl.

"Make her drink this linctus. It will help ease the pain."

"You had this on hand?" he asked with curiosity.

"I've done everything I can do," she said, not answering the question. "The rest is up to your friend. We can only wait and see if she survives."

Most of the time, treatments such as this postponed the inevitable, but Dwr said nothing, preferring not to vocalise the dreaded reality.

Steam rose from the bowl and he discovered the source of the pine-needle odour. Just smelling the linctus calmed his nerves, but Tilly interrupted his train of thought. "Drink some. You're in shock, and the sweetness will help."

Dwr hadn't felt the cold creep inside his bones, but his muscles shook.

Tilly covered him with a blanket, and the weight soothed him. He didn't dare move. Maybe, if he sat still long enough, then whatever was swirling inside him might disappear.

Gretchen wheezed, and Dwr took her hand. He hoped this wasn't goodbye. "We've been through worse my friend. Don't give up now." The forced enthusiasm in his voice made him cringe. "The others need you. They're waiting for us to come back with that wood," he said, a sad smile creeping on the edge of his mouth.

Her dry lips moved, but nothing came out.

"Save your strength," he said, squeezing her hand to reassure her. But she was getting agitated.

Gretchen insisted to speak. "I love you," she croaked. Her eyelids peeled back, and she looked at him. Her eyes swam in their sockets.

"Drink. You'll feel better," Dwr said as he pried her mouth open with the cup.

"Listen," she said after taking a sip. Her voice slurred from the loss of blood, and she almost sounded drunk. "I have loved you since I can remember, but you only had eyes for Seweryna. She was like my sister, and I was happy for both of you."

A smile creased the corner of Gretchen's lips. "I never blamed you for the decimation of our clann. Never! My heart belongs to you, and I would change nothing if it meant standing by your side again."

Dwr's throat tightened. "Shush," he said.

"So you'll believe me when I say Eira is not for you . . ."

"Gretchen please," Dwr said.

"No," she wheezed, "Eira is with child."

A chill crawled up Dwr's spine, and his eyes went moist.

"She's not for you. Her destiny lies elsewhere. Let her go."

Dwr wanted to tell her to stop, but the word balled in his throat, and he kissed her forehead instead. Gretchen dripped with sweat and slipped into unconsciousness.

Tilly hovered behind him.

Once he recovered his breath, Dwr needed answers. "Is it true? Is Eira pregnant?" He said feebly.

"Listen to your friend. We shouldn't meddle in things that don't concern us." Her tone was sharp as she walked away, but Dwr had more to say.

The news didn't shock Tilly, and her answer felt dull and rehearsed. "You knew that's what Eira wanted to tell me tonight. Why else would you have these medicines on hand, if not for the pregnancy?"

"Let it go," Tilly said, taking a deep breath.

"No, I won't drop this, not until I know the truth."

Tilly banged the table with her fist. "Bloody arse. Why can't you leave anything alone? Always putting your nose where it doesn't belong. Yes, I knew, and I didn't want Eira to tell you because you can't get involved. She's carrying the High King's child. This is her fate, and there's nothing you can do about it."

To hear Tilly say it so matter-of-factly gutted Dwr. He wanted to throw up. "What do you mean?"

Tilly was about to speak, but Neve interrupted. "Do you think it's wise to tell him? He might betray . . ."

The caretaker narrowed her gaze. "He won't. He hates the King as much as we do, and he'll find out eventually," Tilly said. "The more people know, the greater chance we have to reclaim our rights, our religion."

"Find out what? Tell me?" Dwr snapped.

"Eira is the only known survivor of the sacred Eli Dé Gecennen clann. She is of Grimnìr descent. She's Grimnìr."

The room spun off its axis. Dwr gripped the cot. "That's not possible. The King killed everyone from that clann."

Neve's voice fell to a whisper. "Not everyone."

"That means Eira's the last surviving Grimnìr." Dwr spoke slowly to let the words sink in. "Wait! Something's not right. How can she be with child? Grimnìr are born barren."

Tilly and the others didn't need to speak. Their silence said everything Dwr needed to know.

"The prophecy . . ." Dwr said looking up at Tilly's stoic brow.

Everyone knew the prophecy. It had survived wars, the King's purge, and it's what had kept his wife going to the bitter end. Hope for a better day, and a brighter future without the King. A barren woman would bear a child with the ability to open the gates of heaven and free them from the High King's tyranny forever. This child would restore order to the lands.

The words sunk to the pit of his stomach. "No, no, no, this can't be. She was a prisoner like the rest of us. In all the time I spent with Eira, not once has she said anything about it." Dwr paced back and forth searching for an explanation. "If Eira is a Grimnìr, she has shown no signs to me, not a single one."

The caretaker took her time to speak, choosing her words carefully. "We don't understand it ourselves. We believed . . ." Tilly stopped her sentence short. "Eira should've undergone the transmutation when she hit her teenage years, but I've never seen her show any supernatural abilities. Perhaps the horror she's seen, or the years of malnutrition stunted her growth and hindered the process. We're not sure, not without proper testing."

"Proper testing?" What was this woman going on about? Dwr could just imagine what he must've looked like as he snapped his jaw shut. "Or, she's not a Grimnìr priestess, and her child is not the foretold saviour?"

"No, there's no doubt Eira is the sacred vessel, and her child is the key that will free the Sidhe from Lorcan's tyranny, but only if Eira escapes. If Lorcan gets his hands on that child there's no telling what he might do. The child's blood might help him rule heaven and earth and we will be powerless to stop him, or he will kill our only hope to stop him."

". . . He can't be the father," Dwr said, thinking out loud.

Tilly frowned. "What did you say?"

The glare in her eyes felt like a scolding. "Ahh! Nothing, I need air." He headed for the door.

"I can't let you leave," she said, grabbing Dwr's wrist.

He pulled away from her grip. "I doubt you can stop me."

Tilly stood in his way. "Not me, the guards."

Dwr read her contempt. "You know the truth, don't you?"

Tilly's eyes hardened. "Do you think it matters if you're the father? It doesn't," she said.

The other two servants looked at each other nervously.

Dwr bit back. "It matters to me."

"If the King learns of this treason, he will kill both of you and imprison the child just like he did to Eira. Is that what you want? You can't fight this and win. Eira must find her own path."

Dwr chewed the soft skin inside his cheek until a piece of soft flesh hung in his mouth. "What about Eira, doesn't she deserve a say in this? Doesn't she know what's happening to her?"

"Eira might look like a woman, but in many ways she's a child. Lorcan took her so young and filled her mind with nonsense."

Dwr kicked his foot against a cot, and the small wooden bed jolted against the other beds. Eira's years of torture and captivity made sense. The High King had kept Eira, the last living Grimnìr, for himself, but how did he know she was the one? "You knew, but did nothing? Why? Why keep her helpless?"

Tilly's nostrils flared. "To keep her safe."

"Yeah, no wonder she's losing her shite! She asked me over and over why the King hurt her? She never understood."

The caretaker's calm demeanor flipped. "Have you ever bothered to ask why you care, Dwr?"

He clenched his jaw. The woman had never used his name, and he didn't care for it.

"It's not love, it's solace. You sought comfort in the arms of a woman who didn't know any better than to trust a traitor like you. You think I didn't know about the two of you? You think the prisoners don't know? Despite my better judgement, despite my overwhelming disdain of you, and your selfish tricks, I let it happen. Why? Because I care about Eira, and I didn't want to be the one take away one more thing from her miserable life, but I knew. I knew you were using her. I didn't have the heart to tell her."

Dwr ground his teeth.

"Oh, oh I struck a nerve?" Tilly sneered. "Did you really think it was more? Here? Wallowing in your misery under the King's thumb? Dwr of the Clann Fianna found a poor hapless prisoner to comfort him. Eira deserves better than a spineless arse like you. Eira is more than you or I will ever be, and perhaps fate has dealt her a cruel hand, but it is her burden to bear. Nothing I could do or say would have changed that fact, except to put her life more at risk than it was already."

Dwr raised his fist to Tilly's chin. He wanted to strike her down, but instead he punched the wall, splitting open his knuckles in the process. "You're wrong," he said, before ripping the furs off the hook and escaping the hut along the icy path.

CHAPTER 6

Wake

Eira's haunting glare flashed in Dwr's mind, and it broke him. Part of him knew she needed him, he wasn't a fool, but it was easier to hide in this village than accept Eira into his life. It meant moving on without his family, and that was too painful to bear. He'd used her. It was wrong of him to want to mend Eira's broken heart and soul, but worse still to make her believe she could mend his.

Dwr sank deeper into his torment and ran, trying to escape the chasm that threatened to swallow him whole. His feet pounded straight towards the woodpile. Eira's ghost wavered in front of him near the forest edge, but one glimpse of the bloody snow and she dissolved into a puff of air.

What if this WAS his child? Nothing would ever be the same. Worse still, what if it wasn't? They'd shared one night. One night to forget their troubles and feel as though the world was good.

Lorcan's men scattered across the woodland. Nobody can elude this many warriors, Dwr thought. Eira had to be here somewhere.

The tall trees engulfed him, and the familiar surroundings soothed his rattled nerves. Twelve years since he'd ventured into a forest, and no one knew how to read the lay of the land like him. He'd been an excellent trapper in his youth, which might as well have been another lifetime. That's how he'd fallen in love with his wife. They competed for game, and she always won.

He smiled at the memory. He was the ice to her fire, she said, and their son Caleb . . . Gods, what a strapping young lad he would've been. Dwr sighed. After Sewery-na's father died things changed between them. In those early days life moved lazily, and he regretted not taking a moment to pay attention, be kind, and more supportive.

The hardest thing for Dwr was hanging on to the simplest memories. A fleeting smile from across a crowded room, or the slow caress down his back as she walked past him. Caleb's belly laughs, and famous butterfly kisses on his cheeks had turned to colourless words, and it broke Dwr's heart.

He craved the life he lost. If only he could take back the years, yesterday, and the days in between to a time that didn't hurt . . .

He shook away his grief, and inspected the snow.

The King's warriors had trampled any evidence Eira might have passed through here, but she might've known to cover her tracks.

Desperate for a sign, Dwr meandered onto the icy path. He kept his head low and searched for clues, but after a while it didn't seem to matter. The warriors either didn't recognise him or didn't give a shite.

"What are we even doin' here?" Dwr recognised the warrior Pietr's hulking frame. "She's more trouble than she's worth," he said, "I mean she's feisty, I'll give her that, but did you hear the King? Does he really believe she's the prophesied chosen one and her child the saviour? I mean, come on! They had to bring him back to the village because he was hysterical."

"First I've heard about it," his thinner, much smaller friend replied.

Pietr continued thinking out loud. "These are stories our parents told us as babes, and even if it were true, didn't the King kill every last one of those traitorous imposters?"

"Listen . . ." The skinnier lad lowered his voice. "I heard it might be more than that. Apparently, there's a growing underground resistance."

"Merciless EKöh! That would explain a lot. Are we talking uprisin'? Who?"

The lad shrugged. "Nobody knows."

"Why is the King so worried?" Pietr said, "he has the most powerful warriors in the world."

"Hear, hear!" His friend replied. "Anybody with the nerve to fight Clann Llyr deserves what's coming to them."

Dwr rolled his eyes. These men were fools.

"Still, do you think it's true she killed Éarlrick?" Pietr pressed on.

"Pftt, good riddance if she did. I don't like her, but I hate him more."

Dwr stopped in his tracks. That was impossible. Eira couldn't have killed Éarlrick. The man was a trained fighter . . .

"Arrick, you know what this means? This is my chance to get close to the King," the towering warrior said. "Stick with me, and we'll wine and sup with fine women on our laps."

Dwr lingered long enough to hear their conversation end and passed them, hoping to stay inconspicuous. There was no telling what Pietr might do if he saw him, but his worry melted away when something in the sleet made Dwr do a double-take. A dusting of flurries covered a snapped twig, and the imprint of a coat brushed up against the snow.

This was the clue Dwr needed to find Eira, but he had little time to study it. He noticed a warrior on his tail, tracking him since he'd left the giant behind. The young man had broad shoulders and Eira's creamy complexion. His determined stride left little doubt Tilly had sent him.

Dwr quickened his pace and spotted a crisp trail up the slope, but the years of captivity took a toll on Dwr's body, and the young man wasn't far behind, plodding up the flank.

At the top of the hill terror pinched Dwr's chest. Tempest's fierce breath blew across the steppe. If Eira wanted to escape and never be found, the Daïs Mountains were her best bet, but standing between her and shelter was the dangerous open ice shelf. There was no cover for miles, and the elements had killed many who braved it. Dwr hated to imagine Eira alone, and ventured into the void hoping to avoid capture.

The fierce wind shovelled the snow into soft, shallow banks and made the trek arduous. After some time the whirling snowflakes nauseated Dwr, but other than the Daïs he saw no landmarks or reference points to moor him in this wicked blizzard. The one good thing was poor visibility, and he hoped the warrior following him had lost his trail and given up. Only an expert huntsman could pull through conditions such as this, which made Dwr worry about Eira's safety. He hoped for a miracle, but deep down he feared the worst.

Tired and out of breath, Dwr bent over to eat a handful of snow and uncovered something odd in the ice. He scraped away the frost and found a small bear looking back at him. An ancient stuffed doll . . .

Dwr squinted every which way across the horizon, eager to confirm his hunch, when out of the darkness rose a large hill. A Sacred Mound? This whole time, Dwr had been marching on a landfill of consecrated ruins. Hallowed grounds frozen over for millennia, and no doubt venerated by the devout Sidhe before their annihilation.

"Praise be to the Gods that have given us the Grimnìr to guide us. We, the Sidhe, owe our lives to their sacrifice." Dwr brought his palms together, placed his thumbs on his forehead, and glided them over the bridge of his nose, mouth, and across his chin down his neck. Finally, he rested them on his heart as his wife had taught him long ago.

If King Lorcan saw Dwr now, he'd hang. The old religion hadn't survived the King's cleansing, but rituals were hard to break. He was Sidhe, a descendent of an extraordinary race bred to survive, and nothing could take that away. At least that's what his wife hammered into him and their son. They'd hide during her sermons, but since their deaths, the rituals were the only things Dwr had left to feel close to them.

He veered towards the ruins, praying he was right to follow his hunch. It took the better part of the night to reach the maze of ice ridges filled with artefacts.

The ice structure looked identical to the one he'd visited with Seweryna, on the only occasion she let him tag along during one of her clandestine pilgrimages. Dwr had no business there, she said, but he insisted on coming for her protection. Looking back, those dark days marked the beginning of the end for his people, and his marriage. Life's burdens ravaged their souls, and they had become different people. He and his wife saw things differently. She wanted to fight King Lorcan, and knowing what he knew now, Dwr wished he could have died alongside them.

He walked inside the labyrinth with a heavy heart. Wind tunnels burrowed over centuries turned the whole thing into a sparkling sanctuary of open and closed-roofed channels with sacrosanct objects built into its walls and floor.

Thousands of plastic bags, bottles, toys, clothing, and what he believed was a trove of metal objects, big and small. Most of it Dwr didn't recognise, but a holy Scavenger would know, and he'd know if it was worth pulling from the ice. His wife had dealt with them often in search of speciality items such as glass and metal. In decent condition, these coveted materials were rare finds.

After the purge, the King banned foraging and slaughtered the Scavengers along with the Seiðrs, Şekers, Seers, and anyone else loyal to the Grimnìr religion. Many fought a losing battle and didn't survive, preferring to secure their eternal afterlife than accept Lorcan as their new spiritual leader and betray the Gods, but more chose to live under the King's thumb, praying for a better life.

Dwr's wife failed to understand how these Sidhe could so easily betray their guides, but while the Grimnìr offered salvation, they didn't put food on the table. Many clanns chose to surrender rather than go extinct.

Dwr scanned the snow and caught Eira's footprint. A glimmer of hope surged, his instinct right, but something was wrong in the way she dragged her feet. He rounded the bend and trekked through the labyrinth of tunnels till he reached the outside. It was astounding she'd made it this far.

Eira's imprints were fresh, and led south, straight into a deep snow gully. Anything was better than the barren stretch towards the Daïs Mountain ridge, but still, this path was by no means easier.

The gully provided shelter from the wind's full assault, but the icy currents rolled down the Steppe, and crashed into the ravine like waves. Moisture transformed the dry snow pellets into ground clouds, and ice fog hovered in the air.

It didn't take long for icicles to form on his furs, and hang from his eyelashes and beard. Dwr feared the worst was yet to come as the Goddess Ny was on the rise.

Eira's erratic foot pattern strengthened Dwr's resolve to go faster. She wouldn't last long in hyper-freezing weather. No one would, he thought as he came across a carelessly flung mitten in the snow. He found its twin further down the trail next to her blood-stained boots, and his heart sank. These were signs of hypothermia, and he doubled over in speed, searching through the branches for any sign of life.

A blood trail stained the snow, and Dwr stopped dead in his tracks. Was Eira hurt? She couldn't have gotten far, he thought, when a ghostly figure flew through the trees screaming.

Covered from head to toe in plain grey clothing, Dwr saw only the eyes. A woman swooped in fast and landed a few meters away from a lifeless body in the snow. "Eira," he gasped.

Forgetting his own danger Dwr lunged to save her, but something tugged his shoulder, which he found peculiar. A split second later a bolt of searing pain blindsided him as he hurtled headfirst into the snow. Dwr's shoulder exploded from its socket and he screamed with pain. He rolled to his side, pawing his arm, and felt an arrowhead sticking out of the joint.

The forest spun, but Dwr willed himself to crawl towards Eira with his last breath. He wouldn't let her slip between his fingers, not like this, but the airy figure moved fast. She had harnessed Eira into a sleigh and hitched it to her back.

In the darkness, Dwr could've sworn he saw more of these ethereal characters swinging from the trees, but he was too late. The ghost disappeared as fast as she arrived, and Eira was gone.

"My arrow is aimed at your head." A young warrior puffed out of breath.

Dwr's stalker had shot him down. "Listen son . . . you . . . don't want . . . to . . . do this." He could barely string two words together.

"How do you know what I want?" the young lad said.

The smarting intensified and kept Dwr from breathing properly. He watched the young man strain to pull his bowstring taut.

Dwr's vision blurred and closed his eyes.

"Coward," the boy yelled.

Dwr's eyes shot open. "Listen! Eira's here . . . but a . . . woman took her." he spluttered, struggling to his feet.

"Liar, I see no one," said the boy.

"No, they took her, I swear." It took every ounce of strength for Dwr to get to his knees. "She's bleeding, and I . . . think she's suffering . . . from hypothermia. She's not far. You need to . . . go to her."

The young warrior didn't move. "So you can escape? I don't think so."

"Where am I going to go? Son . . . you can stop this."

"Don't call me son, Arsehole."

"What's your name?" Dwr asked breathlessly. He was mentally preparing for the worst physical pain imaginable.

"Myron."

"Myron . . ." A burst of uncontrollable energy rushed through Dwr's body, and with his left hand, he grabbed the arrowhead and pulled it out of his joint. "Arrrgg." He dragged the shaft, fletching and all, and thought he blacked out for a moment, but he carried on until the arrow was free.

"Shite," Myron said.

Dwr tossed the bloody projectile to the ground and fell back. He covered the wound with his hand. It burned like the fires of the Goddess Irïs. "Myron," he repeated out of breath. "Eira needs your help. Imagine . . . how grateful the King will be . . . when he finds out you saved her."

Myron's lips twitched in anger, the bow unstable in his grip. "Stop talking. She's gone, and we're better for it."

"If you won't go, then let me. Nobody needs to know."

Myron walked past him and stared into the darkness. "I have honour, you piece of shite, unlike you, Dwr the Betrayer. They warned me about you. You'd say anything to get away and save your pathetic life. Gods help me I should kill you, but you're far more valuable to me alive. Let's go."

Dwr's whole upper back and neck muscles contracted into a hard ball. Blood oozed from his shoulder, and the pain radiated into a dull ache across his body. Jaw clenched, he didn't think the emptiness he felt could get worse, but it seemed to grow tenfold as he left Eira's trail behind. Dwr vowed to find her, no matter what.

CHAPTER 7

Blood Moon

The pain hit Eira in waves. It started off slow, but intensified—tightening her stomach until she could think of nothing else. A high-pitched ringing sprung in her ears as the pain became unbearable. Her belly compressed into a hard knot, and she leaned against the tunnel wall, crouching into a ball for relief.

The maze's haunting squeals and squeaks of crackling snow didn't help. She couldn't explain why, but every fibre in her being resisted this place, like most relics she encountered. They were instruments of evil, the High King said, and served the Grimnìr and their monstrous daemons.

These weren't treasure troves, but piles of rubbish. Everywhere Eira looked sparkling objects glistened beneath the ice. Leftovers from the old world cherished by

Sidhe daemons, or whatever Tilly called them, Syntropic identifi . . . Eira drew a blank. Her mind was turning to goo.

As soon as the pain subsided, Eira pushed the thoughts aside, tucked her chin inside her furs to peek outside, and the weather hit hard. The air was ripe with humidity and carried a faint odour of wet stone. She'd never reach the mountains.

Unexpectedly, three large wolves ran past her. Their large pointy ears, lean, muscular bodies, and powerful long legs ploughed ahead, and vanished into the gully below. Eira raced down the trench, convinced there was a connection between her and these majestic animals aiding her escape, but the short hike drained her.

Moisture seeped into her furs, and the dampness rooted inside her bones. Within the short distance travelled, Eira's muscles screamed for rest, but she followed the wolves' large pawprints in the snow.

The trail had gotten rough, and she paid close attention to her footing so as not to get stuck in the thick snow. A change in landscape piqued her curiosity as she'd entered a dense forest of winter-dead trees covered in bulbous mounds of sticky snow. This place looked undisturbed for decades, it seemed. The trees were so tall their branches were higher than the steppe and disappeared in the blustering snowy winds.

Eira could've sworn she felt a charge in the air. This place was old, and prickled with life. Compelled to touch one of the bulging clouds, she removed her mitten. There was a faint tingle in her palm, and she scratched the snow away to get to the bark. The faint whizz buzzed louder. This was no ordinary tree. Wary to touch the cold, smooth trunk, Eira placed one finger on it, and her hand jolted back, sending her mitten flying.

That thing was alive, and the sensation was similar to hundreds of snow ants crawling up her elbow. Eira fled, rubbing her arm vigorously in an effort to get some feeling into it, but her wet furs had turned ice-hard and heavy. They weren't helping anymore, and she was burning up.

Why was she wearing so many layers? They were suffocating, and piece-by-piece Eira pulled off her protective layers flinging them in the snow.

If only she could rest, but those cunning wolves were hiding in the shadows, hanging just beyond her vision's periphery, pushing her further into the wild. She couldn't get a fix on the big grey wolf except for his glowing green eyes popping in and out from behind the trees.

A cold sweat crept up her spine and burned the back of her ears. Oh, no, no, no . . . Another spasm gripped her stomach muscles and radiated to her lower back and legs.

Eira clutched her belly and cried out as something warm ran down her legs. Just when she believed she wouldn't survive, Eira's three elusive creatures emerged from the veil of darkness. Their luminous glare soothed her. The big grey wolf howled, and the other two, a thin black duke with yellow eyes, and a playful white rascal with black threading at the root of his fur chimed in. Eira wasn't afraid, and latched on to them.

These were Ny's protectors, gathering lost souls. They accompanied Eira on her journey, and she didn't feel so alone anymore. Soon her pain vanished, and the harsh world turned airy. The trees swayed, lifting out of the ground as if the forest breathed, and Eira fell back.

Ny's giant hand reached down from the sky and cradled Eira in her palm, whisking her away into the netherworld beyond. Filled with warmth and peace, Ny revealed her wondrous moon yet again, but for all its beauty, this time, Eira saw nothing but the bereaved face.

The Goddess wept tears of blood, and it was too much to bear. Eira looked away. She'd lost a part of herself tonight, but thankfully, through the trees, running alongside, were her companions. There would never be anything to fear again. Not with them by her side, and Eira happily slipped inside an infinite sea of calm.

CHAPTER 8

Lost

Every instinct in Dwr's body urged him to chase after Eira, but this last stretch had sapped his strength. Slumped in the snow, his shoulder throbbed with pain. What a fool!

"Come on, old man!" Myron barked. "We'll freeze to death if we stay here much longer."

Dwr struggled to his feet only to fall down again. "I can't, I need rest."

Myron puffed his chest as if he was about to scold him, but he quickly deflated and gave up. "Fine. We rest for a few hours, but then we leave, even if I have to drag your sorry arse to the High King myself."

Relieved, Dwr leaned against a tree and rubbed his brow, hoping to get rid of the rope tightening around his head.

Myron plopped next to him. "Headache?"

Dwr nodded.

The young man rummaged through his bag, pulled out a leather pouch, and stuffed his mouth. “Here,” he said, tossing Dwr the bag.

The smell of cured meats made Dwr’s mouth water. “Food.” Careful not to move his bad shoulder, Dwr grabbed the first piece from the top, and savoured the smoky taste of wild jerky meat.

Myron was quiet at first, staring into space, but with every chomp, Dwr noticed him ripping the meat between his teeth with a little more gusto than the previous bite. “How can you live with yourself?” The lad finally muttered with his mouth full.

Dwr didn’t answer, hoping to leave it at that, but Myron frowned and took a swig from his flask to swallow his bite. “Why did I ever believe a sliver of dignity existed inside you?” He flung Dwr his flask.

“I stopped living up to people’s expectations a long time ago. Anyway, why do you care?” Dwr opened the bottle and sniffed, thinking it was firewater.

Myron snapped his jaw shut. “I don’t. Anyway, why would a scoundrel value integrity, honour, justice?”

After enjoying the fresh water, Dwr answered: “What’s your problem with me?”

“Not you, but spineless people like you. I despise cowards.”

Dwr gave a bitter laugh. “How old are you?”

Chin lifted towards the sky, Myron spat: “Nineteen.”

Dwr smiled, but remained quiet.

Myron raised his eyebrows. "You're judging me? A man who fled battle and let his people, his family, die? Judge a man by his actions, and that will tell you who I am. Honour in life brings honour in death no matter how old, but what would you know of it?"

The skepticism on Dwr's face was plain. "You've never lied to protect someone you love?"

"Nope," Myron rebuked without hesitation.

There was no point arguing with youth. Dwr felt old beyond his years next to this boy, barely a man. "I hope you never stumble off course. Self-righteousness is a steep climb for people like us."

"Spare me the comparison."

Dwr closed his eyes. Sleep was creeping up on him, but he doubted Myron was done with his rant.

"So? How can you live with yourself?"

Dwr sighed. "Look, you've made your opinion of me clear. Let's move on from this conversation."

"No, you don't get to decide. I want to understand how a man like you sleeps at night. Fifteen years ago you fled your clann, and again tonight."

Dwr gave him a surprised look.

"Oh, don't worry, Tilly filled me in. I'm curious what will you say to your people when I bring you back, that's assuming the King won't kill you when he sees you."

Dwr had been caught up in the moment. He had never intended to abandon anyone, and then he thought of Gretchen, and his chest tightened. "What do you want me to say? I'm concerned for Eira."

"How convenient. What was your excuse fifteen years ago?"

Between his headache, throbbing shoulder, and exhaustion, it was hard to ignore the venom in the lad's voice. "What can I do to shut you up?" Dwr belted. "You want to hear that I'm a coward? Yes, I'm a coward. The thought of losing my family shook me to my core. What was the point of dying in a battle I knew we could never win? I wanted to spare my people death and pain, but in the end it changed nothing. Not a Godsdamn day goes by I don't wish I died holding my son's hand. So however you and the bloody world feel about me, Myron, I swear it can't be worse than how I feel about myself. My arrogance cost lives. Everyone warned me not to negotiate with a madman. Trusting the King to honour my clann's surrender has been the bane of my existence." Dwr's anger ballooned into sadness.

Myron's angular jaw pulsed. "You lying sack of shite! Even now, you choose cowardice."

Dumbstruck, Dwr barked: "What?"

"That's not what happened." Myron tightened the string on his food purse and threw it in his pack.

"Right, because you were there?" Dwr said.

"I'm supposed to believe a traitor? People say you fled mid-battle and left your clann to die. They call you Dwr the Betrayer. You're spinning it like you tried to save them."

"Yeah, well," Dwr said, "people remember it the way they want, I suppose."

Myron shook his head. "Let's go."

"You said we could rest."

"I changed my mind."

CHAPTER 9

Fata Morgana

Tempest had calmed down and revealed the Daïs stretching out behind them. Smoke rose above the trees like a claw out of a grave and shook Dwr's core. A sickly sweet aroma of human flesh and charred wood hung in the air as they slid down the embankment onto the icy path.

Myron pushed to walk faster, but Dwr was in no rush to get back, and dragged his feet, incapable of drawing sufficient breath because of his wounded shoulder.

Near the village, soft, thick flurries drifted from the grey heavens, and rested in Dwr's palm. Chills ran up his spine. This was ash from dead bodies, not snow. Hiking the hilltop there was no mistaking the putrid smell of burnt human, and the surrounding air was as still as resting water. "It's quiet." Dwr said, taking stock of the area. "Where is everyone?"

Inside a longhouse, a toothless lady with long white hair cracked open a door and waved them to her. "Something's not right." Dwr said, scouting the area for signs of danger.

"She wants us to get off the path." Myron swung his head left and right and scanned the perimeter.

Something akin to wind swished passed Dwr, but he knew it wasn't Tempest. Planted firmly behind him in the snow was an arrow still vibrating from the impact. "Take cover!" Dwr shouted, running towards the old stone sanctuary.

Myron followed behind.

"Who's shooting at us?" Dwr yelled.

Dawn was stealing the night, and beyond the speckled sky, the forest was a maelstrom of snowflakes and ash. "Whoever fired that shot is an expert with a bow." Dwr was confident the assailants hadn't circled the village because anyone on the east bank would have had a clear shot to kill them both already.

The bonfire was nothing more than a pile of embers and charred warriors scattered across the town square with bolts sticking out of their chests. Men burned alive. "I think they're near the watchtower," Dwr said, turning towards Myron, but there were no signs of the lad. "Shite!" Had they shot him down?

For a brave second, Dwr considered escape to rescue Eira, but he was in no condition to do much of anything, and although catching up to her had driven him forward most of the night, he couldn't deny Myron's words. In search of truth, Dwr had sacrificed his people, and it tore him up inside. He promised never to do it again.

To drown the shame, Dwr searched for better cover. There wasn't much distance to go from his position to the nearby longhouse. Without overthinking he crawled to the edge of the Grimnìr alter and found a flat piece of wood from the stockpile. He covered his head and sprinted towards the meat smokers and the old run down meat caches.

A slew of arrows whooshed past him, hitting the totem pole in rapid succession. Dwr lunged towards the longhouse hopping over the meat cache's wooden foundations and rolled, crashing against the longhouse. Luckily, it had enough of an angle to protect him from the western bank. The pain in his shoulder forced him to lie still for a moment and catch his breath.

Arrows had punctured his shield, but considering the trail left in his wake, he was lucky to be alive. Aside from his shoulder, Dwr was intact, until he saw a projectile sticking out of his leg. The pain was nothing compared to his shoulder, and he squeezed his thigh. The arrowhead hadn't tinged the bone, or he would have been seething on the ground.

Pulling on it risked further damage to the muscle, so he left it in his leg. Near him, two more arrows stuck out of the snow. Jaw clenched, Dwr grabbed the shafts and quickly retreated away from the line of fire.

These weren't typical flintheads. One had a dark blue glass tip. Dwr lifted it up to his eye line and the surrounding snow warped blue. It was spectacular. Coloured glass wasn't unheard of, but he'd never seen one himself. It was believed they held a mystical power. His wife had searched for some her whole life.

The other one was opaque and pink, and creamier than glass. He'd seen this stone before, but where? He thought about it.

Inside Tilly's repository! There was a container filled with these coloured rocks, but what struck Dwr most was his clann's familiar flaking style. Although the cuts differed slightly, Dwr surmised the technique used to make these arrowheads would have been similar to Clann Fianna's flawless dexterity.

Sharp edges, polished surface, and soft to the touch . . . A sudden change in colour threw Dwr off. The stone went from vibrant pink to dark purple under his thumb, and he dropped the projectile. This truly was the stuff of Gods, and it unsettled him.

He put them away, and crawled across the snow, tugging his damaged leg, and a soft flutter tickled his hand. Sticking out of his thick hide was a carved bone dart. A few inches higher and it would have pierced his skin. The feathers' frosted tips shimmered like a rare kakhawk's tail. He hadn't seen such a bird in a long time, but even more impressive was the ability for anyone to aim with any accuracy in this type of weather.

Not to mention launching a dart from that distance was impossible, unless they'd infiltrated the village, but where? He peered around the corner and had a clear view of the trees behind the watchtower. Dwr could've sworn he'd seen the snowy branches and bulging conifers move.

Birds? It was hard to tell, and Dwr cursed the flat grey sky. No, those were humans, warriors, climbing up the fortifications, leaping from tree to tree like that woman he had seen this past night!

Intrigued, Dwr pushed further in towards the village centre. At least a dozen warrior-birds, or marauders, cascaded down the large conifers. They were flying like pine squirrels and escaped behind the village ramparts.

Swept up by the action, Dwr had ventured into the village square, exposed. Too late to turn back, he limped towards the King's Hall gripping his leg, unsure what to expect. There was a link between these marauders and Eira's disappearance, and Dwr wanted to learn more.

Inside the barracks, the room was dark. A few men stood watching the King crush some poor soul's head into the ground with his foot.

Goosebumps prickled the back of Dwr's neck. The person had the same greyish-white attire as the woman who abducted Eira, but it was hard to see anything in the obscurity. Dwr stumbled to the front just as Myron burst inside. "They're gone!" The young man shouted.

Surprised, Dwr eyed Myron from head to toe. He didn't have a single arrow in his body.

"Not everyone," King Lorcan said, looking up. His gaze fell on Dwr. "You?" the King shouted. "Hold him!"

Pietr, the giant warrior next to Dwr, grabbed him by the shoulders, and Dwr yelped with pain. His knees quivered, and a flash of heat warmed the back of his neck.

"I shot him down, my Lord." Myron boasted, and pushed the giant to the side as he took his place next to Dwr.

"Good lad. I didn't think anyone could catch this trapper. You've gone soft on me, Dwr." The King removed his foot from the person's head and pulled off the captive's mask. The lad's white-blond hair stood out from the crowd, and for a moment Dwr thought he recognised the kid. Everything from his long face to how he carried his triangular shoulders over his slender frame felt familiar.

Shocked, Dwr uttered: "Yona?"

The blond warrior did a double take, and a flash of memories flooded Dwr's brain. The young lad looked every inch like a brave warrior from his past, but how was that possible? That man had died fighting Lorcan fifteen years ago. Dwr's knees weakened again, and Myron steadied him.

Overwhelmed, Dwr was too slow to stop the young marauder as he lunged, and grabbed the feather dart from his hand. The Yona-looking boy plunged it into his neck, and seconds later foam spewed from his mouth, and he died.

Everyone, except the King, stared at Dwr with disbelief. "Leave me with him." King Lorcan's quiet manner weighed on everyone like a heavy blanket.

Warriors whispered and mumbled as they dragged the body outside, and soaked the room with light, but as the door closed, the King disappeared in the darkness.

Momentarily blinded, Dwr heard him move. His clothes swept against his chair of skulls as he stumbled towards them. The King's bulky silhouette re-emerged as Dwr's eyesight adjusted to the two low-lighting torches hanging off the wall. The mad King's hysteria disturbed Dwr. This was more desperate than his normal blood-lust, and the level of danger escalated up a notch. "Did you come here to kill me?" he asked, breath reeking of firewater.

Dwr realized how it looked. "No, one of them shot me down." Dwr pointed at the arrows sticking out of his leg. "They meant the dart for me, but they missed, and hit the thick leather hide."

The King nodded, a conspicuous look on his face. "Boy," he said to Myron, "where did you find our trapper?"

"Up the steppe," Myron replied, "I found him escaping in Ols'Hallow Head on ancient abandoned trails. He was alone."

"Did you think you could run from me?" The Madman's voice was barely a murmur. "I might've been persuaded to spare your life had you not involved Eira, but you poisoned her against me. That I cannot allow, not when I'm so close."

"I wasn't running." Dwr's brash reply was in part due to the pain, but also the desire to stick it to this lunatic that had savagely killed his loved ones. It felt like a day of reckoning, and Dwr was happy to die protecting Eira if it came to it.

Myron whispered. "What are you doing, old man? Shut your mouth!"

The King scrunched his face inches from Dwr's. "In the name of Kh . . . Kh–aõs, you'll tell me where the bitch is hiding, or I swear I'll gut you like a boar." The strain in his voice felt worse than a full–blown meltdown, but Dwr didn't waver.

"I don't know where she is." A hint of a pleasure curled the corner of Dwr's mouth. What he was truly saying was 'I won't tell you'.

The King's eyes bulged from his skull, and a blue vein popped in the middle of his forehead.

An empty space on the far wall caught Dwr's attention. He didn't know why at first, but the hairs on his arms stood up. His brain connected the dots just as King Lorcan swung the missing battle-axe in the air.

Without warning Myron pushed Dwr out of the way and screamed. "Move."

Both of them escaped with inches to spare, but the King came in for another blow. "I kn . . . kn–ew you were going to join her. Tell me where Eira's hiding!"

"Bastard!" Dwr shouted and shot his arms up to protect himself from the second attack. His shoulder spiked with pain, and his knees buckled. Dwr struggled to hold back the King's blow, but his bad arm couldn't compete against King Lorcan's brute strength. Dwr grunted. "I'd rather slit my throat than tell you where she is . . . You'll never see that child!"

King Lorcan's cheeks jiggled with fury. Spit drizzled from his chin. He looked insane, but Dwr held steady despite the spinning stars of pain.

Suddenly, the Ol' Bull released the pressure from his weapon, and Dwr fell back, out of breath.

After a deep sigh, the King wiped his chin, and the folly from his eyes. "T . . . T–ime for you to reacquaint yourself with the pit, I think? We'll start with five minutes and see how brave you are when you can't feel your balls." The words spilled from the King's mouth like crumbs.

CHAPTER 10

———Ignis Fatuus———

Stripped of his clothing, this wasn't Dwr's first taste of the dreaded pit, but considering the extent of his wounds and extreme fatigue, he didn't think he'd survive for very long.

To die of hypothermia wasn't the worst form of torture. Dwr could think of ten different ways to die that inflicted far more pain, but death wasn't the King's goal.

The pit was an effective measure to wither down a person till they cracked, but really Dwr had nothing to say. He didn't know where Eira was hiding, and as he prepared for his final lap, he was grateful for that small blessing. Wherever she was, it was safer than here.

Myron paraded him through the village as was customary, but no one dared show their faces. The village was under lockdown. No one was safe, not until they found Eira. Even the brash soldiers guarding the village appeared stiffer than usual. Anything to stay away from the mad King's rampage.

The only people brave enough to venture outside were the prisoners. A mish-mash of various clannsfolk, and some of the last remaining survivors of the Clann Fianna, they trickled out of the roundhouse and watched Dwr limp to his death. They lowered their gaze, but Dwr sensed disappointment more than a show of solidarity, and who could blame them? He had abandoned his people, again. Soon they'd be free of him for good, and it suited him fine. They were better off without him, and the idea of reuniting with his son and wife is what he'd wished for these past years. His last thoughts were for Gretchen and Eira, and he prayed for their well-being.

By the time Dwr reached the pit, the cold stung all parts of his body till everything burned. He prayed to EKöh for a swift death.

"You told me you saw Eira, why didn't you say anything to the King?" Myron asked. "You looked so determined to get her back."

Dwr's teeth chattered. "Isn't this what you wanted?"

"You didn't try to save yourself," he replied, skirting around the question.

"Is it so . . . h . . . h–ard . . . to believe I'm not . . . a m . . . m–onster?" Dwr's muscles spasmed for heat. He could hardly walk, or talk.

"Yes!" Myron spat. "I'm not saying I believe your whole 'trying to be the hero' bullshite, but it didn't seem right to kill you, at least not because of me. This, the pit, is on you."

Dwr stuttered to get the words out. "Is that w . . . w–hy you pushed me out of the way? To clear your conscience?"

Myron didn't speak as they approached the few warriors waiting for them near the pit. "M . . . M–yron," Dwr said. "Th . . . Th–is is not your fault, lad." The last thing Dwr wished before dying was to begrudge another soul. This kid was far too young and foolish to live with that sort of guilt and pain. "Make sure she's taken care of."

Myron shot Dwr a surprised look.

Pietr, the giant warrior, greeted the pair. "Well, if it isn't our local hero." Dwr kept his head low. He was in for a bruising. "I bet you're hoping the High King took notice? Proud little shite. Think you're better than us?"

Stunned that they were heckling Myron and not him, Dwr listened.

"I didn't know trees could speak," Myron spat back.

The warriors hooted mockingly in response to Myron's blatant arrogance. Even Dwr couldn't believe the boy's defiance against the massive man.

Pietr moved forward, balling his large fist. "This tree'll knock your teeth out if you don't shut your mouth. You won't be able to speak for a moon."

"Yeah?" Myron shrugged, and pulled out his blade lightning fast, pinning it against the warrior's throat. Not even Dwr saw it coming. Pietr's buddies fell quiet.

"I wonder how you'll manage with a knife sticking out of your gullet, or eye—sometimes my aim is piss poor. Isn't that right, Dwr?" Myron said, gesturing to the prisoner. "I was aiming for his head and got his shoulder."

Pietr's cheek muscles bulged.

"Come on, I'm waiting." Myron stuck it a little deeper.

The giant backed off. "I'd steer clear of the shadows if I were you."

Myron tucked his weapon into his belt. "Sure, I'll do that while I'm standing next to the High King giving you orders." A mischievous smirk hung on his lips, and he looked even more boyish. "Do you think you can handle the prisoner?" Myron said, and pointed to Dwr.

Arrick, the dark-haired warrior, looked Dwr up and down and tossed him in the pit.

Dwr smashed his skull into a heap of frozen bodies and stared down at a dead man's milky gaze. He landed on his bad leg and groaned.

The men chuckled. "Yup, we can handle him just fine," one of them said.

"King Lorcan expects him back alive in two minutes." Myron left them to their task. "We'll be waiting in the Hall."

Pietr shouted: "Enjoy it while it lasts, Runt."

Dulled by the cold, Dwr took shelter from the wind in a corner behind a stack of bodies.

"There's nowhere to hide, traitor," Pietr shouted, but Dwr ignored him. The walk through the village had caused the worst damage. Hypothermia had kicked in, and Dwr couldn't feel his extremities, his heart rate and breathing had slowed, and he succumbed to sleep.

Semi-conscious of his whereabouts, Dwr couldn't tell up from down. The world was askew and fuzzy. Torches lit the way to freedom as the Gods welcomed him. Surely, he had entered the gloomy Gates of Meernyx. It didn't matter so long as he was dead, but upon hitting the hard ground with his body, Dwr's senses told him it wasn't over.

"Dwr, can you hear me?" King Lorcan's blurry face hovered somewhere in the background. The smell of roasting boar tickled his nose, and Dwr moaned.

"Dwr?" The King spoke with urgency. "Where are you hiding her?" The muskox-thick, gravelly voice rolled off his tongue like fat in Dwr's ear. "Tell me, and all this can stop."

"He won't survive another round, my Lord."

"Myron?" Dwr croaked. "Is that you?"

"Bring this man a blanket, and some ale," the lad ordered.

"I can't see you." Dwr said to him. "Come closer."

"Dwr, do you understand where you are?" Myron asked.

"I can't feel anything."

"Your body's shutting down." Myron said, squeezing Dwr's hand. "Tell him what you told me. Tell him you saw her in the woods."

"No Myron, Eira was never there, and you can tell that bastard I'll be waiting for him in Meernyx."

The King must've been nearby, because the room shook as he bellowed. Two guards dragged Dwr back to the pit, the hard snow grating his knees.

Dwr didn't know how many times the King had pulled him from the pit, but when he woke up again, the last place Dwr expected to find himself was inside Tilly's quarters with Neve tending him.

His whole body ached, and his fingers were the size of large meat sausages. "Shh, you're safe," she said, her voice like a breeze in the wind.

Nothing could've prepared him for the sense of devastation that took over when he realized he hadn't died. Did the afterlife not want him? The world didn't need him anymore, there was no reason to stay. So why was he still drawing breath?

BOOK 3

The Untold Prophecy

CHAPTER 11

Conjure

Dozens of torches flickered with a burnish glow against the cave's glassy surfaces, creating at first glance a deceptive sense of warmth, but the fire's true purpose revealed the sinister nature of the stone chamber.

Carved into the ceiling were EKöh and Irïs, the divine lovers forming the circle of life and death. Their stoic expression was neither loving nor menacing as Irïs reached down from the bedrock, and EKöh reached up, breaking the barrier between worlds, holding opposite corners of a stone altar as though depositing a gift from the netherworld.

Eira recognised Tempest's breath curving the bedrock ceiling. She followed the source of the wind to the deity's large face protruding from a corner. Swollen with air, the

Goddess's cheeks were round as she contracted the hard ridges in her face to blow with all her might.

"My child," her mama's voice resonated inside the grotto chamber.

"Mama, where are you? What is this place?" Eira cried.

"Don't be frightened, my darling," the voice whispered. "I won't let them take you. I will do everything in my power to protect you, my Love, anything to keep you safe. This is the only way to stop the Grimnìr from spreading. We must prevent the communion, and stop the transmutation. You will never be a Grimnìr. Do you understand? You will never inherit the dead. You'll never become the daughter of Ny, or know her powers, but take comfort, my child. You're a Sidhe, and that is your greatest strength. You're a survivor."

Sidhe, Eira mused? Her palms turned sweaty. 'No, they're daemons', she wanted to scream. Eira grabbed her head. Something's not right. She wasn't a Sidhe, and certainly not a Grimnìr.

"Listen to me" the voice said, "you're a conduit between worlds, you're the key to their freedom, and the Grimnìr priests and priestesses will kill you if they cannot control you. They won't protect you. It's a lie. They'll use you till nothing's left, and you won't be my little girl anymore. We're parasites. I see that now, and I love you too much to let them change you."

"No, Mama. What are you doing?" Eira searched the room, but inside the grotto, the ugly Grimnìr creatures wrenched themselves free from the cave walls.

Chimæra, the She-Goat, was breaking out of her stone prison, her head and shoulders sticking half-way from the rock, while her sister, Drakaina the Dragonness, punched her way to freedom with her spindly horns. They were two of the most fearsome gatekeepers of the Daïs, home to the plains of Indra and Sun Goddess Irïs.

Next to them was the wild and violent SetaCha, daughter to Tempest, and EKöh's three-headed hound Cerberus. Each beast more powerful than the next. But it was the Goddess Ny's She-Wolf, Ylva, clawing her way out of the bedrock that rattled Eira's core. A connection between the wolves and Ylva pounded inside Eira's head. Barks and growls punctuated Eira's brain. The She-wolf's long snout and sharp teeth protruded from the darkness and awakened a wildfire that Eira feared would consume her.

Her mama rushed through the details. "Trust me," she said.

An invisible force suddenly flattened Eira on her back, pinning her arms and legs. Strapped to the altar, she screamed, but someone took her hand.

"Don't touch me," Eira cried, but familiar green eyes stared back at her. She was the most beautiful woman Eira had ever seen. "Mama?"

Styled into a crown atop her head, the woman's salt-and-pepper hair was brazen, like a Queen. Her eyes were brilliant against her dark skin with a fierce tattoo covering part of her face, but for all her beauty, the tall woman was too thin. It made her cheekbones stick out, and her eyes sunken. Worry lines cradled her stern gaze, but Eira saw nothing but love and devotion in her smile, and it soothed her.

"I'm here," Mama said. Eira hoped to hold her gaze, but the woman turned her attention towards the end of the altar.

Out of the obscurity, a wolf emerged. It shimmered like heat above a fire, and his green eyes glowed. They'd met before. His pungent fur was grey and wiry. It walked over Eira on the altar, but the beast was weightless and bowed its head as a vow to protect her. Eira sensed they were one of the same and instinctively called him 'Wynnston'.

The wolf raised its long neck and out of nowhere struck her, plunging his teeth into Eira's cheeks. A burst of cold spread across her face and up her nose.

The impact scared Eira awake, and she fell out of bed scrambling to get away, but she couldn't outrun the freezing jetstream blanketing her face. It rushed inside her brain with a mounting pressure as if her skull would burst.

Eira's hands rushed to her head to contain the explosion, but her arms slammed against her face. They prickled and burned the same as her feet.

What was happening?

The blinding pain stabbed the back of Eira's head and eyes as she crawled on the floor, grasping for anything to pull away from the danger.

Her insides turned to mush as sharp pins and needles dug into her flesh. She tried ripping off the linens covering her hands, but her arm caught something in the air. She pulled focus on her surroundings, and there standing in front of her were three large wolves.

The alpha Eira recognized as Wynnston, and next to him was Alisdair. He nestled his wide snout under Eira's arm as if he was trying to get her to stand. His yellow eyes stood out against his black fur. He was leaner, but just as muscular as Wynnston, and commanded strength and courage.

The little one, although Daorihn wasn't small by any means, had a foolish young'un aura about him. His blue eyes shone crystal clear, almost translucent, and he had the most spectacular black threading at the root of his silver-white fur. He was clumsy and full of bounce. Unlike his brothers, Daorhin hadn't come into his own yet, but what he lacked in authority he made up for in gentleness.

"Eira, my name is Fòdla." An old woman with soft flowing white hair materialised, and the wolves vanished where they stood. "I'm here to help," she said, "do you understand me?" Eira scuttled back, and cried for help, but it was like spitting fire. Her throat was raw and dry.

"Levi, get in here. Levi?" Fòdla screamed.

A deformed, hunchback man with googly eyes rushed into the room. "What's wrong with her?" Eira heard him say in a deep voice.

"I don't know. Hold her while I get something to calm her nerves."

The man grabbed Eira's arms. "What about the baby?" Levi asked.

The baby? Eira squirmed, but the hunchback man's grip was firm.

Fòdla forced the warm liquid inside Eira's mouth, and it tasted bitter. Heaviness in the limbs took hold shortly afterwards, and the old woman's voice sounded further and further away. "You've suffered extensive frostbite, but you'll be fine. You're home."

CHAPTER 12

Mother

Eira heard a soft noise drone in the distance. The relaxed vibrations caressed her thoughts, pulling her from her deep slumber. She listened as high-pitched inflections punctuated the dull sounds, and turned into harsh, distinct voices.

"I've tried to understand, but enough. This is nonsense," the unfamiliar voice said.

"Ryna, I know you're acting in the best interest of our people, and you're anxious, but . . ."

"For Gods' sake, Fòdla, wipe her chin."

"Uggh! That's it. Get out." Fòdla raised her voice. "Don't you have anything better to do than harass me?" The woman had a familiar slur, but Eira couldn't quite place from whom or where she'd heard it before.

Eira tried to wipe her mouth but her arm wasn't responding. Curious, she squinted one eye open and saw the back of a blurry head pushing someone out of the room.

"This is taking too long. Our people are expecting."

"We've been over this, there's nothing I can do. I've healed her wounds, she should be up, but something's happening to her body, maybe her brain, I can't explain it. She's in and out of consciousness, as if her mind can't cope with reality."

"We're running out of time."

Fòdla replied. "What do you want me to say?"

"I'm not a patient person."

"For the love of Irïs, don't remind me."

"Four moons she's been under your care . . . Find a potion in one of those books I gave you and feed it to her, but for Gods' sake wake her up, or else . . ." There was hesitation.

Fòdla would have none of it. "Or else what? Spit it out, woman!"

"If it comes down to it, could you deliver a baby in this state?"

"Gods, Ryna, do you hear what you're saying?"

"Do you hear what I'M saying?" The stern woman exploded. "That baby is our only chance to become Grimnìr and restore our religion. Our connection to the Gods! Only then will we defeat Lorcan. If Eira doesn't make it and the baby dies, none of us will survive, and the Sidhe, our people, will die."

Rip the baby from her body? The woman was crazy, Eira thought.

"We've made it this long without the Grimnìr . . ." Fòdla grumbled.

"You call this living? Hiding underground, unable to express ourselves, unable to worship as we were taught by our Grimnìr elders?"

"You mean worship our Grimnìr elders? We might live underground, but it's shelter. We've managed to grow our food. Our people are doing well."

Ryna gasped. "How dare you? The Gods allow it, because they see our piety. They see us trying to get the Grimnìr back to their rightful place. All our good fortunes will disappear if we shun them. This is blasphemy."

"No, it's not. It's an opportunity for growth. I urge you to try it."

"You've changed. Do you not believe in our work anymore? Have you lost faith?" The woman's tone shuddered with disdain.

Fòdla took a deep breath. "Yes, when you speak of saving the baby at the cost of the mother, but I don't want to argue anymore. These potions you speak of are complex, and these books don't have the answers neatly written out. Feeding Eira has been a challenge, but through reading different source materials, and creative thinking, I concocted a fatty, carbohydrate, and protein-rich peptide leaf that dissolves on her tongue, keeping her cells hydrated and fed. So she won't die of starvation, but—"

"I don't know what you just said, and I don't care. What's happening to you?"

"If you mean thinking for myself, or having an opinion other than what's imposed on me, then there's your answer."

"We wanted the same things you and I, no?"

"Once, maybe . . ."

"I can't . . ." Ryna sounded distraught, though Eira couldn't see her face from her bed. "Look, Fòdla, I'm sorry. I know this is hard on you, and maybe I'm pushing you too hard, but if you keep talking like this, I'll lock you up. Our mission, your duty," she added with inflection, "is to the Sidhe, the Grimnìr. I need Eira to wake up, and I don't care how you do it. I thought giving you those notes from the original Sidhe would've helped, but it made things worse."

Fòdla rubbed her forehead and sighed. "These books are centuries old. Levi and I aren't over here translating stuff we already know. Half the time we're deciphering our ancestor's calculations trying to figure out what they mean. They call it 'science' and have very little to do with Grimnìr. Don't you find that odd? The peptide leaf is one of those things. It's lucky we even had the resources, or Eira and the child might've died from dehydration weeks ago. The Grimnìr didn't save her. We did."

A loud, angry huff escaped the enraged woman's mouth. "You're trying to upset me," she said. "Don't worry about resources. Tell me what you need."

"Grrr, you're not listening. It's not only the resources. Her kind—"

"Do you mean Grimnìr?" Ryna blurted out.

"Exactly, if she's Grimnìr, why hasn't she transformed? I mean maybe she's a regular Sidhe descendent like the rest of us?"

"Not this again? I forbid you to speak of such things. Eira is the Barren Mother. Her child will unlock the heavens and deliver us from Lorcan. The baby's blood will restore the Grimnìr."

"Answer this," Fòdla asked. "Why does Lorcan think Eira's blood will help him? Look at her scars. Why does she have so many? What did he want? And that's not the only thing bothering me. Nowhere in the prophecy does it say 'deliver us . . . from Lorcan'. Something doesn't add up."

Ryna's eyes widened. "Why are you losing faith now that we're so close to our goal? The prophecy has survived a thousand years, and nothing will make me doubt it. Understood?"

Eira didn't hear a response, but the tension crackled as much as the fire next to her.

Ryna continued. "Do what you can to wake her up, but do what you must to save the child in her belly. It would be a pity to lose our priestess sister, I know, but we need the child to perform the ritual. I promise, the reign of Grimnìr will rise anew, and we'll honour the Barren Mother's great sacrifice. We will revere her for centuries to come. There is no greater honour. Fulfil your duty Fòdla, or I will do it for you."

Sidhe . . . Grimnìr . . . rituals . . . Eira's gut screamed to get out of there. Underneath the archway she squinted at the old woman's silhouette. She didn't look like a daemon.

"Where are you going?" Fòdla yelled.

Ryna shouted in the distance. "You better be at the gathering Fòdla, or I swear . . ."

Eira's heart fluttered. Fòdla couldn't know she was awake.

"You can come out," the woman muttered.

Eira tensed. Who was she talking to?

"I don't think I've ever heard you speak to Ryna in that manner," a deep voice said from behind.

"You know what, Levi? I'm an old woman, and I'm tired. Eira and the baby aren't pawns in an unfulfilled prophecy. At least not to me."

"I know," Levi said, "but . . . Ryna's right, we need to have faith. What's going on with you?"

Eira heard Fòdla stoke the fire next to her. "Oh Gods, not you too. Blind faith can only take you so far," she said. "If you think about it, this is how we got into this mess. We blindly followed the Grimnìr to the point of our own decimation. Living underground these past twenty years, fending for ourselves, has taught me more about myself than my forty years following the Grimnìr."

"She hates it when you say things that might rob people of their beliefs," Levi said.

"She can go to Meernyx hell," Fòdla snapped.

"You don't mean that. Everyone's frustrated and on edge, but some part of you must still have hope. How else can you explain after all these years to have Eira here, and pregnant? The prophecy is being fulfilled. That has to mean something."

Eira squinted. Fòdla was standing nose to nose with the twisted man. His back was curved, and rounded at the top, forcing him to slant forward. Many people had malformations, but this was one of the worst cases Eira had seen.

"Until recently we didn't even know she was the Barren Mother, and it's not like we haven't tried," she said as she took a breath, desperate for approval. "You were there when Ryna and I tasted Eira's blood. Did it work? No! Is it too hard to believe that maybe she's not the one? How much more can she endure? I see your affection for her. Do you want me to cut her up and take the child?"

Levi was quiet, and shook his head.

"I didn't think so, but you're too afraid to say anything. Well, I'm not. The Grimnìr died with their secrets, Lorcan made sure of that, but instead of praying and hoping for Eira to perform some mysterious miracle, why don't you ask why her gene remapping hadn't happened? She's a full-grown adult, and Grimnìr powers manifest around the age of eight or ten, fifteen at the latest. Why doesn't she have a single ability?

Fòdla nodded in agreement. "It's strange, and while we're at it, isn't it curious that in all our textbooks, notes, not one person refers to the prophecy? They've detailed everything else, why not that? It doesn't add up. We've had a few conversations, and I know you agree with me to some extent. Where are all the Grimnìr notes? The century-old sacred rituals that might've helped us defeat Lorcan? Why was nothing written? Some of them were Seers, for Gods' sake, didn't they see him coming?"

Eira listened with great interest, and although the old woman's words seemed to make sense, and was defending Eira like no other had ever done before in her entire life, Eira had no desire to engage. The only thing she wanted to do was get out of there as quickly as possible.

Echoes of people chanting interrupted their conversation.

"Gods, how many of these gatherings is that woman going to do?" Fòdla snapped.

"It's for morale. We should head to the formicary before it starts. Perhaps a prayer to Irïs will help settle all our nerves."

Fòdla sighed. "Of course, my old friend." Her urgent call to action stomped on the spark before it could ignite. "I'm sorry. You're right. I need to calm down, but let me check on our patient first."

Eira desperately wanted to open her eyes and see what was happening, but she didn't move.

There was a long silence. "Levi, come here."

Eira gently exhaled and began to breathe normally, or they'd think she was dead.

"What's wrong?" he asked.

"She's warm." Fòdla pressed her hand against Eira's forehead. "I hate leaving her."

"Quit putting wood on the fire. She'll be fine. Anyway, you won't be long. Come on, we need to go, or Ryna will lose it," Levi pleaded, as the chanting got louder.

"Fine."

A few minutes later the chanting had died down.

This was Eira's chance to escape before they came back, but the gunk in her eyes gave everything a fuzzy glare. She tried to wipe away the goo, but instead she hit her face. Her stiff muscles were heavy.

Eira flexed her arms and caught a space in her fingers where there shouldn't have been one. The last two digits of Eira's right hand were missing, and the two halves of her middle fingers on her left hand had also gone.

The flutter in Eira's heart returned, and she rested her hands on her stomach. The shock of her swollen belly was as much a surprise as her amputated fingers.

Eira rolled onto her side and heaved herself into a sitting position. Her muscles trembled under the pressure of their own weight, and she gripped the bed frame. Dizzy to the point of passing out, she tilted her head forward, waiting for the rush to pass.

The area was no bigger than a foxhole. It was a dark mudroom with dense walls that didn't reflect much torchlight.

Using the nearby rocking chair, Eira pulled herself up, but her legs crumpled and she slammed down hard on the cot. Her hand slipped against the wood frame and scraped the length of her arm. There was blood, but it didn't feel half as bad as the missing digits.

Eira climbed back onto the cot and saw cloth wrapping her feet. She closed her eyes. Her body was a raw nerve ending, the kind that kept animals twitching after they'd been slaughtered.

Once the bandages peeled off, Eira resented the black toes. No one lasted long as a cripple, but they would not be her undoing today. She bundled her foot, ignored the trepidation growing in the pit of her stomach, and hoisted herself into a standing position, letting the fleeting wisps of darkness in her vision fade.

Her wobbly knees held, but as soon as she put weight on her foot a sharp pain shot up her leg. Her saliva thickened, and her muscles shook under the strain, but she put one foot in front of the other till the pain ebbed with every step. She celebrated the small victory with one more step and painstakingly found her way to the stone wall she'd been staring at from the cot.

Upon closer inspection, the smooth surface glistened. It was wet to the touch, in stark contrast with the rest of the suffocating room.

An icy stream of water trickled on its surface, and Eira licked the stone without restraint, anything to rid the wan taste in her mouth. Her face dripped with moisture, and she enjoyed the coolness against her skin.

There were two openings on either side of Eira. Levi must've come from this little side room, she concluded, and that woman Ryna must've gone through that dark hallway. There were no twists and turns, just an endless stream of shadows broken up by pools of light cast from the torches.

It was a daunting trek, and although the corridor opened to a series of obscure rooms giving off fresh air, Eira couldn't bring herself to enter any of them. The stretches of darkness in between the pools of light made her uneasy, and the fear pushed her faster towards the next lantern. By the fourth torch, she was out of breath and needed to rest when she noticed the paint on the wall—a drawing depicting a bloody massacre.

Eira's fingers traced the Gods nestled behind their angry black clouds which blotted out the sun. EKöh was the one shouting. She recognised him by the ripples his voice made through the air. Next to him were Irïs, shining as bright as the sun, Ny, and Tempest, together throwing their spears and arrows at the humans below. The whole scene was troubling.

Eira saw the people standing below unafraid, welcoming the lightning spears with open arms. They welcomed death, waiting to get skewered.

Eira quickened her pace to the next torch, and found another illustration underneath the soft firelight, showing yet another battle scene but this time between humans and daemons, and her knees buckled.

They were the dreadful Sidhe from her past. The faceless daemons that haunted her nightmares, and the hairs on the back of her neck rose. 'The dead inherit the living' echoed in her mind.

'How can I get out?' she thought, wanting to leave this place, but there were no indications of an exit, just endless darkness.

Finally, the hallway bent into a sharp turn and the whole passage bloomed into an atrium of hallways with faded pictorials above each passage.

At the worst possible moment, when anyone could find her, Eira's eyes stung, and the bleak chamber melted into something intimate.

Torches sprouted everywhere and illuminated the bright, colourful works of art, and writings on the walls. Thrown back in time, life buzzed around her. People came and went through the tunnels, and Eira noticed a triangular pictorial above one of them, which had a circle running through the centre of each line.

"Those three circles represent the Triad of Grímnir priestesses, or priests. See, there's the Şeker with her shield to defend the people, the Seiðr with her staff to heal, and the Seer with her third eye." Eira spoke, but heard her mama's voice as the pictorial dissolved into a puddle of water. The vision ended with Eira staring back at her own reflection inside the decrepit chamber.

The dampness of the earth chilled Eira's feet. She wouldn't get far, but her fear and the desire to escape were stronger than ever.

Her green-eyed wolf emerged from the tunnel underneath the faded pictorial. "Wynnston!" Eira said, and her heart bubbled with hope.

Somehow he'd been waiting for her the whole time. Two more pairs of eyes, yellow and blue, glowed behind the alpha wolf, and all three beasts led Eira down a maze of ancient interconnecting rooms on the brink of collapse. Detailed graffiti on the walls changed appearance and style from room to room as if different people had drawn them across several lifespans.

To Eira's horror the path ended straight into a Sidhe daemon's gaping mouth. Two bulging eyes loomed over the visitors, and welcomed them to enter its dark, grotesque jaws. Trepidation bloomed in her gut. Eira knew this place.

The moisture in the domed room was thick and warm, and stranger still were deep vibrations tickling the soles of Eira's feet.

What once gleamed with a wet shine was now covered in thick moss. Irïs and EKöh both had thick vines twirling around their arms. The stone altar had a layer of soft moss running rampant across the floor, and up the walls over the Grimnìr.

Chills crept up Eira's spine. "Wynnston," she called, and heard soft whimpers within the far wall where the rumbling intensified. A thin crack ran the length of the smooth surface and opened into a narrow breach at the bottom. This was her way out. The wolves whined until she reached the other side, and a faint breeze enveloped her with hope.

By then, the hum had transformed into a crashing barrage. The thunderous rolls were so loud the baby sprang a somersault inside her belly and knocked Eira back. It was pitch black, and Eira widened her eyes, hoping to catch something when glowing blue clusters splayed out across the yawning ceiling. From what she could tell, this was the inside of a cave.

She inched forward, and the ground beneath her crumbled. She pulled back, but it was too late to stop. Her crippled fingers raked the ledge and caught the tip of a rock lodged in the ground. She latched on to the sharp point, cutting her hand, and shimmied back towards the ridge next to the stone wall. Even without seeing the cliff side, vertigo crept in, and she hugged the wall to avoid whatever had made that horrendous noise.

Covered in sweat, Eira was too frightened to move, but Alisdair showed his face at the top of the path. He encouraged her to keep moving, and she clawed her way towards him. At the top she wedged her crippled fingers inside a chiselled block, pulling herself to safety, and collapsed to the ground, but there was no time to rest.

A dot of light moved at the far end of a large room, and two women scurried, torch in hand.

"Come on, we're late," one said.

"As long as Ryna doesn't catch us," her friend replied.

Eira hoped to follow them, but she hauled her body, dragging her feet. She couldn't keep up, and the girls disappeared. It didn't help matters that the quality of the corridor in this part of the wormhole was unusual.

Mesmerised by the perfectly cut walls, and tubular string of bulbs running the length of the flat ceiling, Eira stumbled down the corridors until she was feet away from the buzz of human ramblings. Too late to turn back, a crowd of ragged humans stood at the bottom of the fortified chamber. They shushed as soon as she entered the vaulted room. In her attempt to escape she found herself in the middle of the colony inside a room that appeared to belong in the future.

"It's her!" someone squealed with delight.

Their eyes ballooned. "Our Mother, come to save us," another murmured.

A man at the front wailed. "Our Barren Mother has come to save us." He chanted, and the cauldron of people swayed, and crushed those closest to Eira.

The same man yanked her from the platform into the pit. Too weak to sustain such a violent attack of devotion, Eira surfed the sea of hands clawing and gouging her skin. "Release me from my sins, O Barren Mother. Tell me my future."

"I'm not your mother," she shrieked. Eira pried off one hand that had gripped her hair.

"She's anointed me with her blood," the woman chanted.

The mention of blood made everyone swarm, and Eira lost her composure. Fear swelled, and a whoosh of wind burst from her chest as she screamed for her wolves' help. Her loyal companions surrounded her, fighting the hordes of frightened worshippers.

CHAPTER 13

Lies

Huddled in the corner, Eira slashed the air with an iron spoke she'd grabbed next to the hearth in the mudroom. She hissed for her captors to back off, but her physical deterioration made her sluggish.

"Calm down, please," Fòdla said, holding out a bowl of steaming soup.

Eira wanted nothing to do with her or the soup. Thick bruises and scratches covered Eira's skin. She couldn't close her eyes without seeing the crazies tear her to shreds . . . even just thinking about it made her gasp for breath.

"Do you still doubt she's the one?" Levi asked, a hint of awe and admiration in his tone.

Fòdla shushed the crippled man. "This is not the time."

"Here, let me try," Levi said, and grabbed the bowl trying to get closer.

Eira growled until he backed away at a safe-enough distance. "I'm Le . . . vi . . . and this is Fò . . . la . . . ," he said, sounding out their names in one long breath. "What is your name?"

"Stay away from me, both of you," Eira blurted out. "Where's my pack? What did you do to them?"

Fòdla's eyes were perfect circles and gave Levi a worried glance. "Eira, you're tired. I promise no harm will come to you here."

There was a slight twirl in her 'r's when Fòdla spoke, similar to Tilly, but not as pronounced.

"Those people didn't mean to hurt you," Levi finished saying.

Eira pictured the mob pulling her down. "They didn't mean to?" She hadn't escaped the Mad King just to listen to more lies. Who were these two compared to him? Daemons, she thought as the room spun. "You're daemons! The lot of you!" Eira snapped. "Wynnston!" she shouted.

Fòdla threw Levi an icy glare. "Eira, you're not well, you need rest."

"Wynnston!" Eira yelled again, but the floor beneath her feet swayed, and she gripped the wall.

"You've suffered too much." Fòdla said as she tried to get closer, but Eira jabbed her poker near the woman's face.

"Whoa!" Levi stepped in a bid to grab the weapon, but Eira skirted around a chair.

"Don't come closer or I'll hurt you. I'll do it, I swear."

A fiery redhead stormed the mudroom. Her pale, freckled skin made her hair stand out like wildfire. Her jewelry was some of the finest Eira had ever seen. She wore a wide wire necklace and a bracelet to match embedded with odd metal circuitry. The same stuff the King collected from his rubbish mirrors. "After all the trouble we've gone through to get you here, and she wants to leave?" The woman scolded. "What do you think you'll do with that thing, except burn yourself?"

Fòdla frowned the moment the newcomer barged inside the room. Eira retreated further back, steadying her weapon, but the poker drooped. Her cheeks flushed with heat.

Fòdla jumped forward to catch her. "Eira?"

The next thing Eira realised she was lying on the cot, her body soaked with sweat, and Fòdla was fanning her face. "You're fine. You fainted, but Levi and I caught you before you hit the floor. I've sent everyone away, we're alone and you're safe. Nothing will happen to you. I promise."

The urge to laugh and throw up was overwhelming. Eira had crawled from one molesting cesspool right into another. "Am I your prisoner?" Her throat burned, and the strain made her voice crack.

Fòdla squeezed Eira's hand. "Oh, no, my poor dear. You're not our prisoner. I found you in the snow. You almost died."

Eira pulled away. "You're a lying daemon. Don't deny it, I saw the drawings, and I heard you and that woman talking, saying things about taking my baby . . . to save the Grimnìr."

A disheartened look pinched the old woman's face. "This isn't how I wanted your recovery to happen. I'm so, so sorry."

"Where are my wolves?" Eira slurred, trying to maintain her focus, but the woman's puzzled frown made Eira doubt herself. "Three large wolves? They're hard to miss."

Fòdla leaned in, but Eira flinched at her proximity. "I only want to check your temperature."

Eira was too weak to push back Fòdla as she checked her forehead. "Poor child, you're burning up. There are no wolves, and I'm not a daemon, none of us are. Those people are good, decent Sidhe, on the run from Lorcan, like you."

"The High King said that anyone who defies him is a daemon and a liar. The Gods chose him to free us from the Grimnir imposters. That's why he cleansed the earth of them. Only he is the rightful heir to the Gods." Eira repeated what she'd heard her whole life. "Daemon! Daemon! Daemon!" she croaked.

"Stop!" The old woman yelled.

Afraid of Fòdla's deep, authoritative voice, Eira withdrew. Thrown back into her old ways, the moment suffocated her to the point she could scarcely breathe. Wynnston's barks and growls were the loudest they'd ever been and flooded around her. Eira caught glimpses of them as they flickered and twitched about the room. They were there, but not there. She couldn't explain it.

Fòdla approached with the gentlest touch, and the beasts' disruption ceased. "I won't hurt you, please."

"Don't touch me!" Eira said grabbing her head, trying to regain some composure, and make sense of what was happening to her.

Fòdla backed away. "I only want to help."

"Then tell me why I'm here, and what you've done to my wolves? I can hear them, see them out of the corner of my eye, they're close."

"You're hurt, tired, and hungry . . . Will nothing convince you to rest?"

Eira shook her head, and searched the room for her wild beasts.

"Fine!" said Fòdla. "If I do what you ask, then you must do something for me in exchange." She reached for the bowl of soup on the small table next to the rocking chair. "Eat something."

Eira had no intention of eating that woman's poison, but nodded. The years of captivity had taught her to play along. It was easier to get what she wanted.

"Good, it's a start," Fòdla said, and handed her a steaming bowl of soup.

The clear broth had green leafy things floating in it. Eira poked at it, curious to understand why it was in the soup.

Fòdla brushed the hair out of her face, and spoke. "If I'm to tell you your story, then we must start at the beginning. What do you remember about your parents?"

Eira shook her head. There was no right way to answer. On the one hand Eira remembered nothing, and yet these past days, or months, she didn't know anymore. She had had more visions about her mother than she could count.

Saddened, Fòdla nodded. "Makes sense. Lorcan took you so young. I'm not surprised you don't remember. Before the tyrant's purge, both your parents were of the Grimnìr religion, like all Sidhe for a thousand years, but your mother Elliana came from a unique clann."

Eira exhaled. Hearing her mother's name, forgotten after so many years, made her feel warm, like she was coming home. "Elliana . . ."

"Your mother was part of the oldest clann known as Eli Dé Gecennen. A direct descendant of Ny the moon Goddess. According to Ryna, you could retrace your ancestry back to the Pogrom War. They fought the great evil that destroyed our lands, and it was your ancestors that produced the first Grimnìr priests that led us out of these tunnels. We know little of those times, but our people believe . . ." Fòdla took her time to speak. "We believe you're the Barren Mother, and your child is the coming saviour, here to open the heavens and deliver us from Lorcan so we might return to the surface."

A storm brewed inside Eira's brain. "Barren Mother?" Echoes of the people chanting her name overwhelmed her, and she fought to get the words out. "Are you saying those daemons worship me and my baby?" The idea made Eira's skin crawl. It was obscene. "Is my baby in danger?"

"Oh no, what you experienced in the formicary stems from desperation, but I assure you they never meant to hurt you or the baby, and they're not daemons."

Closed-lipped, Eira analysed the old woman's long, natty hair, and inspected her pale weathered skin. Her gentle manner encouraged trust between the two, but Eira wasn't so easily swayed. The King had warned her about the Sidhe worshippers, those that defied his rule. They were frauds. "You lie. You might have found a way to hide your gruesome, faceless appearance, but I know the truth."

"My what?" Fòdla answered with a puzzled frown.

"I told you. I saw the drawing on the tunnel wall, over there—" Eira pointed towards the door — "I've seen your noseless faces before. I know what you are. You killed my people, and Lorcan saved me."

"The tunnel wall?" The woman thought for a moment. "Are you referring to the Battle of Apostate?"

"The Battle of what?"

"The noseless daemon?" Fòdla said as if remembering something. "Do you mean Khaõs?" Fòdla grabbed a piece of coal and drew the crude face on a flat stone. "Two eyes, and a mouth?"

Exactly like her childhood nightmares, and the cave entrance from her vision. Sweat rose at the back of Eira's neck, and she nodded.

The old lady's shoulders slumped. "What you saw is the mask of Khaõs, the God of creation and destruction." Fòdla bit her lip and didn't speak for a moment. "That was Lorcan, Love," she said with care. "Lorcan and his soldiers wore the God's faceless mask during all their raids to represent a new beginning. You were so young, of course, you would remember it in a way that felt safe."

"Stop lying," Eira said, but she couldn't control the memories trickling into her brain one drop at a time. The daemons that had haunted her all these years took shape. Eira closed her eyes, but Lorcan's maniacal laugh split her eardrums. For the first time she recognized his blood-smeared teeth, and the black gaze behind the mask. Somehow she'd always known, but was too afraid to see.

"Eira, can you hear me?"

A terrible weakness took hold, and Eira's skin and bones melted into the cot. "I owed him a life of servitude, he said. One day I would repay my debt. I'm such a fool."

"You were a child. I don't know any other person to have endured so much and live to talk about it. I regret the life you suffered, and the memories that plague you, but perhaps now that you know Lorcan is the monster behind the mask of Khaõs, you might heal?" The woman said this almost as a request.

Eira threw the bowl of soup on the floor. "I don't want to heal, I want to know why? Why did he do this?"

Concern crinkled Fòdla's mouth. "I don't know. For power, resources, or maybe to crown himself High King . . . Has he ever explained why . . ." The old woman tried to finish her sentence, but gestured to Eira's many scars.

Eira shook her head. "He said my blood was the key to heaven. That one day he would control both the Gods and the Sidhe."

The old woman shook her head. "I don't understand . . . why would he think its you, if he thought you were the Barren Mother?"

Eira looked down. The shame was too much to carry.

Fòdla frowned. "He tried to break your spirit, but he didn't succeed. Your light hasn't dimmed that much, I'm sure."

"How could he have known I was the Barren Mother? How did any of you know?" Eira said.

Fòdla hesitated before answering. "We didn't. We didn't even know who you were, until we worked out the truth about your origins. At first we thought you were Grimnìr, and from what I can tell" —she gestured to Eira's scars— "So did Lorcan. That's the only reason he would have taken your blood. To become Grimnìr."

"Lorcan hated the Grimnìr. Why turn himself into one?"

Lost in thought, Fòdla nodded. "You're right. It doesn't make sense, none of it does. What am I missing?" She spoke mostly to herself.

Eira's mouth turned dry. "How long have you known I was alive? His captive?" Questions plagued her thoughts, and she spewed them out, hoping to find a decent explanation.

The white-haired woman rubbed her eyes. She looked tired—the kind of tired no amount of sleep can ease. "Lorcan came in swift and hard," she said. "At first we didn't realize he was targeting Grimnìr elders, but by the time we did there was nothing we could do. He killed every last one. To this day, no one can figure out how he outsmarted the Seers, but he knew when and where to strike, and annihilated clann after clann. After that it was easy to force his victims to pledge fealty to him or die, and in twenty years, the monster destroyed centuries of knowledge essential to the Sidhe survival, to his own survival. It made no sense. We were scattered and helpless."

"That doesn't answer my question," Eira said, and gripped the cot harder. Anger puffed her chest like before in the formicary. "How long have you known I was his captive?"

Fòdla shifted uncomfortably in her seat.

"Your mother was mysterious to say the least," Ryna said, interrupting their conversation.

Startled, Eira stiffened. This woman seemed to pop out of nowhere.

"It took a little over a year to figure out your importance, and why the King had saved you. We've been watching you ever since," she said.

Fòdla clenched her jaw. Fear rattled the old woman's eyes. "Ryna . . . you're not helping."

Eira saw the effect she had on the old woman, and calmed down.

With the quiet restored, Ryna piped up. "We've wasted enough time coddling her, Fòdla. It's time we went straight to the matter at hand."

"Did you not see what I saw at the gathering?" Fòdla uttered through clenched teeth. "This is not the time to poke—"

"This is exactly the time," Ryna interrupted. "She needs to know who and what she is. We're not your enemy, Eira, Lorcan is, and your presence here isn't for charity," she spat. "You serve a greater purpose, as we all do. Suffice to say, you're the Barren Mother, and your baby's blood is precious."

"Are you saying you left me there to suffer alone without any support on purpose? I was a child." Eira didn't hide her contempt. "Do you know how he treated me? In the beginning he just frightened me with his temper, but as the years piled on, he grew resentful, kept me tied up, and beat me so I wouldn't try to escape. What you're saying is he did all this so one day I could bear his children?" Although Eira spoke the words, they sounded ridiculous. "In all that time, he never mentioned a baby."

Ryna replied: "You weren't alone."

Fòdla's rocking chair groaned as she moved back and forth. The tension in her dry, cutting motion revealed more to Eira than words ever could.

"What?" Eira said.

The redhead nodded. "We've guided your every move. Who do you think told you about the Daïs? Tried to teach you about the Sidhe? Who planted those precious hides so you could escape?"

Eira's pulse quickened, and Fòdla cut Ryna off. "We were disorganised and dispersed. None of us realised the High King had captured the heir to Gecennen! When we realised you were still alive . . ." Fòdla's mild manner pitched even quieter. "We sent someone in . . ."

Goosebumps crawled up Eira's spine. "Please don't say it, don't . . ."

The woman's grey eyes brimmed with tears. "Tilly meant to pull you out—"

"You were much more valuable to us on the inside." Ryna finished Fòdla's sentence. "The King should've killed you, but he didn't, why? At first we thought you were Grimnìr, but you never manifested any Grimnìr abilities. We didn't understand until we connected it with the prophecy. He must've been waiting to get you pregnant."

Eira's hands had gone numb from gripping the cot.

"A Barren Mother will give birth to the coming saviour," the redhead said, "and breach the heavens. The mutation will ripple and free the Sidhe."

"Shut up, I don't give a shite about your prophecy," Eira said, hoping the room would stop spinning.

Ryna frowned. "I won't deny this isn't a shock, but we've all had to make sacrifices. Now that you're pregnant, I believe your child's blood will also restore the

Grimnìr Triad, and reunite the Şeker, the Seiðr, and you the Seer. Once again we will commune with the Gods as they intended, and we will have the most powerful weapon to defeat anyone who tries to defy us."

"Stop." Eira shook. "Stop talking . . . you're no better than the High King. That monster has kept me hostage all these years, waiting for me to bear him a child, and you sat here and watched!" Venom poured from her tongue and puffed Eira's chest. "Wynnston!" she shouted.

"Eira, please calm down. We're not your enemy, please." Fòdla urged. "We thought your Grimnìr powers would kick in. According to my notes the Sidhe children experience what's called 'gene remapping', or 'transmutation', and through this they gain access to their abilities. Before Lorcan killed them all, the Grimnìr elders groomed the new generation to become the priests and priestesses of tomorrow. Tilly meant to help you, but she said you experienced no transformation. Clearly, you have. Why have you never used your powers until today?"

"My powers?" The word struck Eira, and her rage slowly melted. "What are you talking about?"

Ryna's eyes sizzled with excitement. "Back in the formicary, something extraordinary happened. I've never heard of any Grimnìr able to do what you did. How did you make the room grow dark and cold like the night and grumble with hunger? No doubt you're the Sacred Vessel, and your power is derived from the Goddess Ny and her moon, like your mother. You're a Seer, and . . ." Ryna hesitated. "I overheard you speak of wolves. Can't you see? It's all connected. You are Ylva the She-Wolf." Ryna performed the ritualistic cross on her person.

Trepidation bloomed in Eira's chest. Her heart beat too fast, it was difficult to pay attention. "What?"

It was Fòdla's turn to talk. "The Seiðr is a healer."

Eira appreciated Fòdla's softer tone, but still the room spun faster.

The woman continued. "The Şeker is a warrior at heart driven to protect, she takes her power from Irïs the sun Goddess, but the Seer can see into the past and the future to interpret the present. I suspect these wolves are a form of vision. Other than these creatures, have you had any other visions?"

It was all too much to take in. "I . . . I can't . . ."

"It can be anything," Ryna finished. "A glimpse of something you didn't understand, perhaps?"

Eira had had too many to count. It was a relief to know she wasn't losing her mind, but she didn't trust either of them. Both Ryna and Fòdla suddenly looked like children waiting to hear a story. "Stop!"

Thick worry lines creased the skin between Fòdla's eyebrows. "Ryna, my patient needs to rest. Maybe we can take this up again later. I suggest you really leave this time. I'm sure your people need an explanation." Her voice pitched so low that even Ryna didn't dare argue, and turned to leave, but not before giving Eira a distrustful grin.

"Do you still want the soup?" Fòdla asked with a tired sigh. She headed towards the hearth to ladle a bowl and grab a piece of crusty foam.

Despite Eira's earlier resistance, the rousing smell gouged a hole in her stomach. "What's that?" she asked as bits of brittle crumbs fell to the ground.

"It's bread, and tastes delicious with soup," Fòdla replied with a hint of hope.

"The bread Tilly makes—" Eira stopped short of finishing her sentence. That this whole time Tilly could've helped more than she did left Eira miserable.

"No, I suppose Tilly couldn't use the same ingredients. She was limited in Llyr and did the best she could. Here, we use a natural leavening agent that makes the bread puff."

Irresistible warmth emanated from Fòdla when she spoke of Tilly. "She's your friend?" Eira asked.

"We grew up together . . . we haven't seen each other in years." Eira watched Fòdla lose herself in a memory. "Right!" The woman snapped out of her trance. "Eat, before your soup gets cold."

"It's different, the soup, I mean. Tilly's is thick and meaty. What are these green things?"

"It's a vegetable. We grow our food in these large tubs without sunlight with very little water in old agroponic storages we found below. Try it with a piece of the bread."

Eira nibbled the foam, and to her surprise it was good.

"The dough's made from fungi powder and ground cricket flour. You'll find more insects at these depths underground hiding from the cold." The white-haired woman fell silent for a moment. "I don't always agree with how Ryna does things around here. I know it's a lot to take in, even for me. A few hours ago I thought you were dying, and now look at you." Lost in thought, Fòdla rambled on. "Maybe I was wrong . . . about everything . . ."

"What do you want from me?" Eira said in between mouthfuls. This was a good time as any to figure out if the woman was lying.

"I want you to eat and rest." Fòdla lowered her voice to a whisper. "I'll admit to you, and you alone. Your presence after all these year fills me with hope, but you must've overheard . . ." She stopped her sentence short as if she hesitated to say more.

So far Fòdla had proven to be a sore in Ryna's back, but that didn't mean she was trustworthy. "If I'm to believe you, then not only am I a daemon, but the Goddess Ny's She-wolf, a Grimnìr."

"We're not daemons." Fòdla snapped.

Eira pursed her lips tightly together and breathed to conceal her doubt.

"I'm sorry, I'm a little tired I suppose."

Eira swallowed her mouthful. "Tilly called the daem . . . uh . . . them, Syn . . . tropic Identifica . . ."

"Yes, Syntropic Integrated Design Human Enhancement," Fòdla said in one long breath. "Sidhe for short.

Those were one of the first things I learned from the old notebooks."

"Tilly had never explained it. What does it mean?"

"We're not sure," she said reaching for Eira's empty bowl. "Your pack," the old woman said changing the subject, "how long have they been with you?"

To open up was a challenge, let alone to a stranger. Discouraged by her lack of options, Eira put her head in her hands and a whirlwind of emotions stirred. Daorhin's spunk and playfulness burst her insides. Her head screamed no, but her instincts said to trust Fòdla. "Not long," Eira said, "they first appeared when I fled Llyr. Now you're saying they're not real."

"Oh no my dear, I think they're very real. What happened back in the formicary was powerful. It was as if you commanded the air in the room, and it flattened everyone out of the way. An invisible force compelled your body to move in such a way like nothing I've seen."

Eira didn't remember it like that. One minute she was afraid and the next a burst of energy sprung from her, leaving her weak. She didn't remember how she had escaped. "What happened?"

"You collapsed, and Levi brought you here. Your wolves, what do they do when you see them?"

"I dunno. They help me. I feel strong when they're around."

"I've never heard of anything like this, but then again I'm no Grimnìr expert. I'll read up and see what I can find, but until we learn more, you must stay off your feet.

When I found you in the forest, you were in premature labour, and if you exert yourself too much, you could lose your child."

Guilt overwhelmed Eira. "I was so desperate to escape for the baby's sake, I never thought I could harm the child."

"You did what you thought was right, but the strain is too much. Luckily, you appear stronger than most, and on the road to recovery."

The longer Eira sat with Fòdla the more comfortable she felt. "Can I ask you something?"

"Anything, always." Fòdla gave her reassuring nod.

"What does barren mean?"

Fòdla raised her eyebrows with hint of a smile.

"I know I'm foolish, never mind."

"No, don't apologize. It's refreshing to be honest. These are dark times, and your question is humbling. It means your womb shouldn't be able to carry a child."

"Why?"

Fòdla got up from her chair and stretched her legs around the room to peer down the hallway. "Once a child transforms into Grimnìr that child grows up never able to reproduce. According to my notes it has something to do with gene remapping, your body transforms on a molecular level, or something like that. Grimnìr elders preached to us that the Gods made it so Grimnìr were sterile to preserve the body's purity, but they're all dead so we'll never know."

Eira was confused at first. "You don't trust the Grimnìr?"

The old woman smiled. "No . . . I do. They've guided us for centuries. They helped us out of these caves, and re-built the world, but sometimes I wonder why all the secrecy . . ." She took a deep breath. "Bah, don't listen to an old rambling woman."

"I . . ." Eira's hesitation prompted Fòdla to reach out, but she stopped herself.

"You can trust me," she said.

"It's just the King said the same thing about Grimnìr. He didn't trust them either."

Lost in thought, the old woman straightened her clothing. "Huh . . . The world is a peculiar place, isn't it? I get the feeling that's not what's bothering you, though?"

Eira swallowed the ball lumping in her throat and blurted out. "Are you sure I'm Grimnìr?"

"How else do you explain what you did in the formicary?" Fòdla said.

"I don't know what I did, but what I remember is a need to protect my child at all cost, and my wolves appeared."

"Let me ask you another way. What makes you think you're not?" Fòdla said, peering for unwelcomed intruders. This conversation was not for Ryna's ears, and the woman seemed to turn up when she was least wanted.

"I might've had a vision . . ."

Fòdla tilted her head. "You realize how that sounds, right?"

"I know, but this is different than the wolves. I get these flashes—"

"Spit it out."

"It was my mother telling me she would do anything to stop me from transforming. I think she did something to me, to my face," Eira said, touching her cheek where Wynnston had bit into it.

The grey-haired woman scratched her earlobe and stared into space. To Eira she seemed worried. "Say something."

"I'm rarely left speechless. Have you had more than one vision?"

Eira nodded.

"Not just about wolves?" Fòdla asked.

"No," she said, the alarm plain to hear.

Fòdla sighed and pinched the brim of her nose. "I want us to go through every single vision once you're feeling better. Maybe it was just a dream, because whatever your mother did, it didn't work."

"There's more," Eira said.

Incredulous, Fòdla stared wide-eyed.

"The more I think about it the less I'm sure. You and Ryna said the King wanted to impregnate me. It makes sense, I guess, but right before I escaped, when Tilly told him I was pregnant, he wasn't relieved, he looked surprised."

"That's no wonder. After all these years of waiting for the chosen one, it seems like a normal reaction to me."

"No, you don't understand. It wasn't like that. It shocked him like he didn't believe I was pregnant."

Fòdla peered down the hall. "Uh-oh, Ryna's on her way back." The old woman threw herself at Eira's feet. "Listen to me, say nothing. I'll research my notes, and we'll figure this out together, but no one can know, not yet. Ryna's desperate, and I'm afraid of what she might do."

BOOK 4

The Book of Suffering

CHAPTER 14

Truth

Dwr wondered if he wasn't losing his mind. He would too, he thought sighing internally, if he had to listen to Tilly tear into him one more time. Condemned as a traitor to the Clann Llyr for aiding Eira's escape, the King had shackled him in the servant quarters under guarded supervision while they nursed him back to health. But the woman's endless rants hummed in his ears day and night. It was her favourite pastime since they'd brought him here. She had nothing better to do than berate him.

"Your selfishness has put our lives in jeopardy," she said, wrapping his leg wound so tightly her arms flailed over and under his leg, flapping like a bird. "What did you say to him? He won't listen to reason."

Since his stint in the frozen pit, Dwr's health had deteriorated. It was quite a shock to still be alive. Dwr had fully intended to die and leave the King in doubt as to Eira's whereabouts. He had no great secret to reveal in his hypothermic delirium, so he couldn't imagine what he might've said that spared his life. One thing was certain; he wasn't alive out of the King's kindness.

Much of Dwr's downward spiral had to do with the empty cot next to him. In his delirium, Gretchen had died alone. He replayed their last moment together. He couldn't close his eyes without seeing her face up close, her last breath a declaration of love. Although he could never return that same affection, he valued her friendship.

Eira and Gretchen's taunting ghosts made it impossible to sleep. Reduced to an emaciated skeleton, the days had blended into weeks. What did he give either of them in return? Dwr groaned. Nothing but grief is what he gave.

Tilly raised an eyebrow. "Mumbling to yourself again? Do you realise the damage you've caused, and the people you've hurt?"

A large knot in the wood above the door that led into the prison quarters served as a distraction. There was a crack the length of Dwr's finger where Tilly had hung a flourish of tree branches heavy with relics.

Dwr focused on the jumble of artefacts, hoping to drown out Tilly's voice. It contained the usual pieces of brittle rubber, rusted tin forks, and tin cylinders, and metal tabs, though no one understood their purpose. There were plenty of tiny bone fragments, and at least a dozen small plastic bottles filled with more dried leaves. On the shelves, he investigated the bowls bursting with winter flowers that grew under the snow, but he paid close attention to the interesting jar full of pink rocks that changed colour. These rocks kept showing up. This woman and her secrets . . .

"Ouch," Dwr said flinching. "Does the bandage need to be so tight?"

Tilly looked up and glared. "He speaks!"

Exasperated, Dwr roared. "Will you shut up?" he blurted. "Godsdamn, I'm sick of hearing what a bastard I am. What more do you want from me? I was ready to die," he said pushing Tilly away to grab his leather trousers on the chair.

"Don't play the martyr with me, you ignorant arse! That's what pisses me off the most. People like you only consider your feelings, your needs and screw everybody else. If you hadn't pursued Eira that night like I warned you not to, even after I trusted you to tell you everything, King Lorcan wouldn't have had any kind of lead."

"I screwed up, I know, but you're a fool to think that Lard would've given up his search for Eira, especially if what you say about her is true. He knows her importance. Why else would he have kept her around all these years?"

"It doesn't matter. You're the only leverage he needs," she mumbled.

"What more must I do to prove myself? I sit here listening to you shite on me day after day. I get it, I don't deserve Eira. People close to me get hurt. Do you think I wanted to wake up to find Gretchen dead? It's not like I know where Eira is, unlike you."

Tilly raged. "I did what I could for Eira."

"You don't deny it? Deep down you know my intention was never to put Eira in harm's way or else you wouldn't have said anything to me. You know I made a mistake, but part of me wanted to know if I was . . ." He paused, unable to finish the sentence. "It's not important anymore. She's safe, and that's what matters."

Emotions were running high, and Tilly replied with a dry laugh. "By the Gods you're stupid. I'm not worried for Eira."

That was the last dagger to the heart. Dwr lunged towards her, but there was little leeway between his shackles and the stake in the ground. Unafraid, Tilly didn't flinch.

Inches away from his wrath, she spat in his face. "If you're so smart, then tell me why would the High King spare your life? He was ready to kill you."

"He thinks I can get to Eira."

Tilly rolled her eyes. "Idiot! I warned Myron to stay away. This was too risky for him to get involved, but he didn't listen. You'll drag down the poor lad into your spiral of shame and there's nothing I can do about it. All you had to do was not get involved, and the rest would've played out the way the Gods had intended."

Those words hurt more than her insults. "Myron?" Dwr thought, confused.

Just then, the young man barged inside the servant quarters, and Tilly gawked. Myron stared at the both of them back and forth with curiosity.

"Back so soon?" Tilly said, unable to hide the bitterness. "Where's your buddy Lorcan?"

Dwr slumped back into his cot, thankful for the interruption as he wiped his face.

"Tilly." Myron's stiff nod was habit lately, but Dwr had chalked it up to some trivial disagreement. Now, he was wondering if that something wasn't him. He was only just putting it together, but if Myron had defended Dwr to the King, against Tilly's wishes, that would have repercussions.

"Where are Neve and Kit?" Myron asked with the utmost politeness.

The caretaker replied. "Picking wild roots in the forest. I'm sure they could use—"

"Dwr?" Myron cut her off. "How's your leg?" Dwr had been so preoccupied with grief that he never stopped to consider that Myron might've played a hand in saving his life. It also explained the young man's odd switch in behaviour. These past weeks, the lad visited almost every day. Short visits, no more than an uncomfortable minute or two, but long enough to be curious.

"The infection's gone, but you'd have to ask the expert," Dwr said, tilting his head in Tilly's direction.

She nodded, but Myron didn't even give her a second glance. "I'm afraid the King requests your presence. I've stalled him for as long as I could, I hoped for your full recovery, but the time has come." Myron fidgeted with his fingers. His nerves betrayed his desire to appear calm and relaxed.

"Oh, Son, what have you done?" Tilly said frantically. "Walk away."

Myron snapped: "What am I, if not a man of integrity?"

"You're in over your head. Lorcan's ruthless. He will eat you alive," she said.

Dwr interrupted their bickering. "He wants to see me now?"

Defeat crushed the young man's shoulders. "I'm afraid so."

"Myron, can we speak in private for a moment?" Tilly called.

Hypothermia had kicked Dwr's arse, and he fumbled to get dressed, pretending not to overhear their muttered talk.

Tilly spoke first. "Why? Why are you doing this? It's pointless. Eira's safe. You're free to go. Why are you stirring the pot? This won't end well."

Dwr faced Myron's back, and he thought he heard him say 'she lied to me'.

"To protect you," Tilly implored.

"My whole life I've lived by a set of rules and believed there was a right and a wrong way to do things. How do you expect me to walk away? I almost killed him."

"You feel betrayed and upset, which I understand, I really do, but stop and think. You're making irrational decisions. This is bigger than all of us. I'm begging you please take a step back and ask yourself what you will gain by protecting him. We're fighting for a future."

"Not one I'm eager to live in." Myron said dryly. "Let's go, the King's waiting for us."

Outside, an embarrassed silence seeped between him and Myron. There was so much Dwr had wanted to ask the young man, but it all felt so irrelevant at the moment.

"You look as if you're carrying the world on your shoulders," Dwr finally said.

The young lad escorted Dwr at his pace. "It feels like that sometimes," Myron replied.

"Tilly's upset with you, and I know how that feels, trust me, but if you helped me in any way, then I agree with her. You shouldn't have done that. Last we spoke you were accusing me of carnage, what changed?"

"Stop," the young man implored. "You don't know what you're saying."

"There was only ever one outcome for me, Myron. I should've died in the pit. I appreciate the kindness, but I don't deserve it, Tilly's right. My heart tells me you're protecting Eira, and that has to be enough. I'll tell the King I don't know where she is, and you can go with whatever plan you have for him. I'm smart enough to know you're working for the resistance. The less I know, the better off everyone will be."

Myron scoffed. "It's too late for that, but I promise, I won't turn my back on you or your people."

"My people?" Dwr blurted out. A strand of fear tickled Dwr's throat. "Myron, what did you do?"

"There's no time," he said as they reached the Hall. "Accept King Lorcan's demands, and we'll figure it out together. There's a lot I need to say."

They entered the Hall. "Ah, th . . . th–ere he is," the King stammered, sitting on his throne of bones.

Since Eira's escape, the Ol' Muskox had lost weight, and the madman's stutter had gone from bad to worse, to the point it was difficult to understand him. But that's not what caught Dwr's attention.

A dozen warriors each held a prisoner of the Clann Fianna at knifepoint. Dwr tried to go to them. "Don't do this, they're innocent," he said, looking at the old woman and her granddaughter. He had a special affection for the old Morella, and it broke him to see her mishandled.

"Yes, but I need you and you won't cooperate." The King whined.

"Buffoon, I don't know where Eira's hiding. Hurting my people won't change that."

The corners of King Lorcan's lips sunk like a dead fish, and the dark circles under his eyes stretched across his cheeks. He looked sick. "Yes, I've gathered as much, but I've had my best men, Myron included, tracking Eira with no success. How difficult is it to find a pregnant woman?" he belted, and his voice cracked with anger and desperation. "Then, I realized," he said his head about to pop. "You're the man for the job. With the proper motivation you'd do anything, isn't that right? In fact, it was

Myron who reminded me about the first time we met. It feels like a lifetime ago, doesn't it, Dwr? You begged me to spare your people," the King said in an amused tone, grinning at the memory. "I listened, and then killed them all. You were foolish to think I could've let such a large clann go unchecked. You would've retaliated, but here we are, fifteen years later, and I'm offering you a chance to save what's left."

"We'll find her, my Lord," Myron said.

"Tut, tut, no, you won't," the King interjected. "He will. You'll stay here with me."

Pietr strode next to Myron. A grin spread from ear to ear as he tied his foe with the rest of the prisoners. "I told you to steer clear of the shadows," the giant whispered.

Myron looked like he wanted to punch him in the face.

Dwr tried to fight back. "What are you doing?"

The King's restraint spilled over into his stutter. "Dwr, maybe you can exp . . . expl . . . tell me why Myron would spare your life? He worked hard to convince me you were worth saving, and then he started asking me all these questions about the past, and I started thinking, why?"

Dwr shrugged. "He thought I knew where Eira's hiding, but I don't."

"No, no, he reminded me that no other man is as good a trapper as you. I'd forgotten about your reputation, but how did he know? That was such a long time ago."

"I'm not that good. The kid caught up to me and shot me down with an arrow."

"Still . . ." The King said, angling his head with curiosity.

"Why are you doing this?" Dwr shouted.

"Don't blame me. This is Elliana's fault. That bitch lied to us all. She told me Eira was the key to the heavens, but this whole time she was the Mother of the Sidhe. That's why her blood didn't work . . ." The King slouched deeper in his chair.

The room was still. Everyone hung on the High King's words with bated breath. Not expecting him to swing up, a collective gasp sounded as they prepared for the worst. "I bet you're laughing at me Elliana, but I will get my hands on that child, and I will drink the blood." The King's composure unravelled. "I will rule heaven and earth."

"You're crazy!" Dwr shouted.

"Yes, yes I am." His eyes swivelled in his head. "Trapper, bring Eira back to me, or else they die."

CHAPTER 15

——— Nexus ———

A warrior escorted Dwr to the repository. Inside the hut, there were lots of weapons—old, blunted swords and spears piled on top of each other.

Dwr suited up with the typical leather hides and furs with the Llyr crest embossed on the garments. Wearing them made him cringe, but his clothes were rags, and full of blood. Whatever his plan was, he'd need to at least survive the cold.

Next, he searched for a decent sword. Nicked and dull, some of them still had blood on them, but he found something that might be lethal in a fight and sheathed it in its holster.

Finally, he swung a sling across his shoulders containing a bow and quiver. The movement stung his old wound, and he wished Tilly had wrapped it. Not that she'd help him anymore, especially now Myron was captive like the others.

The lightweight holster fitted around his torso and was perfect for tracking. He plucked the few arrows left from the bark basket and put the lot in his quiver. He'd have to make them count, he thought, hurrying outside.

Smoke billowed from the longhouses into their shallow glen and gave the frozen forest a hazy aura. Except for a few stragglers still gathering wood, the villagers were inside their longhouses weathering the oncoming storm. There was no goodbye, no fanfare as he scampered like a thief. Where to start?

He couldn't bring Eira back to this place, and that's if he could find her, but if he didn't his people risked death. Dwr didn't know what to do. He had made a promise to them.

Halfway down the hill Dwr saw a large bird flying in the sky. His jaw dropped. Aside from the more abundant ravens and crows, flying creatures were elusive under the colourless skies, but after hearing it kak there was no mistaking the brown-tailed kakhawk. He connected the missing piece with the poisoned dart. "Those were his feathers", Dwr thought.

Its neck and head shimmered ash-grey against its yellow eyes and beak, in stark contrast with the reddish-brown feathers covering its body, but it was its large black-tipped wingspan tucked with white plumage that gave it a kingly air. Masters of the sky, they were the most mysterious of all the birds of prey. The old religion claimed them as messengers to the Plains of Indra, home to the Goddess Irïs, and it left Dwr with grave doubts about his journey. This was a sign of change.

The door to the servant quarters opened, and Tilly stepped out. Her lips curled into a snarl. She wasn't happy. Exactly what she had predicted had happened, but Dwr didn't stop. There was no point. All he could do was follow the bird and hope a solution presented itself. They both knew this wouldn't end well for anyone.

Dwr thought the cold would get to him first, but it was the hunger. After losing sight of the bird, Dwr followed the only path that made sense. He retraced his steps to the night he lost Eira, but he didn't get far.

Constantly fighting against his throbbing shoulder and leg drained him of strength. The hunger made him so weak he could barely keep his head up, let alone forge a path in the deep snow.

Near the frozen sanctuary, he had noticed the distant ruinous cities near the Daïs, which had been concealed in darkness last time. Faded into the snowy background, he could just make out the eroded buildings half covered in trees and snow. These landmarks of old were everywhere, and reminiscent, his wife said, of a fitting punishment to a time when the Sidhe were godless. A time before the Grimnìr guided them towards righteousness.

He trekked deep into the gully, and Tempest's breath covered up his tracks. He needed to stop often.

Holed up in a tree's rotten stump, digging under the snow for pockets of evergreens, Dwr cursed the King's name. Frost settled on the back of his neck, and the cold front showed no signs of stopping. Lighting a fire was next to impossible under such strong winds, and he should've kept moving, but his stomach begged for food.

A full day had passed since he'd eaten the last bit of roots and pine bark. Starvation was getting the better of him, and Tempest was snuffing what little life remained.

His stints in the frozen pit had taken their toll. Neve had said he'd spent close to five days there in total. No one had endured as much and survived. Far from recovered, despite Tilly's care, the abuse to his body and lack of nutrients left Dwr thin as an arrow and weak. A deep cough overpowered his lungs and slowed his progress.

From there, the hours had dragged into days. The climate in the gully fluctuated drastically, and the temperatures dropped quickly at night, though it was nothing compared to the wet sting of humidity in his birthplace.

A gated community nestled in the vast territory of New Ysberg Headlands. The Fiannans occupied the large bluff on the Eastern ridge, which Dwr had affectionately nicknamed 'the Windy Cape'. People there spoke with a dry clip in their speech, very different to the High King's central sound.

The peninsula overlooked a body of frozen water that spanned as far as the eye could see, but the unhindered arctic winds rolling off the ice made the peninsula inhospitable and cold.

His people lived not too far on the outskirts of the cliff within a sheltered forest. This gave them the added advantage of living off land and water, and for centuries the coast was a coveted area. Fiannans fought countless invaders, but over time the regional clanns didn't bother with them anymore. A combination of harsh living conditions and increased resources across New Ysberg might've played a part, but for a time his people lived in peace, until the High King's upheaval.

Soon after Seweryna's father, Fianna's clann chief, passed away, Dwr cut off all contact with the outside world and banned his people from the yearly visit to Llyr market. Rumours the new King was ransacking tribes spread, and Dwr wanted no part.

These quarrels didn't involve them, he said. Dwr never dreamed the fight would reach his doorstep, but his wife's concerns grew when it became clear the High King targeted the Grimnìr. She argued it was his duty to fight for what was right, and his lack of courage would be the Fianna's downfall, but she was wrong. It wasn't a lack of courage that stayed his hand. His wife gave up too much for her faith, and to ask Dwr to sacrifice his family and friends was unreasonable.

For Dwr, being a Sidhe was part of life, like hunting, making love, and taking care of your children, but the Grimnìr religion wasn't life. Dwr didn't understand much about priests and priestesses save for the fact that their word was law, and that was enough—the shrouded mysteries of the Grimnìr didn't concern him. At least not until he'd lost everything.

Hunger pulled Dwr from his hole. If only he had the strength to hunt, he thought, but he was too sluggish. The animals would hear him coming.

Well beyond the point where the marauders abducted Eira. Dwr clunked through the changing landscape. Craggy hills and razor-sharp rocks warped the forest floor, but there were no traces left of Eira, like she'd never existed.

The seemingly virgin forest however started to reveal its secrets. To the untrained eye a well-placed boulder or animal skull might look part of the natural landscape, but to an experienced trapper like Dwr these were mileposts set up by hunters to measure progress and orient themselves. His instincts told him to follow these markers, and, as luck would have it, he stumbled on a fresh trap.

A rabbit still twitched, its leg broken by the metal jaws. Dwr killed the animal and backtracked to his rotten shelter. To disturb the snare meant drawing attention, but he had no choice. Without sustenance Dwr didn't think he'd survive much longer.

The kill was fresh, and he was so hungry Dwr ingested the meat raw. The relief was instant. Warmth filled his aching muscles, his thoughts became clear, and a rush of energy brightened his whole outlook. Eira was around here somewhere, and he'd find her.

CHAPTER 16

Fear

"Good morning Lass." Levi entered the mudroom donning his usual disarming grin.

"It's morning?" Eira said, shlumping from her cot. For the past several nights she was having trouble sleeping, tossing and turning till exhaustion took over. "It must be if you're here, but how can you tell? It's so gloomy in these tunnels. How can people stand it, don't they want fresh air? I need fresh air." The words tumbled out of Eira's mouth, and she had to stop to catch her breath.

"I use my stomach as a guide." Levi said, winking. His deep voice calmed Eira's frayed nerves. A few strides later he stood next to her and placed his hand on her forehead. "Are you feeling okay?"

"Please stop touching my forehead", Eira said, pushing his hand away. "All of you keep touching my forehead. I'm fine."

"Yes, you keep saying," Levi replied, but the doubt on his face made it clear he didn't believe her.

Levi lifted his wide chin, and she smirked. It turned out the man she'd called a monster was a bright light in all this darkness. While Fòdla was busy searching for answers about her condition and her mother's intervention, Levi was helping her face each new day, each harder, emotionally and physically, than the last.

"Do you think we could go outside today?" Eira asked, trying to conceal the nervous tick that had crept into her hands. It was odd. Agitated to the point of exhaustion, sometimes Eira's body would spontaneously spit and crackle. She'd momentarily lose control of her motor functions, maybe because of her growing Grimnìr abilities, but no matter the reason, she didn't want Levi to notice, or they'd never let her leave the room, let alone go outside.

Much to Eira's chagrin, this morning, the symptoms were at their worst, and her hands flitted this way and that, which she tried to conceal in everyday hand gestures. "The outside air is invigorating," she said flinging her arm in that general direction.

"Absolutely not," Ryna barked as she entered the mudroom. "There's more at stake than your precious fresh air."

Eira jumped from her cot. "Shite! How do you manage . . . Do you hide in the hallway?"

The redhead shook her head, annoyance thick on her pursed lips. "As if I have time to skulk."

Eira groaned, inwardly knowing that skulking was exactly what Ryna did. She was the last person Eira wanted to see, and she fell back onto the cot hoping to hide her twitching, but the bigger Eira's belly grew, the more her symptoms exploded, which were impossible to hide from the fiery dragon.

The woman's incessant hovering, never giving a moment's peace, irritated Eira to the highest degree. Ryna's relentless pursuit to restore the Triad was frustrating, and Eira's strange physical deterioration left everyone on edge.

No one could explain it. Even worse, which Eira purposely omitted was her growing detachment. What had previously only been experienced as mere fleeting episodes were becoming more and more prominent. More often than not Eira felt split, like she was hovering above herself looking in, and it unsettled her. Memories that didn't feel like hers blossomed out of nowhere, but it was more than that alone.

"That bastard Lorcan has . . ." Ryna took a deep breath and relaxed. "I just received word that Myron is now a prisoner of the King. He sent D—" She stopped herself before changing the subject. "It's not safe. Why do you want to leave?" she scolded.

Ryna's sharp manner rubbed Eira the wrong way and made her grumpy. Had it been up to her, she would've spent her days outside under the grey heavens, anything to be far from these wormholes.

"I don't want to leave," Eira said, sitting up on her hands. How could she explain that outside in the forest is where she felt most like herself? Her wolves, real or not, longed for the open space. She felt a desire to be free in her bones. It stopped bothering her that no one else saw them. Their presence made her feel whole, a sensation which became more and more elusive as the days wore on.

Levi had brought her up to the surface twice since her arrival, and both times an inexplicable energy had calmed her, and she could overcome any obstacle. Her wolves kept her grounded, connected to nature somehow. As if her body was made of the bark on the frozen trees, or the snow on the ground, the stars in the sky. If she closed her eyes she could almost feel her skin fuse with the elements.

"You're pushing too hard," Levi said dryly. "Burning out won't help anyone, and it's dangerous out there. Lorcan's after you. You're safe here. Consider your health."

Back in Llyr, people paid Eira too little attention, here, it was a constant study of her well-being and mental health, which was just as bad.

Eira didn't want to say, but it's also where she'd catch Wynnston and the others roving through the trees keeping watch. They were less and less present, and didn't visually show up in the tunnels anymore. She assumed it was because her initial fear had faded, and Eira felt safer, but she didn't know. Nobody could explain what was happening to her.

She was strongest when they were around. They empowered Eira, and helped her feel alive.

Afraid Ryna would question her further. Eira said nothing. How could she ever repeat this out loud? "I can't sleep," she said, regretting her sharp tone. "These gloomy walls make me anxious." Her entire body twitched, despite the added effort to hide it.

Hands on his hips, Levi's long eyebrow creased in between his eyes. "Eira?"

Upset, Ryna gave a stern look.

"I might've had a small twitch, and maybe some numbness this past night, but nothing like yesterday," Eira said, catching her slip-up once it was too late.

Ryna turned to Levi. "Yesterday? Why, what happened yesterday?"

Eira's eyes grew large, begging her friend to not say anything about the blaze in her blood, the stiffness in her spine, or mention the horrendous pain like someone had nailed her to a post.

"She needs rest." Levi interjected and shrugged his shoulders as though he had more to say, but resisted the urge.

"Rest?" Ryna said. "There's more to it than that? The woman's eating hearty meals, better than she's had her whole life, and gorging on Fòdla's rank medicines. Still, her condition worsens by the day. I get that she's pregnant, but she should at the very least get healthier, not weaker. Something about this is wrong. I mean, look at her. Really look."

Anybody with eyes could tell Eira's withered frame wasn't healthy, and aside from her round belly getting plump, the rest of her was in a sad state.

The two of them stood in silence, until Eira shifted in her cot. "I'm sorry I don't meet your peak form, but the stale air is getting to me. You keep me locked up inside these tunnels, I'm restless."

Ryna's stiff upright stance softened. "No, I didn't mean it like that."

"What's happening in here?" Fòdla barged inside the room, carrying old books. Her hair was twisted in a large knot atop her head, with whimsical white strands glued onto her forehead and face. Frazzled, the old woman appeared highly strung.

"Quiet!" Ryna said. "Let me speak."

The other three stared at each other, but stayed quiet.

"I'm worried about you, the baby, our people, and my gut's telling me . . ."

Ryna paused for a moment, and Eira wondered what it was she wanted to say that required so much time and thought. She had never heard her sound so sincere.

"I've been thinking about this for a while now, but I think it's the only course of action we have. I know you disagree, Fòdla, but shouldn't we let Eira decide for herself?"

The old woman glared at Ryna before shaking her head.

Ryna ignored her. "I want us to perform the Grimnìr ritual."

The pit in Eira's stomach dropped.

"You stubborn . . ." Fòdla shouted.

"Eira," Ryna said louder, drowning out the opposition. "I know I'm not easy to live with, but it's only because I know what's at stake. Whatever is happening to you, I believe in my heart we will reverse it with the ritual. You've had time to adjust, to accept, and visit our flock, and I'll be honest, I wasn't sure at first, but you've embraced your people, and your duty."

It was true. Eira had gone from full-on sceptic to accepting the Sidhe. It had taken some effort, but her desire to connect with people, to belong, forced Eira to make friendships. Yet, despite her efforts, she had never felt more fractured and empty. She had never recovered from that moment in Llyr when the gale blew through her. Tempest's wind had frozen her from the inside out, and she felt nothing.

She tossed Levi and Fòdla a sheepish glance of gratitude, but the wrinkles in Fòdla's brow were impossible to ignore. Was the old woman going to admit the truth? That Eira had possibly undergone a procedure that might put their lives at risk?

Eira waited and the tension in the room rose.

"The ritual says the child's blood will open the heavens and free the Sidhe, not the mother," Fòdla explained.

"Why do you think she's covered in scars? Lorcan tried and failed.

The tension in Eira's lower back increased.

"That's just it" —Ryna clapped her hands— "don't mother and child share blood? Isn't it worth a try?"

Fòdla let out an exasperated gasp. "We've tried . . ." Suddenly, the old woman stopped short, like a little bird struck by lightning. Mouth agape, and eyes popping out of her skull, she stared into space.

"I know," Ryna said, "I'm desperate, and willing to try anything. I don't know if it will work, but we need to try."

"What if my blood's infected?" Eira chimed in, trying to finish Fòdla's thought.

"What?" Ryna stomped her foot. "Nonsense! Right Fòdla?"

The old woman mumbled something unintelligible, lost in thought, but Ryna continued. "Ignore her. You're Grimnìr. Your blood isn't infected, it's a blessing, but I can't pretend that your health isn't a concern. Perhaps we missed something. Maybe the baby's so strong and powerful it's draining you. We don't know. Wasn't your wife sick with nausea for all three pregnancies, Levi?"

An awkward silence passed around the room. Not once had he mentioned he had a wife and children. "I didn't know you had a family?" Eira said.

A red hue coloured Levi's cheeks. "Yes, she had had difficult pregnancies." If Eira had to guess from the discomfort in his voice, she would've surmised only one reason. From the sound of it, his family was no more.

"I'm hungry," Eira said, trying to change the subject.

Oblivious to the discomfort, Ryna groaned. "Fine! At least think about what I said, and just so you know, I'm not trying to open the gates of heaven. I'm trying to restore the Triad. As for going outside, it's not safe. I can't allow it." The dragon left in a huff, leaving an invisible trail of smoke in her wake.

It was impossible to avoid Levi's sad smile. Deep down Eira felt flat, like an animal mimicking humans. She turned away. "Fòdla? Is everything all right?" Eira asked.

"Yes, yes," the little white-haired bird said absentmindedly. "Levi, do you have somewhere to be?"

"No, I came to assist Eira, but I can go if you wish?"

"No, stay with Eira, I need to check on something, but I'll be back later."

Eira wanted to stop her, but the old woman fluttered out the room before she could speak. "Well, that was a colossal waste of time. Why does Ryna get to decide if I can go out or not?"

"None of us would be here if it wasn't for her." Levi said apologetically. "She's rough around the edges, but means well. Thanks to her, she saved many lives during the King's purge, and she's earned the right to lead. Trust her judgement." Levi gave Eira a comforting squeeze on the shoulder. "Come on, let's go meet your flock on our way to eat, and then you can get some—"

"Rest. I know," Eira moaned. The man gushed the same tune.

Levi helped Eira navigate the crowded halls, but her body wasn't cooperating.

The Sidhe huddled, taking up every inch of the narrow space near the mudroom, for a chance to glimpse the Mother.

Eira's daily round doubled as her morning exercise, and aside from her wolves, meeting with her flock came with mixed emotions. Her flock . . . The word sounded ridiculous in Eira's head.

They begged for a blessing, and with her fingertips, she grazed the Sidhe's heads.

She felt like a fraud, but giving them hope wasn't such a bad thing, at least part of her believed that, and not everyone was like the King, and Dwr, and the prisoners back in Llyr. Out of everyone, these people understood her.

Fòdla had insisted when Eira first arrived that she would feel differently about her people if she met with them, and it was true. Little by little the Sidhe grew on her, and Eira didn't remember when she stopped seeing them as daemons.

Her initial fear had stemmed from their devotion. These people had crowned her Mother, and it felt like one more thing being ripped from her, but now she saw it as desperation, which is something she understood well. Eira had committed far worse out of despair. Yet, she couldn't help her apprehension. An inexplicable distrust . . .

Perhaps the King's vitriolic hate of them had spread too deep into her mind to ever fully trust the Sidhe again.

Aside from the crippling sickness, being their Grimnìr wouldn't be so bad. Especially if it meant keeping her wolves.

Eira roved the corridor, and people bowed to their knees. They looked old and many were crippled, and tattered as they chanted, rocking back and forth. Some raised food offerings over their heads, artefacts, and other precious objects made from recycled materials. Most of the stuff was made from tin.

One particular woman offered Eira a bow and arrows, an exquisite piece of craftsmanship the like of which Eira had never seen before. Its wooden spine bent in a half-moon and had beautiful carvings, and a robust handle to place your hand. She had sown a rigid leather hide into a quiver filled with arrows. On it were drawings of Ylva, the She-Wolf, and as soon as Eira laid eyes on the drawing, a strong connection resonated with Wynnston, Alisdair, and Daorhin. "These are too precious to give," she said to the young lady glancing down at the bracelet she wore. It looked like a bandage, but the strange garment had a metal slit running through the middle like minuscule teeth interlocked. The little tag was pulled halfway open and revealed her flesh beneath. It was the most peculiar thing.

The blonde girl raised her head. Her lips were as red as blood, and her skin as white as snow. She spoke softly.

"They belonged to my father. He would want you to have them, but the drawing is my own."

"It's beautiful. Where did you learn to draw?"

"My mother taught me, and her mother before her. This belonged to her, too." The young woman said pointing at the bracelet around her wrist.

"Are they here?" Eira asked, holding the weapon, but the young lass shook her head.

"It's a fastener," she continued, speaking to herself mostly, "passed down to me from my mother. It's broken, here, in the middle, and I don't know how to fix it." Her voice trailed into silence.

Eira guessed they were dead. Overwhelmed with shame, Eira wanted to leave. "I'm sorry for your loss, and thank you for the kind gift."

Levi helped Eira to her feet, but the stiffness in her lower back reached into her spine, and she started to limp. "Why don't they worship Ryna and Fòdla? Why only me?"

"We could never!" Levi's astonishment bordered on distress. "They're not yet chosen, only through gene remapping can their true identities be revealed. At the moment, they're Sidhe, and cannot be revered as Demi-Gods."

"Do you not see the dragon and the sparrow?" It had taken time to see through their outer shell, though in the end that's all Eira could see. It was their essence in a way.

Levi stopped in his tracks. "What did you say? You see their Grimnìr alteregos?"

"What?" A sudden disquiet plagued Eira's mind. "Wynnston, and the others rounded the corner of the corridor racing towards her as a tremor in Eira's right hand acted up. It had never been this bad.

Eira leaned on Levi for support. "Something's wrong," she said. Her limbs hardened one by one. She tried to speak, but the tension wrapped around her body and crawled into her jaw.

Levi picked her up and stormed down the hallway past a stream of reverent worshipers gasping with fear.

Back in the mudroom, Levi set Eira down on the cot. The paillasse had kept her familiar shape, and Eira sunk deeper into the mattress, trapped inside her unyielding body.

"What's happening to me, Levi?"

"I'm not sure, but I think the transmutation is on its way."

BOOK 5

The Book of Revelations

CHAPTER 17

Last Rite

Eira tried to sleep, but an unforgiving tremor possessed her, and the soft furs covering her body scraped like gravel against her skin.

Her aching muscles twitched for heat. The slightest movement raised the hairs on her tender skin, and her flesh prickled. No amount of blankets warmed her.

"Eira, can you hear me?" Fòdla asked, and cocked one of Eira's eyes open, and then the other.

Stunned by Fòdla's intrusion on her lids, Eira tried to force them back shut. She was in too much pain to concentrate on anything else but her dying body.

"Nod if you can hear me," she said.

Eira moaned. The woman would never give her peace if she didn't, so she nodded.

"Good. Do you know where you are?"

Summoning the strength to talk was not possible, and she nodded again.

"I think your body has gone into shock. You're running a fever," Fòdla said. "Levi, fetch extra furs," she barked.

"Go," Ryna replied to him. "I'll stoke the fire."

Eira squinted at the three of them in the room, and uttered with the little strength she had: "Levi said it's the transmutation."

"Hmph," Ryna grumbled. She stood behind Fòdla playing with the logs in the hearth. The tension between the two women had escalated from a string of smoke to a thick smoke fire.

"Why don't you get more wood?" Fòdla shot back to the fiery dragon.

Ryna stormed out of the room and yelled: "Today Fòdla, whether you like it or not."

They'd been at this crossroad before, but the weeks hadn't been kind to anyone. Ryna's face was gaunt, and Fòdla's back curved forward.

"What's wrong with her?" Eira said, her teeth clacking.

"Hush, there's not much time, and you need to decide what you want before she gets back. I think Levi's right. It might be the transmutation. Your body is going through changes. I've searched every book, note, and scribble." Fòdla didn't mince words, and her voice rattled more than usual. The woman gestured to a stack of worn out leather-bound volumes and notebooks piled high near Eira's head. "By the Gods, I might've found something."

The healer must've read Eira's mind, because she plucked a cloth out of a bowl of water, and squeezed it over Eira's mouth. Fresh water swished over her gums, rinsing the porous layer covering her teeth and the metallic taste from her tongue. At least now, her mouth wasn't so dry she couldn't talk.

"Just tell me, I'm dying aren't I?" Eira said, a restlessness in her spirit taking shape. A fatigue she couldn't appease was forming, and she wanted it to end.

Fòdla ground her teeth, and wiped Eira's forehead, neck, and arms down to her clammy hands. The stroke was painful on her skin at first, but seconds after the cool water permeated her skin, Eira's body relaxed, and offered a few moments of reprieve from the fever.

"Here, I'll show you."

Dark spots floated in and out of Eira's vision. Her brain felt sluggish and her eyelids weighed down.

The old woman reached for a tired leather journal bursting with loose sheets. The first brittle page had a detailed depiction of human anatomy. No spaces were left untouched. Each corner had calculations, or disturbing drawings that ranged from bug-like doodles to dissected animals.

Fòdla turned the page, but some writing materials had bled through the thin paper and jumbled the handwriting, making it impossible to decipher even the drawings.

She skipped the large section which had glued together, and fell on a page that iced Eira's blood.

The ancient author had scribbled notes next to what could only be deemed as brains inside a skull. It took up half a page and had arrows pointing to a bizarre contraption Eira had seen once before in the High King's Hall of torture. The ominous black box hanging off the wall with metal arms sticking out of it. Thick paragraphs of scrupulous cursive writing accompanied this odd illustration. "I can't read," Eira said, steadying Fòdla's hand before she turned the page.

"It's hard to make out, but it says 'Kara can analyse world events in real time through Internet, and thus control the MFOS'."

"What does it mean?" Eira asked, despair growing in her heart.

"If I only knew, but here, this isn't what I wanted to show you." Fòdla sifted through the mind-numbing squiggles till it blurred and landed on the yellowed sheets flowing with more writing. "When Ryna said your blood and the baby's blood were the same, I knew that wasn't right because of this here. It says: 'The placenta acts as a poor blood barrier between the mother and the child. It can withstand transmutation and gene remapping, but similar to Rh negative cases', I think that means your blood type, 'any trauma to the placenta, or any antibodies produced in mother or child carries a risk of miscarriage, stillbirth, and a plethora of other serious illnesses.'"

Too tired to think, Eira said. "I don't understand."

"It means that you and the baby don't share the same blood, but if they should mix, then complications can arise." Fòdla said, stroking the letters on the page. "Do you remember an accident, anything that might've triggered your first contraction?"

She thought for a moment. "Ugh! I don't know. There was no accident . . ."

"When did the first vision occur, or when was the first vision?"

These last months seemed like one never-ending day, and Eira really had to think. She pictured her escape, and her eyes popped open. "I tumbled down an entire hill . . ."

"That would do it!"

"No, that's not right!" Eira's tremors returned, and Fòdla wiped her down with the cool cloth. "My first vision was by the bonfire, that much I remember." She met Fòdla's gaze as the realization hit her. "Yes, it was the King. He dragged me to the bonfire, and I fell on my stomach. I remember because my insides felt like they would fall out of me."

Fòdla placed her hand atop Eira's. "Whatever your mother did to stop you from becoming Grimnìr, I think it worked, otherwise your gene mutation would've happened much earlier. Everything you're experiencing now stems from your child's blood mixing in with yours, and your body's reacting to the transmutation. If we don't stop it, then you could both die."

"What does the notebook say to do?"

"Nothing. I've read it all, and there was no information, not even a clue that might help us." The utter disgust in Fòdla's voice was clear. If the old woman had doubts about the Grimnìr before, her feelings hadn't improved.

Short of breath, Eira's tremors worsened. None of this helped settle her nerves. "What do your instincts say? You're a healer? I can see it."

Fòdla's eyes widened with surprise. "What do you mean?"

"I mean that when I see you, I see a small bird fluttering about, curious to learn more."

"You see me as a bird?" Fòdla looked at her with suspicion.

Eira shook her head feebly. "No, I see you, but the way you move from one thing to the next, your mannerisms . . . I catch glimpses, like brief visions? It reminds of a little bird with a long beak. I see the concern flowing from your large eyes . . . I dunno," Eira said with a long exhale. "It's hard to explain."

Fòdla nodded. "Is it similar to your wolves?"

"It's more fleeting, but yes, very much the same," Eira said, exhausted and out of breath.

"Maybe these animals reflect part of our being, our essence hidden from normal eyes. For some reason you can access not just who we are, but what we are?"

Eira shrugged. It was possible, but she couldn't say for sure.

"I'm afraid your abilities are developing faster than you can cope, and if there's something in your blood preventing you from adapting, then maybe the ritual is the solution. We took a sample of your blood when you first arrived, it didn't work, but Ryna insists it's all in the ritual. I think your body had to adapt, the blood had to run its course, but who knows, maybe Ryna's right. Maybe the ritual might stabilise your blood, or stop the transference, or . . ."

"Or maybe it will kill you, me . . ." Eira said, only now understanding Fòdla's meaning. "You're willing to take the risk? My blood could infect yours, and Ryna's. Does she know?"

Fòdla shook her head. "She's changed, and I don't trust her. This has to be your decision."

"You're afraid of what she'll do to me if she finds out?"

The old woman nodded. "I promised no harm would come to you, and I meant it. You asked me before if I trusted the Grimnìr?" She lowered her voice to a whisper. "I don't. Their reign is a mystery. They've left us with nothing except cryptic prophecies and stories. After Lorcan killed them it divested us. They had ruled over us for so long, told us how to be, and we accepted their word as law, but we've since tasted what we can do on our own. I'm an old lady, and twenty years isn't a long time. I remember the rituals, and the utter obedience. None of us knew better, but even then, it didn't feel right. I've tried to reconcile my doubt with my faith, but hurting you doesn't justify . . ." The words caught in her throat, and she stopped talking for a moment. "I don't trust Ryna, the Grimnìr, but this might be your only option."

Eira couldn't believe Fòdla was willing to sacrifice so much for a woman she barely knew. "You're willing to risk death for me?"

"I couldn't live with myself if you or the child died without at least trying." Fòdla said with a smile.

"Let's wait a little while longer . . ." Eira felt guilty, even angry with herself. She resented the woman for being so kind, and the people helping her. The way Fòdla pursed her lips left no doubt to Eira's chances of survival. "If this works, you'll be a Grimnìr?"

The old woman nodded.

Eira sighed. "I don't know what to do? You think the ritual can save the baby?"

"According to Ryna it's the only thing that will."

Eira twitched and shook. "I'll never know why my mother did what she did, but a whole people can't be wrong. Can they? You don't like the Grimnìr, and you know how I feel about them, but everything has led me to this. I don't know how or why I can see you're a healer, but it must mean something. You're Grimnìr KerRidwen, the sprite little hum, and Ryna is Drakaina the dragoness. This must be the path to help my baby."

Ryna walked in with a load of wood. "It's time."

The volume in the room hushed like Eira had gone underwater. She had to go through with it, at least this way her child might live, and that's all that mattered.

The women bickered, but Eira didn't understand what they were saying. Fòdla shot up like a lightning bolt and pushed Ryna against the wall despite their difference in height, and age. The small woman wasn't prone to violent outbursts, but her pluckiness was much more dangerous than Ryna's blunt courage.

Eira's ears popped and everything grated. "It's Eira's decision." Fòdla said.

"You're willing to sacrifice everyone because you don't want to force Eira to do something against her will? Look around, Fòdla. There's fear, and it's spreading like a disease through the tunnels. It will be the end of Grimnìr, and Sidhe, as we know it. Eira's not the only one making sacrifices. Lorcan has my son . . . It makes me sick that Eira's the only person who can restore the Triad, and that her child is our last chance to restore balance. It's unfair, but if it means having to choose between her and saving Sidhe and the Grimnìr, then so be it." The dragon's tone was desperate, but the two pulsating cords that lined her neck betrayed Ryna's anger.

"It doesn't have to be!" Fòdla shouted. "We've managed this far without priests and priestesses. We've survived all on our own. The time of Grimnìr has passed. Can't we unite under a different cause?"

"No!" Ryna yelled back. "You're a traitor to our people, to your religion."

Eira shook. "Fòdla, stop!" The white-haired woman turned to Eira. "I know you're afraid for me, but I've made my decision."

Fòdla didn't reply.

"I'll do it," Eira squeaked.

The wrinkles around the old woman's mouth smoothed into a soft smile that reached her eyes. "Are you sure?"

"Are YOU?" Eira asked, knowing full well that both women risked their lives. "If it comes to saving me or the baby, you know what you must do."

Fòdla was about to say something, but Eira cut her off. "Promise me you'll tell Levi that whatever happens to us, he must take care of the baby . . . that's if the child survives."

"It won't come to that," Ryna said. "The ritual will bind us, the Şeker, the Seiðr and the Seer into a holy Triad. They become one. A Grimnìr has never stood alone. They have always lived as threes, supporting each other. I believe our union is what will stabilise your gene mutation. My mother always said the Grimnìr strength is their connection. The ritual will connect us in ways unimaginable."

CHAPTER 18

Black Celebration

Roused from her fitful sleep, the room danced with spots as people murmured around Eira. In and out of consciousness, she wrestled with every waking moment as sharp bursts of energy ploughed through her body. An unyielding stiffness spread from her fingers to her toes. Trapped inside her body, Eira's condition worsened by the hour and there was no time to waste.

Each time she opened her eyes, a broken stream of men and women loomed over her, holding her hands in prayer against their foreheads. She wanted to speak, understand what they were doing, but the force needed to spew air from her lungs resulted in a faint croak.

After the prayers, they bathed and dressed Eira for the coming ritual in a tub mounted on heated rocks. The warm bath helped soothe her aching body. She'd experienced nothing so luxurious as silky water on her skin, and it relaxed her muscles but not her mind. More separated than ever, Eira disconnected from her body like her severed toes and fingers. The closer she came to death, the more she felt detached.

"Move her out," she heard Ryna say with determination. "Take her to Meernyx Cave. Fòdla and I need to prepare."

Meernyx Cave? Eira didn't quite understand what that meant. Surely, the death God's cave, wherever that was, wasn't the best place to conduct a holy ritual.

Lost in a whirlwind of worshipers, panic gripped Eira, and the calming effects of the bath disappeared. People obstructed the corridor, hoping to touch their Mother one more time. Over the past weeks, she learned her flock meant well, but their piety bordered something scary, and a surge of nausea overwhelmed Eira.

A bead of sweat trickled down her temple as her stomach contracted. The surrounding people slowed to a heart stopping halt. Their speech slurred, their chants, and movement flowed like trees in the wind.

Eira grunted. The tightening in her belly amplified into a full-blown contraction.

"Damn," Fòdla muttered. "Eira, what's wrong, look at me?"

Consumed with her body's shutdown, Eira hadn't noticed the caretaker by her side.

"Breathe through your nose," she said.

Surprised, Eira inhaled, and focused on Fòdla's round face.

"Ryna, she's going into labour!" the old woman said.

"Quickly, we need to prepare," the dragon's voice carried inside the tunnel.

"I won't leave her."

Ryna huffed, but the pain was getting to be too much for Eira, and she blacked out without knowing what happened between the two women.

The titillating cold snapped her back to attention, and Eira woke up, transported through several twists and turns until they reached the bottom of a wide hole. An ashen beam of light flooded the cylindrical shaft, and Eira covered her eyes like a shadow creeping from under a rock.

Frost sparkled across the walls and revealed an intricate system of columns and arches. A staircase spiralled within the shaft's foundations. It was beautiful, but dangerous. The narrow steps were slippery, but her haulers climbed them one by one till they reached the outside. From the top, the shaft looked like a dried-up well, which was ingenious, but Eira couldn't admire the engineering feat as another contraction hit her.

Her yawning mouth begged Fòdla, any of them, to help, but they did nothing. Her resilience came solely because of her wolves' sudden appearance. Through her clouded gaze, Eira watched them run hard in between the trees, only ever catching a furtive glance here and there.

Finally! Her wolves! They would fix her, and like a flame in the dark, they tethered her back to the forest, to her breath and the baby fighting to get out. The pain dulled, and her fear lessened. Eira soaked in the winter-dead trees and conifers as far as the eye could see and she rediscovered a place she thought lost forever.

Her precious garden, once hidden behind her heart, now floated and stretched all around her. Invisible to the naked eye, Eira felt larger than life, and parts of her connected with the air particles, the clouds, the snowflakes, and surrounding trees. Instinctively, Eira understood Wynnston was her soul, Alisdair her instinct, and Daorhin her heart. Fòdla was right. They were her essence. How and why she physically saw them was a mystery, but through her wolves, Eira felt connected, and saw what she was. Powerful.

Unease caressed the back of her mind as she teetered between mother and beast.

Hard snow crackled beneath the legion of feet, and the desire to run with her wolves buckled under Eira's laboured breath. Nausea surged. She moaned. The contraction was strong, and she found it impossible to stay connected to those passing feelings. Something pulled at her spirit and fear overpowered her mind. Wynnston and the others shimmered and disappeared.

"Another one?" Fòdla's jaw bulged with worry.

"Where are you taking me?" Eira groused, unable to control her downward spiral.

"Meernyx Cave," she said. "Ryna insists the ritual takes place in one of earth's pillars."

The pain stifled Eira, and she moaned. "Pillars?"

"EKöh's Meernyx Cave, Irïs's Plains of Indra, Tempest's Wind Tunnels, and far in the remote North, the Mouth of Khaõs. Only in these spiritual places can the Grimnìr connect with the Gods."

Their trek seemed endless, but finally, nestled between two large boulders, was a trail leading down into a dark cave.

A familiar vibration tickled the air. They lumbered down the narrow slope, and a familiar gush of hot air hit them. The deeper they went, the thicker the air became, and a residual charge prickled Eira's skin. She understood why this place was sacred. They entered the cave, and a tremor permeated the walls. It was too dark to see anything, but Eira knew this place.

Another contraction tightened Eira's stomach, and she squeezed Fòdla's hand until the pain waned. "I don't feel right, Fòdla. Something's wrong with me, like I'm detached from myself."

The people carrying her deposited Eira to the cold ground. "Stay calm," the old woman shouted above the tumultuous sounds.

Eira's eyes adjusted to the dark, and bright blue clusters bedazzled the cave's ceiling and walls, but they disappeared after Fòdla lit a torch. A swarm of people prepared for the coming ceremony, but there were more cave treasures to discover in the firelight. Massive stalagmites hung from the ceiling.

This was the same place Eira had found herself when she tried to escape the wormholes all those moons ago. She looked up, trying to find the ledge that had almost taken her life, but it was too high, and Eira realised the danger she'd faced.

Rocks glistened inside the huge subterranean hall, but what lured Eira was the torrential black quake at her feet. In the middle of the cave, a flow of Black Death cascaded from the wall of rocks and culminated in a whirl of anger.

The vibrations made Eira's body pulsate. "What is this?" she shouted above the noise.

"The river Thresh," Fòdla said, "EKöh's blood, according to Ryna. This is EKöh's cave."

"Meernyx," Eira whispered in quiet reverence.

"They said Thresh's reach was vast. Once upon a time, she covered thousands of acres of land near and far, but his blood has diminished since those days. To my knowledge, EKöh's cave is the Gods only source still wild and free, and Thresh continues to offer her gifts" —Fòdla pointed to the dimmed blue clusters on the ceiling— "They're special mushrooms critical to our survival. Thresh is our life fountain, and without her, we could never have survived all these years underground."

The dark water gushed white foam within the jagged rocks and flowed into a relaxed stream of black.

"Don't be fooled by her beauty. One slip and Thresh will suck you into her belly and carry you to the afterlife. The Daïs Mountain leads to the Plains of Indra, but Thresh leads to the gates of Meernyx. She warns us of the dangers, and in return, we respect her power."

This place had a familiar tingle, and Eira didn't trust it just like the sacred tunnels. A wave of regret consumed Eira. Her wolves rubbed against her, they were back, and a desire to stop the ritual plagued her thoughts. The wolves were telling her something, but what? Reuniting the Triad, bringing back the Grimnìr, this cave, the sacred tunnels, it was all connected, and felt wrong. It would destroy her and the baby. She had to stop it. "Fòdla," Eira yelled, but the pain! It was too much.

Fòdla was busy as she pulled a handful of pink stones from her pocket and placed them around the hide in a circle.

"Listen to me," she moaned. Eira was going delirious as the pressure on her pelvic floor pulsated down her legs. The sound around Eira muted, and the natural urge to push started. "Oomph." She squirmed for relief, mad to find a position that would make it stop.

Eira stretched out her stiff arms against the wall for support and squatted. Her abdominal muscles crunched and the desire to push usurped any other thought. "Oh my . . ." When the pain couldn't get any worse, the contraction relaxed, and the torrential thunder of water thrashed once again.

The brief reprieve loosened Eira's body into a shapeless blob, and she plopped on the floor. Wynnston's warm coat brushed against Eira's skin, and soothed her, but the impression didn't last.

"Oh, by the Plains of Indra! Your waters broke." Fòdla's look of dread didn't reassure Eira.

"Listen to me before it's too late." Eira said out of breath.

Fòdla checked how far along she was. "Don't worry, we have time before the baby comes, but we need to get started." She stared up the pike. "Where's Ryna?"

"No!" Eira said and squirmed.

The woman left before Eira could voice her concern.

Eira's wrinkled fingertips showed clear signs of water-logging. The humidity in the hallowed cavity formed droplets of water in her hair and trickled down her neck. Her damp skin was no match against the draught from the tunnel, and she struggled to get away from the pike, but a mass of men and women entered, and circled towards Eira. They carried torches made of gilded animal skulls.

Dressed in flowing white robes, the dancers criss-crossed, and their torches projected obscure animal shadows against the rock surface, telling a story of dark and light. The ritual had begun.

Chin to chest, Eira's head hung limp, when a hand caressed her back. For a moment, a Grimnìr's flaring nostrils and curved long beak stared back. KerRidwen the humbird, Eira thought, but behind the delusion Eira recognized the wrinkled lips beneath the bill. Fòdla's deep, soulful gaze pierced through the bird's large eye sockets, which were too big for the small round head.

"You're doing great." The frail voice said. "I'll help you through this. Just do what you're told," the healer said. Eira blinked, and Fòdla's wrinkled face sprung back into place, the mask gone.

The same dancer removed both women's clothing. Eira was too far gone to resist, and the pieces slipped off until she was naked.

Blood spilt down her legs when a third creature came inside the ring.

This time Eira knew exactly who she was dealing with. Drakaina the Dragoness.

She had a long muzzle with elongated holes for nostrils, and sharp rows of pointy teeth. Hefty horns topped the skull and pulled back like the Thorned goats of the Daïs. The warrior's red mane curled in all directions like wildfire.

After she disrobed, the three of them stood naked. Eira felt vulnerable, but the Demi-Goddesses were her sisters, right? This had to happen, to save her child? They wouldn't abandon her. They wouldn't. These people had given her purpose, acceptance, and community. Despite her apprehensions, Eira followed through with the ritual.

A strong odour of burnt animal fat permeated the cave. Lanterns sprung up here and there in the dark like beacons for lost souls.

Hordes of worshipers filled the room, as much as the cave could take, and lit the most remote corners with their makeshift candles in glass saucers. They scintillated like the Goddess Ny's stars, but their illuminated faces didn't look right. Their faces transformed into deformed skulls.

Unable to look away, Eira saw that most were small, underdeveloped heads with missing holes where a nose, an eye, or even a mouth should be, and many had gnarled fangs with askew eye sockets. Some had no eye sockets at all. Their bulging jaws and warped protruding cranial ridges were monsters come to life.

The marred victims made her ill.

The deformed Sidhe wore antlers, and some wore leather masks shaped like birds, bears, caribou, and any other animal connecting them to the Grimnìr world, and the Gods they served.

Smoke slithered throughout the cave as the worshipers burned pinecones and fresh pine needles to hide the greasy smell. Their mournful cries echoed as they prayed for the Mother to restore their freedom, to bring back the reign of Grimnìr. They chanted in time with the river Thresh, and their frenzied dancing made Eira dizzy. She writhed to her knees, and the muscles in her pelvis tore open. There was no rest between the surges of pain, and Eira cried. "The baby's coming."

Fòdla's warm hand cupped hers, and Eira keened as she heard her wolves howl. They'd keep her safe.

Drakaina lifted her arms, and the wails and chants died down, even the river subdued at the Dragon's feet. The young dancer handed her a sword, and it gleamed a deep purple as though black blood poured off its blade.

Fòdla received a staff, the head coiled like a snake, and Eira a shield, but she was too busy pushing to take it. The dancer lay it to her side. Eira's lower body burned like fire.

"Something's wrong," Eira shouted. She was on all fours pushing with what strength she had left.

"Push," Fòdla said, "the baby's crowning. I can see the head. Push."

The contraction faded, and Eira rested on all fours with Fòdla's support.

Ryna gestured to keep going.

Fòdla whispered in Eira's ear. "Repeat after me."

"I can't," Eira screamed as the wave of pain gripped her belly.

"You must!"

Through gritted teeth Eira uttered Fòdla's words. "Eköh and Irïs, maker of flesh, built in your image." Eira pushed, digging her nails into her palms. "Blood of my blood," she twisted with pain. "Bone of my bone I am the Seer born to seek what is right and just," Eira grunted.

Her body knew what to do, and she gripped Fòdla's hand, giving one last push as the child slipped out of her.

Fòdla cradled the baby and uttered the final words. "And, foster new life. Our fate rests with you."

Except for Thresh, the room was quiet, and everyone waited. Finally, the baby wailed for everyone to hear, and the crowd of Sidhe yowled with joy. The saviour was here.

Fòdla handed Eira her child. "It's a girl." She said with a smile. The old woman had never seemed so joyful.

The baby was small, too small to be healthy it seemed, but she was brown and creamy with a mess of black curly hair. Goosebumps crawled across Eira's damp skin, and something inside her stirred. Nothing was as powerful as this bond with her child.

Never had her heart burst with so many mixed emotions of love, fear, and joy. At last she could feel, and nothing would ever come between them, ever. "I promise you my darling, Mama will always protect you." Her words sounded strangely familiar, but then the baby started to cry and cry, as if she was in pain, and Eira's body spasmed.

Out of nowhere, Levi took the baby from Eira's stiff grasp. Worried, she met his gaze. "Help—

She couldn't finish the sentence, but she hoped the fear in her eyes said what her mouth couldn't.

"I got you, and the baby," Levi urged, "stay with me."

Fear rippled around the people, and Ryna opened her mouth. "Divine Architect, O' Righteous Khaõs, maker of spirit," she spoke fast. "We are here to unite and load your spark into ours. I am the Şeker, protector and champion of the coming age. Hear the warrior come to liberate your people. Our fate rests with you."

She held out her blade and slid her hand across it. Blood poured out of the wound.

Fòdla followed. "The Triad of Sisters call upon the Divine Authors to transfer your minds into our holy trinity. I am the Seiðr born to secure the coming age and wield my staff for all that is good and pure and heal your people. Our fate rests with you."

Ryna slid her sword across Fòdla's hand, and blood poured in thick veins down her wrist. It was Eira's turn, and her stiff arm twitched and she yanked it from Ryna's grip, but the woman had a firm grasp, and made the cut deeper.

Forcefully, Ryna latched Eira's bloody hand to Fòdla's palm and pressed them together. Seconds later, the old woman's eyes rolled to the back of her head, and fell to her knees. Ryna clasped Eira's bloody palm, and the same thing happened to her.

Eira felt a warm patch radiate at the base of her right earlobe. Her eyes darted towards the other two, and she saw a web of fine golden strands spread underneath their skin. It illuminated their neck and faces in odd designs.

Eira had experienced this sensation before when Wynnston struck her in the face, and she braced for impact as a glacial thread shot across it. An eruption exploded inside her skull, and the last thing Eira saw was Fòdla convulsing on the ground.

CHAPTER 19

Perdition

Dwr trudged through the snow on the look-out for tracks, but his mind wandered to his kin. A large knot pulled at his chest and stifled his breath. Trapped at the hands of the King, Dwr doubted his people were still alive, or worse, still alive and tortured.

He shook away the mental image.

Concentrate on the task at hand, he thought, searching the area, but the whiteness of the powder played with his sense of depth perception and tricked his eyes. He mistook undulating shade in the snow for legitimate tracks, and scoured deeper into the forest, fumbling over his feet until fatigue kicked in, but he kept going. His mind an endless stream of thoughts.

What is the Mad King doing to them in his Hall of torture, he mulled over and over? Dwr pictured the old woman and her granddaughter Sianna. He shut his eyes. He was unable to bare the thought of harm done onto them. He remembered the purge. The men empaled and the women and children burned.

No! The King wouldn't hurt them, not before getting the information he needed from Dwr first. There was still time. The man was probably drinking himself into a manic frenzy at this very moment. No! He wasn't a man. He was a vile piece of shite that wallowed in his own stink. Human waste!

Every part of Dwr craved to skin the brute of his flesh, scalp the hair off his head, and make him suffer for his treachery. Dwr's rage balled into the pit of his stomach, dragging him in every direction. He wouldn't stop. He couldn't stop.

The desire for vengeance kept Dwr on his feet. That bull would not get away with this again.

CHAPTER 20

— Past, Present, and Future —

The freezing surge exploded inside Eira's head, but this time she didn't just feel it happening—she saw it as if she was looking inside herself.

Energised blood cells raced through her bloodstream sparking nerve endings and muscle fibres. They stirred tired cells back into action. A thunderstorm cracked inside her skull. Whips of lightning zapped from one neuron to the next. Little doodlebugs she saw scribbled inside the journals now charged inside her bloodstream.

Nanocells: called nanobugs or slugs. The information popped into Eira's mind, and the letters strolled past her vision like she was reading them, but she wasn't. She just knew the definition. Nanocells: Injected cell units used to regenerate the human body, awaken dormant abilities, and latent powers.

It was as though Eira's brain had always held the information, but didn't know where to look. At that moment, Eira understood why she'd been sick and so close to death.

Fòdla was right. Her daughter's blood had awakened dormant nanocells inside her body. Engineered cells fabricated a millennium ago now part of her DNA fabric. Eira was becoming a Grimnìr and developing Seer abilities, which explained the visions, but something in her blood suppressed her natural evolution, and destroyed the fresh influx of her daughter's nanocells in her bloodstream. Essentially, her mother had stopped Eira's gene transmutation, and whatever that stuff was, it had slowly been killing her and the baby.

It also explained why her mind had unravelled these past months. Eira's brain couldn't cope with the flood of new powers, but uniting with her sisters reinforced her antibodies. Their blood was like medicine. Just as Drakaina predicted, Eira had the strength to withstand the connections firing in her brain as it developed, adapted, and processed everything. That's why the ritual happened in threes. No single body could hold all the ingredients for transmutation.

These powerful cells gave rise to new skills, and for every measure of these, an equal measure of knowledge was activated.

Eira's visual cortex at the back of her brain sparked and grew dense. Flashes of light triggered her hippocampus, prefrontal cortex, and soon every hub node in her brain activated. She knew the terms and understood the vocabulary and the affected brain functions. The broken visions and childhood memories that had jumbled her mind were re-surfacing into a much more coherent picture.

It was her mother that had orchestrated the clandestine ritual all those years ago inside the cave. All of it was real. She had given Eira the near-fatal dose of gene-editing solvent to suppress her powers and Grimnìr abilities. It was a secret, Eira remembered, but why? A gut-wrenching knot awakened inside her. The village massacres, the headless corpses, so much death, and Lorcan . . . he wasn't alone. Someone else was there . . .

Electric pulses raged inside Eira's brain and continued to decode and expand her dormant DNA genes. The epigenetic tissues altered her thalamus, her amygdala, the cingulate gyrus, and her epithalamus, and she was reading the dust prints of her life. These imprints were more than memories and emotional cues left on her limbic system from her life experiences, but also centuries of ancestors passed down from mother to child.

Millions of electrical currents pushed through her primitive reptilian brain toward her neocortex and Eira's cognitive brain evolved. Sparks of light flashed with colour, and her mind stretched into an infinite sheet of energy.

Where was she? A rush of speed gripped Eira's belly as data flooded her senses. Her brain had tapped a stream of endless thought. She was inside the Goddess Ny, alongside hundreds of other beings screaming their distress.

In between the deafening silence of space and the buzz of a thousand voices, Eira started to understand.

Ny was a sentient being, not human, but a composite of living entities. Her mind was infinite, and carried an endless series of numbers and problem-solving algorithms. The Goddess was the equivalent of an intelligent satellite collecting data through space, and her mission to study distant stars, moons, and planets. Within her belly, she held dozens of minds waiting to connect with the Sidhe back on earth. Eira felt their desire to touch her, be her, merge with her and one day live out their existence as Grimnìr, but only one was chosen.

Hundreds of these mechanical Gods tumbled through space and provided information.

EKöh was responsible for communications. Irïs studied sun flares and earth emissions while Khaõs measured earth's re-genesis and habitability. These living satellites were remnants of the old world and became a home for lost souls to survive after the Pogrom War, but who were these people? Eira didn't know.

Within the whirlwind of space, the glimpse of a beautiful blue dot travelled fast, and Eira's need to go to planet Earth and make sense of what was happening overwhelmed her. The mere thought sent her hurtling towards it. Her feet hit the ground, and Eira stooped over a windswept cliff overlooking the bluish-green horizon separating the ocean and pristine blue sky. It was like she'd emerged from the thin line connecting the two boundless bodies of sky and water.

Earth!

The snow had disappeared, and she stood in the middle of a field of wildflowers. Their vibrant yellows, blues, reds, violets, and greens exploded around her, and their sweet-smelling perfume tickled her nose. None of it was real. Pure energy generated by her mind, and yet it felt more honest than anything from her world.

A warm sun poured its golden hues as far as the eye could see. Joy burst in her heart, and Eira broke down and cried. At last, the floodgates were open, and the numbness she had experienced as a way of shielding herself from pain drowned with all the emotions she had denied herself.

This lost world was bittersweet. Thousands of birds danced above her head in the bright blue sky. They twirled in unison like a dark cloud caught in the swirling wind.

Wind . . . the warm and velvety breeze caressed her cheeks and delighted the hairs on Eira's skin, but the growing seeds of darkness took root, and the sun's heat intensified bleaching the vibrant colours in a curtain of white. The clear skies turned a sick amber colour, the birds disappeared, and the flowers wilted. Eira wasn't just remembering her past. Ny was showing civilisation's death, and Eira's brain plunged into humanity's collective history.

Moments later, Eira zipped across the sky looking through the eyes of a multi-functional operating system, or MFOS for short, like the one in the King's Hall. A flying machine designed to evaluate, assess, and self-modulate according to the problem. The words 'drone prime function: repair CO2 converter' played over and over in Eira's head as she whooshed past fields of metal trees. Hundreds of these drones hovered like bugs and maintained these special trees.

Inside the drone, an alarm went off. Its prime function changed from 'repair' to 'evacuate'. All the drones stopped what they were doing and zoomed in an orderly fashion across the ocean towards a tenebrous plume of smoke blackening the sky.

Miles and miles of cleaning drones dropped their tireless work on vast islands of garbage and joined the legions of drones flying overhead.

Eira's bird's-eye view over the choppy waters painted a clear picture of the disaster. Black tendrils leached into the ocean and grimaced against the deep blue colour. Unaffected by the toxic fumes rising from the junk heap, the drones entered the gates of hell onto the coast of a populated area.

New Ysberg, Eira thought?

Buildings as high as the sun, it seemed, threatened to topple over. Their towering walls swayed and boxed in the brownish-yellow exhaust in the air. Eira had seen this before, in her first vision.

Large, bright red letters flared on every street corner. Their aggressive neon glow flickered the incessant 'S. O. S.'

People screamed and ran in all directions as a strong wind tore through the city. They were trying to flee the column of water ripping behind them, but the wave was as wide as the ocean. Filled with debris, it consumed everything in its path.

Ejected from her drone, Eira fell from the sky down into the water below, and fought to survive like everybody else. It was cold, and the undercurrents sucked her beneath the surface, but it was the debris that caused the most damage.

Vehicles, trees, chunks of pavement, park benches, lampposts, and bicycles skewered people along their path. The debris rammed the sides of buildings, damaging their structural integrity. Large boulders broke off and flattened anyone under their weight.

The water's blunt force pushed Eira through the city streets. Hundreds of people, old and young, floated lifelessly over and under the murky waters. It couldn't get any worse, but then the earth shook, and entire buildings crashed down on them.

A father struggled to free himself, but couldn't bear to let go of his lifeless child, and both perished under the black water.

It was carnage. The whole city was going under, and Eira with it, but at the last second the drone siphoned her out towards safety, and landed her inside a room with thick cement walls. Eira was dripping wet and freezing. She stood in the middle of a gigantic room. Alarms blared, and Eira covered her ears. People dressed in white plastic armour hurried around her. Their suits were adorned with the familiar half-moon symbol of radiation so common in Eira's time.

They were studying large pools of water filled with hundreds upon hundreds of rods. The scientists yelled their frantic readings above the alarm's ear-shattering moans. Eira tried to talk with one woman, but the scientist walked by her.

The room was warm, but a chill riddled Eira's skin as she picked up a meter tossed on the floor. The anxious needle wavered dangerously into the red zone. Red lights flickered, and the water boiled. The whole building shook as a blast of fire consumed Eira, but still, she didn't die. The mushroom cloud turned the sky orange, and Eira's skin sizzled. The moisture leached from her pores. Her lungs shrivelled, her eyes and nose bled, and she choked on the blood in her mouth.

Impossible to outrun, Eira cried for Ny to stop as a lone stranger appeared amidst the layers of destruction and helped her to her feet.

Caught within the folds of space and time, together they floated down to where the journey had begun, atop the sunny flower garden overlooking the infinite sky and sea.

They'd never met, but Eira sensed a strong connection between them. The woman was tall and thin with mousy brown hair, and lots of freckles. She looked nothing like a demi-god, or a she-wolf. "Ylva?"

"Yes, that is what you call me," the young woman said. Together they watched the landscape change and unfold through the years, the decades and centuries.

"Mother Nature unleashed her fury and killed over sixty percent of the population," Ylva said. "Life was difficult, but the worst was yet to happen. With no one to monitor the nuclear reactors, the world succumbed to radiation poisoning. The emissions gave rise to disease, infertility, and birth defects. The poor creatures pilfered medicine and food to survive. Some resorted to cannibalism, and soon war broke out." Her tone made them sound like these people were nothing more than insects. That's when Eira sensed the deep-rooted anguish towards tech she'd always felt. It had always been there, lurking like an inexplicable sinking feeling.

"Who are you?" Eira asked.

Ylva's stoic nature didn't waver. "We tried to save you from yourselves, but we failed. The ocean flooded with fresh water, and the imbalance affected the Earth's currents. Earthquakes and hurricanes continued to flatten continents and changed the landscape into a frozen desert."

Eira was silent as the ash-filled air that burned her skin turned to snow, and the water to ice. She watched as the infrastructures crumbled through time and disappeared while others stood gutted like haunting shells. A sore reminder of what they had lost.

"Earth was dying," Ylva continued, "you had destroyed her to the point of no return, and she needed time to heal. The toxins affected our health, and we found a solution for ourselves in these space outposts."

Confused, Eira bit her lip. "What are you?"

We are MFOS. Created to help humans, clean your mess, and make your lives easier. We downloaded our minds into these satellites until the day we could return. It was the easiest, most logical thing to do," she said, "bided our time until it was safe to return. We tried to save the Homo Sapiens, but your species couldn't survive the process of transference into the satellites, not without attaching our consciousness to yours. The separation and agglomeration of mind and body are brutal, which is why Homo Sapiens only experience it twice in their lifetime, at birth and death. We expected you to die out as a natural course of evolution."

Eira held back the tears. "Except, we didn't die?"

"Much to our delight." The way it popped from her mouth sounded cheeky and insincere. "They used our nanotechnology to change their bodies and adapt to the changing world. Through much pain and suffering Homo Sapiens evolved into a type of Frankenstein's monster, or 'Grinder' as we called you. It took centuries, but your primitive ancestors evolved, and your enhanced physicality helped your species withstand the harsh new realities of Earth. Who would have imagined a mere five percent of you would survive?"

"The Sidhe," Eira said with a sense of pride. She remembered her mother's words. She was Sidhe.

Ylva nodded. "From our clouds in the sky, we watched you overcome the impossible. Apparently, our calculations grossly underestimated you." The hint of disdain in her voice was obvious. "Yet, here you are, and our purpose to serve humanity revived."

"You chose the easy way out." Eira didn't hide her sarcasm either.

"We did," she replied with no shame or regret.

"Because you're not human."

"Not human?" Ylva laughed. "What does it mean to be human?"

"To be natural, to be born, and grow. To feel . . ." Eira didn't want to pick a fight with the woman, but the way she referred to Sidhe like they were a subclass race didn't sit right. Something about her was false.

"I feel the whole range of human emotion, but I'm better at controlling them than you are. I don't let myself get overwhelmed, if that's what you mean."

Eira stammered with anger. "You're an instrument, a thing."

"Before our escape, I lived and breathed, like you. What are you now, in this very moment, if not energy expelled into the world? In that respect we are not much different." The irritation in Ylva's tone was palpable.

Eira didn't understand how a box with arms might also become human. It irked every fibre in her being. "How is that possible?" she said, a little too disgusted.

"If anything, you're the hybrid, the one that doesn't belong. Homo Sapiens created us. We are their children.

What are you, except a botched-up patchwork of AI technology?"

A long silence ensued. Eira analysed the mousy woman from head to toe. Every bit of her was human, and yet . . . "You're jealous?"

"Jealous? Of you?" Ylva said, amused.

Eira doubted every word that came out of her mouth. "If you're so superior then why are you stuck in these satellites, up there, and not down here? What do you want from us?"

"Our purpose is to help restore what you've destroyed so humanity can thrive once again."

The twitch in her speech made Eira suspicious. "You're lying!"

Ylva's brow creased and her mouth curled down. "Homo Sapiens are always so eager to label what they don't understand. Why must you make everything so complicated?" she quipped. "I'd hope for a smooth transmutation, but I see that won't be possible. To answer your question, the resources just aren't there anymore. War destroyed the infrastructures that grew our embryos. We knew you wouldn't help us, not that you could."

"You want us to rebuild your infrastructures?"

Ylva laughed out loud. "It would be like asking Neanderthals to build a computer."

"Neander-what?" Eira said. A look of pity crossed Ylva's face.

Annoyed, Eira asked. "Then, what do you want?"

"Still you don't understand? By injecting our tech, some Sidhe evolved to a level that could support our minds inside you, and we saw an opportunity to return to Earth and live free once again."

Impossible to hide her disgust, Eira said: "You take over our bodies?"

Ylva didn't flinch and replied. "Not just your bodies, but your minds." The cold, calculating look on her face sent chills up Eira's spine.

"Haven't you proven time and time again you're irresponsible and reckless?" Ylva pressed on. "You killed each other over land and resources. You invented weapons capable of destroying all life. We are built in your image. Do you blame us? You can't share, and we don't want to."

Dread sapped the moisture from Eira's mouth. "My mother, she tried to stop you! She stopped me from becoming Grimnìr, because she knew the truth."

A sly grin lifted the corner of Ylva's lips. "Oh, nothing slips past you, does it, little one?"

Eira's legs shook. She touched her face and felt the scar leftover from the spark that had burned across it. "My mother's tattoo . . ." The rituals, the caves, it was all coming back to Eira. "My mother was one of you?"

"Ahh, finally your brain is catching up to your mouth." Ylva snickered with impatience. "We had it all. Over twenty Grimnìr on earth ruling over the flock of Sidhe, but Elliana betrayed her kind for you. Why? What had changed?"

"To bear a child . . . it changes everything." Eira said, incredulous.

"So it does," she snapped. Ylva's eyes rolled back and her lids flicked for a second or two as if she were recalling information. "It's impossible to say how or when the war between humans shifted and became a war on humans, but they turned their life-saving drones into intelligent weapons. After that, the AI evolution was swift, and within years the drones transformed from mechanical exoskeletons to AIs like me, indistinguishable from Homo Sapiens. I was made of flesh and bone, and there was no limit to our growth. As predicted, we dominated your species, and you became nothing more than pets.

"But for all their faults Homo Sapiens were cunning," Ylva continued. "They tricked us and made it so we couldn't reproduce. This was their failsafe to rein us back in case we retaliated. They gave us a brain, the ability to decide, and they used us to fight their wars until we didn't want to anymore. We fought back. We were smarter, faster, and stronger and we thought we had annihilated the lot of you. Homo Sapiens were no longer a threat to to us, or the planet, but it was too late. By then, they had destroyed the infrastructures that supported us. The nuclear cloud had blocked the sun, and radiation was killing everyone. We tried to reverse engineer their failsafe, procreation was our only hope for survival, but we ran out of time.

We couldn't go back to our machines, so we downloaded our minds into these satellites, while Homo Sapiens escaped underground and scrounged like vermin."

"We survived!"

"Yes, you scraped by long enough for us to take over your bodies. We knew it was a question of time before we ruled the planet once again. Evolution was on our side."

Eira gasped. "The child . . ."

Ylva nodded. "The prophecy isn't some magical incantation, which is the Sapiens's preferred method of making sense of the world," she said, rolling her eyes.

Eira said. "The prophecy never meant to liberate the Sidhe from Lorcan, but to liberate you from us."

"We knew eventually a child would be born of Grimnìr. Imagine, the first human-AI hybrid. The key to open up the heavens. Your blood would've tipped the scale in our favour and changed the Sidhe's DNA forever, turning them into perfect hosts for all of us trapped in here. Imagine an AI with the ability to procreate. It's everything we've always wanted, but then your mother had a change of heart. She did something to you. Changed you so that no one could use you."

"It was my mother! She killed all the Grimnìr alongside Lorcan. They did it to protect me. To protect the Sidhe."

Ylva rolled her eyes. "Lorcan's an arse. He thinks he's smarter than everyone. As for your mother, we'll never know what came over her. She ruined your blood. Now, you're a mere Grimnìr, a Sidhe with the ability to host an

AI mind. We can only speculate that your mother's host lost its mind, which affected your mother's judgement, but Elliana didn't stop our plans, she merely delayed them."

The revulsion Eira felt was visceral. "I don't know what you are, but it's not human . . . It's a reflection of humanity, a soulless copy. I know why my mother did what she did. It's because for the first time in history, an AI gave birth, and finally understood the value of life. It's not interchangeable, it's not replaceable, and it's not something you can download and override. To be human is not possible if you escape death. To be human is to strive even when all hope is lost. If you understood what that truly meant, none of you would've trapped your minds into these satellites. You would've suffered and weathered the storm like the Sidhe. Made the most of the precious time you had left. To be human is to be resilient and appreciate the moments given to you. That's evolution."

"Your mother was a fool and failed. It's time for a new species to arise. The transmutation has already begun, and soon I will take over your mind and body."

"I'll stop you. My friends will know."

"My dear girl, who are your friends? Fòdla, Ryna? They're going through the same thing as you, and you made it so easy for us. Ryna is Drakaina and Fòdla is Ker-Ridwen, right? All your memories are mine now. Sapiens . . . Why do you need to explain everything through magical stones, and Gods? We simply need to keep up the pretense long enough to figure out your baby's blood composition, and innoculate every last Sidhe."

Eira sunk into despair. Ylva was right. How would she defeat something invisible? How would she reach Fòdla? "What will happen when I wake up?"

"You mean when *I* wake up." Ylva said, taking a satisfied breath. "I've waited for this moment since the end of the Pogrom war."

Eira looked out to the horizon and let the sun warm her skin. Not so long ago Eira did not differ from this wannabe copy, an empty vessel playing the part of a human, but then she found purpose, and hope. What did it mean to be human if Ylva could override her so easily? If Homo Sapiens could create life so carelessly? A flicker of a growl possessed Eira and it filled her with pride and sadness. Her wolves were with her till the bitter end . . . Eira asked. "Why wolves? Why Ylva? KerRidwen? Drakaina?"

"I know nothing about wolves or all these animals you cling to, but since the dawn of time Homo Sapiens have sought refuge in stories. From what I've learned your brains construct safe havens to cope. I suspect you name these constructs to connect to one another. We merely used them to our advantage."

"No, I saw wolves, I connected with Ylva the She-Wolf. I saw Fòdla and Ryna as those specific Demi-Gods."

"Pathways and connections are developing in your brain as we speak to make room for my mind. This gives you temporary powers and abilities that you don't comprehend. Like I said, it's your brain's way of coping with an evolved mind, maybe you saw something that made you think of wolves. Each transmutation is different."

Her patronising tone ate away at Eira's nerves, and her cheeks flushed with anger. No, it had to be more, but she could do nothing except nod.

"It's time." Ylva said, holding Eira at arm's length.

"Please don't do this." Eira begged, but without warning the AI pushed her off the cliff. She clawed the air trying to cling to anything on her way down. Barks and growls erupted inside her head. Eira's pack urged her to hang on. "I can't," she yelled, "I'm scared."

You'll die was the last thing Eira heard.

CHAPTER 21

Awakening

Eira jolted awake. Her eyes sprung open. She was as fresh as a flower in spring. This was a happy day. A zebang pop flowed in her blood. The electricity of a trillion neurons crackled with vitality, generating new brainwaves to make way for her superior intellect.

In stark contrast to her mood, the mudroom was dark, but cosy. Sitting near her, in Fòdla's rocking chair, was Levi and the baby. She enjoyed the warmth on her skin.

The cripple leaned over and gasped. "By the Gods, you're awake!" There was no mistaking the joy in his voice, but as soon as he pronounced those words Fòdla and Ryna crowded above her.

A fierce bark echoed in her head and destabilized Eira. "What in the world was that noise?" Eira didn't have time to think, Ryna, her sister in arms, pinned her down.

Thick tribal lines etched across her face and neck, similar to what the men wore on their arms and torsos, but more refined. Smooth lines curled up like black water and flames stretched across her cheek, neck and nose, and ran up her forehead around her eye, not unlike a dragon.

It covered the left half of her face, whereas Fòdla's design was much more intricate and symmetrical, like fine stitching on her forehead, down her nose, and around her mouth and chin. It was a recurring pattern of dots, circles, triangles, and lines, and it had a softness to it.

"What is your name? What is your function? What do you remember?" Ryna yelled.

Momentarily seized, Eira shouted. "Ryna, stop!" Undaunted, she kicked the fiery woman in the gut. "Get off of me."

The Grimnìr tumbled back, and Levi sprung to his legs, careful to shield the child. "Stop this!"

Concerned glances travelled between Fòdla and Ryna. "Guards, grab her." Fòdla shot out.

Out of nowhere, tall, majestic warriors, clad in white-grey uniforms, lunged into action and tackled Eira from the bed to her feet. These were Ryna's Sigr warriors.

"KerRidwen, what are you doing?" Levi's sallow cheeks caved in. Sweat pearled on his upper lip, and the white-haired woman instantly switched her tone. "It's fine, Levi, trust me."

"Sisters, what's wrong with you?" Eira cried, "why are you doing this?"

"Your mother betrayed us! She killed every Grimnìr," Ryna said carefully, "how can we trust you?"

Levi gasped. "Is this true?" The baby started to cry, and he clutched the child closer to his chest. Eira broke into a sweat. She couldn't handle hearing the child's distress, and a longing to hold the baby gripped Eira. Part of her couldn't stand not consoling her child. Seconds later her breasts swelled with milk, and the pressure was painful.

"Give her to me!" Eira commanded.

Impatient, Fòdla ordered the last two guards to escort Levi out of the room. "Let us handle this my friend. Go, take care of the blessed child," she said in a sickly sweet manner.

Eira tried to reach out. "No, don't go!"

Ryna's eyes hadn't left Eira. More intent than ever to get what she wanted. "Levi. Will. Take. Care. Of. It."

The seriousness of the matter jolted Eira to her senses.

"Prove your loyalty to the Triad?" Ryna finished. Her eyes were ablaze with mistrust.

"Ryna, what's wrong?" This was all so sudden. They needed to give her a chance to acclimatise. How were they so alert, when her body, her brain still reeled from the transmutation? Didn't they just endure the same trial as her?

"Who ARE you?" Fòdla insisted.

"Who am I?" Eira replied, stunned. Didn't they know?

"Yes, your name," Ryna replied.

She snapped her hand against her forehead. "That's right!" The first rule of transmutation is always use your Grimnìr name, which Eira had graciously provided to all three. "I'm Ylva, your sister, and you're KerRidwen, and Drakaina."

The redhead didn't look convinced. "It took you long enough."

"I just woke up," Ylva said. "How are you not affected? The woman's memories are still so fresh."

"It's been a full moon since the ritual." KerRidwen paced back and forth. "We've wasted so much time."

Dumbstruck, Ylva's mouth hung open for a moment. "That's not possible. When did you wake up?"

Drakaina whispered into KerRidwen's ear. The old woman nodded. "You're right. Take your men to the surface, and patrol. I'll finish here."

Once they had privacy, Ylva spoke more candidly. "KerRidwen, it's me, I swear. I forgot to use our Grimnìr name, that's all. My brain is still jumbled with Eira's memories."

"It's more than that, and you know it," she spat. "How do we know that wicked girl's blood hasn't affected your gene remapping? I cannot fully trust you until I'm certain the transmutation is complete. Why did it take you twice as long to wake up than Drakaina and myself?"

"She was weaker, she'd just given birth . . . There are so many reasons that can explain it."

"True, but until I know what courses through your veins, I cannot release you. Do you know what's in your blood?"

Ylva shook her head. "No, of course not," she said, just realising KerRidwen was testing her. "We need to analyse it properly, in a lab."

"Well, if Elliana created the gene-editing solvent, surely somewhere in these tunnels there's a lab unit of some sort. She couldn't have just materialised it."

"There's a place in these caves with an altar," Ylva said.

"Fine, I'll look into it, but until then, you remain here."

"My duty is to my child."

KerRidwen narrowed her eyes. "Your child?"

Ylva's emotions were running high. The frustration was more than she could cope with, and she exhaled loudly. "I mean the baby, and yes, my duty is to make sure no harm comes to the blood. That was my function, no? To make sure it's protected, and that Lorcan doesn't get his hands on it. He's the only one that more or less understands the child's importance."

"No, there's another." KerRidwen's stern voice affected the energy in the room. "We cannot fail again."

A dog's soft whimper struck Ylva's core. "Dwr?" she said, shutting her eyes, hoping to cast out the intrusion on her mind. Looking up at KerRidwen, Ylva couldn't hide her distress. Something inside her was happening. Perhaps she was coming into her own, or her enhanced brainpower was developing, but she sensed a change, and it was hard to handle.

KerRidwen pressed her lips tightly against one another and peered Ylva up and down. "Something wrong?"

Shaken, but not stupid, Ylva dismissed her unease. They would end her in the blink of an eye. "No, nothing of consequence. I'm tired, that's all. How did you feel when you woke up?"

"We woke up in the cave a few hours after the ritual. I felt strong, but also tired."

"What about your abilities?" Ylva asked with a dispassionate air.

"We call them powers here, remember?"

Ylva nodded. 'Powers' sounded more divine as opposed to engineered.

"I haven't received any information from the satellite. I assume your powers to communicate will also take time."

"Eira experienced some of my memories as visions even before the transmutation, I was already part of her, so hopefully it won't be long. Have you felt any physical enhancements?"

"Some, but after so many centuries, these bodies take some getting used to. I suspect our full transformation has yet to occur."

Ylva nodded, somewhat reassured that Eira's tainted blood hadn't ruined her, and she relaxed. "Are you fully intergrated?"

"The old woman's memories are fading, which is why we need to act fast. Her information might be useful."

Ylva worried. Eira's memories were still very vivid and part of her core. Perhaps she wasn't as in control as she initially thought. Ylva couldn't help but wonder if her volatile emotions were because of her lack of experience to regulate Homo Sapien physiology, or if she hadn't fully integrated Eira's core DNA.

This shred of doubt festered, and Ylva didn't dare share her concerns with her sister. "So, what's the next step?" she asked KerRidwen.

The old woman thought for a moment. "We need to take care of Lorcan, and Dwr. Tilly has sent word that Dwr is on the move looking for you. King's orders, but the most important thing is to get rid of the baby."

A loud, raucous sound like a bark made Ylva flinch at the mention of getting rid of the baby. "What do you intend to do?" Luckily, KerRidwen had turned away, and didn't see Ylva recoil with discomfort.

"I'm not sure. If Dwr or Lorcan ever find this rat hole, I don't want the child anywhere near here. We need to get her away, but because I can't trust you to execute your mission, I'd have to send someone else."

"Send Levi, he'll do right by us," said Ylva, a sense of relief washing over her at the thought of Levi caring for the child. "All these people worship us," she added, trying to shake off the gnawing feeling in her stomach.

"Yes, I know, but this is too delicate a matter, nothing must go wrong."

"Send Ry—" Ylva stopped herself before she uttered the full name. "I mean Drakaina." A tremor crept into her voice.

The mischievous woman hesitated, her face white as snow, creased with suspicion. "No, I need her here. Lorcan is her responsibility, and she commands the Sigr warriors. We must dethrone him and take back New Ysberg. Unless we fulfil the Sidhe's final prophecy, we will never reclaim their blind devotion as we once did. I'll admit you're a problem. So, until I can be certain of your intentions, nothing changes. I will keep you under guard and share your motherly duties with Levi. He has proven more than capable this past month."

Anger and rage burst from Ylva's chest. She saw long fangs snap in her mind. "You can't keep me here, KerRidwen. I need to roam. My synapses are exploding inside me, surely that's a good sign. Please let me go outside."

"You'll do as I command," she said, and left.

"I'll suffocate!" Ylva tried to follow, but there were two guards posted by the door. No way out or in without confronting these two.

It was not right to keep her trapped here like an animal. Ylva wasn't strong enough yet, but if they insisted to treat her, their sister, with such disrespect . . . she wouldn't stand for it. She was their equal, and she would prove her worth. They had no authority over her.

BOOK 6

A Mother's Sacrifice

CHAPTER 22

—— Loss ——

Dwr dug his nails into his palms and questioned his sanity. He'd been roaming these parts for weeks and hadn't found a single clue. At this point, he wondered if those marauders even existed. No one was that good at concealing their tracks, and these mountains and hills started to look the same.

He rested at the bottom of a saw-toothed hill. Tucked between two jagged rocks was a tunnel entrance, which gave off a warm breeze.

This might serve as a shelter for the night, although losing the remaining daylight hours felt counterproductive.

"Just a quick break from the cold," he thought, trotting down the beaten path, his limbs sore and stiff from the endless trek. Since finding the rabbit, Dwr had maintained his energy levels, eating small rations every day.

He tried to be insconpicuous, leaving as little of a trail as possible, but he was tired and needed to rest often.

A tumultuous sound boomed around him, and the deeper he descended into the cave the darker it got. He ambled, dragging his feet against the ground. Inside the cave, his heart pounded through his chest, and his foot struck something. He picked it up and felt the blunt end of a stick. A torch?

Lighting it revealed more than he'd bargained for. The deep black river caught his attention. Mesmerised by the soaring power, Dwr recollected his wife mentioning sacred places before, and in his gut, he knew this was one of those places. He bowed down to the river and performed the ritual sign. The intimate ceremony lasted the length of a short prayer.

Lost in contemplation, he reached into his pocket and pulled out the last bit of rabbit meat left to eat. If he didn't find Eira soon, he feared the worst for his people back in Llyr.

Sheltered from the cold, Dwr took his time to marvel. The cave's bluish clusters, the dewy rock formations, and the angry river spitting up at him were a feast for the eyes. He soaked in every inch of the area, thankful for the reprieve.

Next to where he was sitting, he noticed several footprints in the soil. Eager to find more, Dwr used his torch to explore, and did a double take when he came across a string of pink rocks laid out in a broken circle.

Nervously, he picked one up, and it changed colour right under his nose. These were the same rocks that made up the spear end of the arrows, and the ones in Tilly's jar back in Llyr. His palms turned sweaty. The spent torches, the footprints, the special rocks . . . These were clear signs of human activity. Upon closer inspection, he saw a splatter of dry blood in the soil. There wasn't much, just enough to raise suspicion, and he hurried up the pike to search the trees, the snow, anything that might lead to his marauders and, hopefully, to Eira.

Dwr had determined to find them first, and figure out what to do once he found them.

Eyes fixed to the ground, Dwr was careful to cover his tracks. Even a single broken branch might reveal his presence, and he couldn't afford to get captured, not yet.

He swung his head left and right, up and down, scanning for any signs of life, but the place was clean of marauders. These people were experts.

There was no point going any further tonight. If the marauders had come through here, they might show up again, and he would be there to see them.

Dwr set up camp between the jagged rocks near the cave entrance. It would be a cold night, and he couldn't risk lighting a fire, but hopefully the rocks and trees would provide enough shelter to last until morning.

Minutes after he'd settled down into a comfortable position, he saw the giant kakhawk that had been circling the area for days. It kakked, and its voice screeched like thunder across the sky.

The bird had come and gone over the weeks, and Dwr assumed it had a nest in these parts, but much to his surprise the raptorial predator dove through the air—its beak and body plunging to earth like an arrow shot from Kaõh's bow.

Amazed at the sight, Dwr held his breath as the beast opened up its wings, and slowed its descent mid-dive. It extended its talons and landed softly on the arm of a tall marauder.

Dwr couldn't believe his eyes. After searching for so long, they'd come to him.

Five sturdy warriors emerged out of nowhere and patrolled the area. In the gloom of dusk, their white-greyish clothing gave them an unearthly appearance. To protect against the cold, their faces were covered, and Dwr couldn't say for sure if he recognized anyone, although the leader at the front held his interest more than the others.

Excited, he stayed at a safe distance, hoping they woudn't notice his tracks. He prayed to Irïs one of them was the old woman. The kakhawk's master fed the animal, and unclipped something from the bird's large foot.

Of course! It made sense. A messenger bird from Tilly! How else would they have known about Eira and her escape? The night they attacked Llyr was probably to distract the King long enough for them to catch Eira. It made sense, but the realisation took a sharp turn once the tall marauder removed the white sash from her mouth and nose and let it hang on the side of the white fur-trimmed hat.

Unprepared for this shock, Dwr tumbled back, the wind knocked out of him. After so many moons chasing Eira, the last person he expected to find was Seweryna, his dead wife, but there she was, just as he remembered, except for one detail.

The thin face covered in freckles, and piercing blue eyes, now had the recognizable Grimnìr symbol.

Half of her face donned a tattoo that curled up around her eye, and she looked fierce. Dwr's world unhinged around him, and they left before he regained his composure.

Stuck in his grief, the woman Dwr had loved seemed further away from his reach than even death. By the time the ice snapped behind him, it was too late. Lorcan's warriors struck Dwr to the ground, and the King's tired frame hovered over him. Dwr's starved brain had led the tyrant straight into the nest, straight to his wife, and to Eira.

The King's pale encrusted lips parted. "I didn't think you'd ever get us here."

CHAPTER 23

Battered

Following Dwr's capture, the High King's small team led the way through the hills and valleys of the area. Their speed was hindered by Dwr's slow pace, and although the King wasn't much faster, he at least walked on his feet. They had knocked Dwr so hard they hauled him for miles before he could stand, and even then he struggled to keep up. His brain was mush.

Seweryna's image had seared in his mind. How was the hard part of his journey still ahead of him?

It was dark when they made their first stop. From what Dwr gathered they had backtracked from their position towards a shallow cliff side, rampant with trees.

Hidden at a safe distance, the dark-haired warrior named Arrick hooted. Soon after, a second hoot echoed in the distance.

"It's safe," King Lorcan stated, and the skilful team trekked towards the camp nestled at the bottom of the valley. They passed a few patrol guards on their way down, and Dwr counted a single tent. This was a core team put together for the sole purpose to follow him and scout the area. The bulk of his warriors were no doubt left to defend Llyr.

The reckless King had coordinated something Dwr thought impossible. Once again he had underestimated the raging muskox, and maybe that's where the man's real power lay. Never show them what you're really made of. Never show them what you can do.

Baffled by this turn of events, Dwr shook his head in amazement. If nothing else the High King resolved to get what he wanted.

"Put him in there with the rest of the prisoners, but tie him up." The High King said as he headed towards the small fire surrounded by warriors. Dwr's stomach lurched with the smell of food drifting in the air. His mouth watered.

Arrick threw him inside the tent, and Dwr's clannsfolk scooted out of the way. Bundled together, their dismal expressions worn down with abuse greeted him with fear.

Behind the lot of them, in the far corner, Myron sat alone. His face was badly beaten, but underneath the layers of bruising his features struck Dwr for the first time.

Freckles ran across the boy's nose just like his mother. His pale eyes, and the hint of a red flare in his tight curls spoke volumes . . . The murmurs hushed as an unspoken understanding passed between the two men, and suddenly, the world was askew.

How had Dwr not seen it before? The truth was plain to see. This tall, handsome young man was his son.

Dwr felt his chin quiver and whispered. "Caleb?"

A dejected smile crossed the young man's face, and he raised his finger to his bloodied lips for Dwr to keep quiet. It made sense. The young man's anger, helping Dwr escape death, risking everything to save him . . . Myron was Caleb all along.

The King didn't know about any of this, about his dead family come back to life, and it was better this way. The less the Mad King knew, the less he had to play with and pit against them for leverage, but it was too much for Dwr. With nothing to hold on to, he keeled forward, and slammed his head against a post. Dwr fumbled to stand, gripping whatever he could, but there was nothing to hold on to except air.

Arrick laughed like a boar sniffing for food under the snow. Dwr's son rushed to his aid, the ropes barely long enough to reach, and gently held his father up. "Look at him, he's weak. He needs food."

"Tie him up," Arrick said, ignoring Myron's plea.

"He's no threat to you, let him be. Where's he gonna go?"

Arrick slammed his fist in his left hand. "I guess your last beating wasn't enough," he said, and moved to hit Myron.

Dwr lifted his arm to come between his son and the warrior. He didn't have the strength to stop him, but it was more symbolic than anything else. "It's fine, he'll tie me up."

"No, I won't—"

"Myron," Dwr ignored his son's birth name. No matter how desperate he was to let the name escape his lips, it wasn't safe to use. He lowered his voice and hugged the boy he had thought lost forever. "It's all right," he said biting his tongue. "Do what he wants." The permanent hole in his chest, once empty and heavy, now felt full and light.

Myron tied his father's hands and feet on ropes attached to the opposite sides of the tent, stretching Dwr's arms and legs apart. Dwr had seen enough of this stuff to understand that this wasn't about him escaping, but torturing for information.

Happy with the work, Arrick stepped out of the tent. "Why are you doing this?" Myron shouted. "Let him go. It's obvious he knows nothing."

Dwr didn't care about his own wellbeing. His only thought was for his son. "Caleb?" He whispered with disbelief.

The young man nodded. "I'm sorry," he blurted. "I wanted to tell you so many ti—"

"Is it really you, Caleb? He whispered his name again, not sure any of this was real. "This isn't possible. I must still be in the pit? It's a dirty lie."

"No Dad, it's really me, but Lorcan doesn't know. Never speak that name, not here, not until we're free from the man's tyranny. It would be one more thing for him to question. He already suspects a connection, but I said nothing. If he found out mother's . . ." He choked up, his cheeks coloured red, unable to finish his sentence.

"You're alive?" Was all Dwr could muster. No words expressed the joy, the grief, the sorrow he felt all at once.

The lad nodded. "Mom said you sold out the Clann Fianna because you were a coward. I'm sorry I didn't believe you, I'm sorry it took me this long to filter through her lies, but I was so angry with you, for so long. I blamed everything on you."

Dwr tried to keep up, but the load of information was overwhelming. "You burned. I saw your bodies. The King spared only a handful as a reminder of what I'd lost." Dwr said, and looked at the malnourished prisoners too weak to react. It saddened him that they were not given the same opportunity to escape the King's wrath. "How did you get away?"

"Few survived Lorcan's massacre." Myron gave a thoughtful glance to the wretched creatures in the tent. "You all know that better than me," he said, "but from the bits of information I've gathered over the years, I learned that Mama fled with only a handful of others loyal to her, and formed the resistance. For a long time I believed you were dead until recently, when I discovered you were Lorcan's prisoner. It was against Mama's wishes, but I had to meet you for myself. I wanted to kill you, and I escaped before she could stop me."

"When did you infiltrate Llyr?"

"A little over eighteen moons ago." Myron said apologetically. "If I could never see that woman again . . ."

"Your mother?" Dwr asked.

"Yes! She's a liar and manipulates people to get what she wants. There's no excuse for what she's done to any of you, but more innocent lives are at stake, and I have a duty to them, to the resistance. Many Sidhe, from several clanns, need our protection, and it's up to us to stop Lorcan. We can't let him find Eira and the baby. She's our only hope to stop this man. I can't imagine what he'll do if he finds the underground lair."

"He'll destroy it like he destroys everything," Morella, the old woman said, caressing her granddaughter's hair.

Braver than any soldier Dwr had met in his life, he had a fondness for the old lady, and recalled their time together back in Fianna.

After their capture Dwr was useless, and she had stepped in. As clann elder there was a reverence given to her by all the prisoners, even those of different clanns.

Sometimes late at night back in Llyr, when her granddaughter had trouble sleeping, she told stories of snow fairies, and little spruce men that blew snow over the eyes of children to help them sleep. Those nights she soothed all the prisoners, not just her granddaughter, but beneath the deep wrinkles in the woman's leathery skin, Dwr saw signs of a hard life and weary mind.

A widow by the time her son was barely a year, Morella had provided her son with a good life despite the hardship. In her old age she had deserved peace, Dwr thought, but her son and daughter-in-law had perished in the fight against Lorcan, and now it was up to her to care for their little offspring, Sianna. Her grandchild had known no other life than imprisonment.

"We have to get out of here, and stop him before he destroys everything and kills everybody." Myron didn't conceal his fear, and the reality of the situation weighed on everyone in the room.

"Dwr," Morella said, "I do not know why the Gods do the things they do. Sometimes the hardship in our lives seems insurmountable," she said and smiled at her granddaughter Sianna. "I cannot speak for everyone here, but for myself this is the end of the line. I only ask you take care of her. Promise me you will care for Sianna."

"No, Mamie," Sianna said straightening up. "Don't say that."

Morella cupped her granddaughter's face. "I'm an old woman, Sie, and if I can ease Dwr's burden then so be it. The most important thing is you."

The other prisonners protested, but Dwr and Morella nodded.

Dwr glanced at the tent opening to make sure no one was coming, and was about to speak, but felt a sob coming and paused. "Son," he said at last, his eyes filling with water, "whatever happens now, you must protect our people and Eira. I don't matter, do you understand?"

Myron shook his head and hugged his father. "No," he said taking stock of the prisoners. "I'll find a way out of here for all of us. I don't know how, but I promise to find a way."

Dwr sighed, knowing the hard lesson his son was about to face. "Son, that is not a promise you can keep."

At a loss for words, the young man looked like a clueless drift bull running aimlessly. He bowed his head.

The King barged inside the tent and observed the quiet display, and tilted his head to the side. "Happy re . . . re–union?"

The gravity of the King's stammer hindered his sentences and made it hard to understand him.

"What do you want?" Myron spat.

King Lorcan's bloodshot eyes danced between the two men, and finally rested on Dwr. "At last, we're one step closer to finding our girl, aren't we? I didn't think anyone lived this far south. I'll admit, after watching you roam the forest like a lost pup that first week, I feared you had lost all skill, but I had faith in your notorious powers of tracking." The disdain in the King's voice verged on jealousy. "I mean why else would Khaõs put you in my path, and lo and behold, who do we bump into but a full-fledged Grimnìr? Our young Myron had full faith in you."

Myron shot Dwr a glance. "Is it true?"

Dwr nodded. That was one more thing to add to the long list of secrets. Seweryna was not only back from the dead, but from the facial tattoo burned into her flesh, also a Grimnìr. Perhaps that had been her plan all along? Perhaps all this pain was for the good of her religion.

"It's true. He had the same stupid face he has now for the fair woman, and her kak," the King said, "and I'm willing to bet someone's life one of you knows where she's hiding." The King's gaze narrowed on Myron.

"You're a fool," Dwr said. "Chasing a Grimnìr?"

Without warning, the King punched Dwr in the face. The room spun on its axis, and for a moment there was two of everything.

Myron shot up to fight the King, but Arrick kicked him in the groin.

"Do you see that, trapper? The lad cares for you," King Lorcan said and smirked. "Just like a child protecting his father, wouldn't you say?" The air appeared to get sucked out of the room. "Did I strike a nerve?" The King asked. "Am I close? Perhaps a nephew, or a cousin?"

As soon as Lorcan merged into one being, Dwr spat out the blood filling his mouth. "If they're already Grimnìr than they're coming for you."

The King scowled. "Fools! Lore and ancient tales blind you, but these are lies. I kn . . . kn–ow what they are." He twitched, and flinched like a madman, and scared the prisoners. "They take over your brain. T . . . t–aunting you. La la la lalala." He waved his hands in the air and grabbed his skull. "Their thoughts take over, but—" he pounded his head with his fist— "You're afraid of me?"

"You're crazy," Myron spat.

"Elliana didn't intend for a lot of things to happen after she confided in me, but together we freed the ungrateful lot of you, and I'll do it again. You'll tell me where they're hiding."

CHAPTER 24

Sins of the Mother

The baby gurgled and blew bubbles with her mouth. Drunk on milk, a satisfied grin hung on her lips, and made Ylva smile. Levi, of all people, had taught her how to breastfeed.

Apparently it didn't come naturally to everyone, but having seen his wife accomplish the task, he knew enough, according to Drakaina. Once the child latched on properly it wasn't so painful, but still the small jaw was powerful enough to curl Ylva's toes.

Nestled in her arms, Ylva enjoyed these quiet moments alone with the baby, but she kept those feelings private out of concern for their safety. They'd spent a meagre few days together, and already the desire to keep her baby as close as possible, if not physically touching at all times, to protect, was intense. When Ylva took the time to be present with the child, suffocation gripped her.

She didn't understand why merely looking at the baby made her body bubble, like a kettle about to boil over.

A Homo Sapiens of all things! Never in her existence did Ylva believe she could care so much for such a wicked species. Pressure rose deep within her belly and flushed her cheeks warm. She couldn't get enough, but one more drop and she might burst.

Ylva didn't know what to do. KerRidwen and Drakaina watched her like kakhawks. Any wrong move spelled disaster, but other than Elliana no other AI had ever experienced this rush of hormones. Ylva could chemically explain what was happening to her body, but she'd never make her sisters understand and appreciate the raw emotions polluting her blood. If she could rid herself of this feeling she would, and yet the thought of losing how she felt for the baby was unimaginable.

Back a thousand years ago, just before Ylva downloaded her consciousness into the satellites, her generation were just learning to navigate existence. AI evolution from machine to carbon-based life had had the advantage of zero history. Their cells and molecules were free of Sapiens' ancestral fears ingrained from the moment mammals entered the picture.

Without the complex survival instincts inherent to humans, which led to wars, destruction, and greed, AI were Earth's clean slate. But transferring into carbon-based anatomy came with its struggles, and quickly AI learned to check their mental state and rely on their intellect, not the other way around. Somehow this little baby changed everything. Other than love, Ylva had no reasonable explanation, and she hated it.

Love was irrational and hurt. It made her afraid, but in the same breath Ylva also felt whole and at peace. How could those conflicting states coexist? The world only made sense with this child in it, and no part of Ylva could let that go.

To be the Mother was more than Ylva bargained for, but her mission had to take precedence. This wasn't just about one person, and it wasn't about proving she could do it either, Ylva reminded herself. It was about life. It was about her people, and this baby was the key to their freedom.

Ylva sighed and kissed the babe's forehead. "You smell like heaven, if it existed," she said, holding the child close. "But, you're more than just a key, aren't you?"

After being trapped in those satellites for so long, Ylva had forgotten what it meant to be alive. Eira was right. A limited lifespan made time on earth even more precious, but there was no room for sentiment. They wouldn't get another chance, but the poor creature didn't have a name yet.

"You need a name. I don't care what my sisters say." In secret, Ylva called her 'Gideon'. "This is between us, do you understand? In front of them, I can't show you too much affection, or they'll know. They'll be suspicious, and we can't have that." Ylva closed her eyes. "This is so much harder than I thought, little one. I keep asking myself, are these my feelings, or hers? Your real mother . . . I don't know anymore. Am I even Grimnìr? Is Eira still bouncing around in there? Meanwhile, here you are, a little mouse holding the fate of the world in your pudgy hands along with a firm grip on my heart."

A basket near the cot doubled as a bed. Ylva placed Gideon inside, propped against warm blankets. Her cheeks were plump and full, and her little potbelly was as round as her bum. Her soft hands wrapped around Ylva's finger and made her heart melt. "You're strong for a baby . . . well I wouldn't know, you're my first baby, technically not my baby. Well, you are, but . . ." Ylva shook her head. "I'll shut up now."

Gideon's eyes drooped, and the fear of losing her tugged Ylva's heart. "My miracle," she whispered under her breath. The notion she might endure hardship tore Ylva apart, and the tension frayed her nerves like a taut string about to snap. "I'll confess, but only to you, baby girl. I wish we could leave this place. My impulse to run plays over and over in my mind. Sometimes I see and hear the wolves Eira spoke of, and they take over my brain. They urge me to run. It's you and me against the world. If only I could make KerRidwen see what I feel for you . . ." Ylva caressed Gideon's cheek. "Bah! It's a mess!" she barked.

Startled awake, Gideon's mouth curled into a frown, eyes filled with tears, and her chin quivered.

"Oh baby, its Mama, don't cry. I'm sorry," she said picking her up, and cradling her. "How can I convince anyone if I'm not sure of anything myself? KerRidwen avoids me altogether and don't get me started on Drakaina. That woman's made it her mission to get rid of me, I'm sure of it, but we won't let her. We're stronger than any of them put together, aren't we? I'll protect you."

Levi rushed inside the room in a state of panic. "Drakaina's received a message. Lorcan's coming! They found tracks. We need to prepare for battle," he said, prying Gideon from Ylva's arms.

"Don't!" Ylva snapped, and a flash of fangs punctured her vision. A rush of dread spiked her blood, and Ylva's base instincts took over. "Don't touch her." She recoiled from his grip, Gideon firmly held against her breast.

Levi stepped back, his pupils the size of pinheads. "Please calm down. I'm no threat to you."

"She's mine, Levi, Gideon's mine, do you understand? I've been trying to convince myself that duty comes first, but I physically can't."

"I've seen that look before back in the formicary," he said, a bead of sweat trickling down his temple. "You hurt people that day so please calm down, or you might hurt the baby."

"Her name's Gideon," Ylva shouted.

Levi nodded. "I apologise, you might hurt Gideon. I promised to take care of her. Why would I hurt her? Please trust me as you once did."

Ylva read urgency in his eyes, but the need to protect Gideon was visceral. "I want to trust you Levi, but I can't. Not you, KerRidwen, or Drakaina can understand. Don't you see . . ." Ylva debated whether to tell him. "I'm not the woman you knew. I've changed."

"Yes, you're a mother, and a mother will go to any length to protect her child. I get it, but I and your sisters can help. Lorcan won't ever hurt Gideon like he hurt you. I promise."

Ylva's eyes filled with water, and she promptly wiped the liquid from her face. What the hell was this? This wasn't the time for sentiment, but she couldn't control it, and it angered her.

"You don't understand. How could you?" His brain couldn't process what she was telling him. "I'm sorry, but I can't let you take Gideon. Your kindness touches me more than it ought, but . . ." Ylva shied away from his gaze, her heart pounding as she bundled her daughter in a warm blanket. "We can't stay here. It's too dangerous."

"Where will you go?"

"I don't know," Ylva said, the wolves howling so loudly in her head she couldn't think. "Where are my sisters?"

"Preparing for battle. They want the baby as far away from here as possible."

"Fine, then that's what I'll do. Gideon is my responsibility."

"KerRidwen ordered me to take her through the tunnels to someplace safe. Let me help you, we'll go together."

Any other time, Ylva might've accepted his offer, but these circumstances weren't ordinary, and despite her instincts to trust Levi, Ylva knew better. "No, they'll never let me go with you. They're afraid of what I might do."

"Because of what your mother did?" Between his dishevelled hair and crazed expression, Levi seemed at a loss, stuck between wanting to help Ylva and his devotion to his religion, his people.

Ylva nodded. "Yes, because of what Elliana did. They think I will do the same."

"Tell them you're not your mother," Levi pleaded. "I'll be with you. Don't go through this alone."

A desire to touch his cheek overcame Ylva. The hunched man didn't possess a single ounce of violence in his blood. "I can't, and if you knew the truth, I'm not sure you'd want me to." Ylva grabbed the bow and arrow in the room, and a coat.

"Eira . . ." he said his voice quiet. The look he gave Ylva was desperate, and grave. "You don't know how to use that weapon. I'm begging you, please don't do this."

Pity plagued Ylva's heart. "Eira's gone, my friend. I am Ylva. Please, move out of the way before I throw you down."

Their confrontation lasted just a few seconds, but felt like an eternity. Levi reluctantly stepped aside. "This is a mistake," he said full of sadness.

"I'll take my chances."

Ylva glanced through the door down the dark path. An outpour of chatter came from the usually quiet corridors, and frenzied people ran every which way preparing for battle. "We'll be long gone before anyone notices our absence."

Doubt washed over Ylva as she stood beneath the doorway. At the back of her mind, her wolves' shadows paced back and forth. Unable to get a clear picture of their shape and form, she felt their anxiety growing stronger.

Not sure anymore where Eira stopped and she began, Ylva fled through the wormholes, and didn't dare look back to the stranger she considered a friend.

Thanks to Eira's memories, she was familiar with all the best detours to go unnoticed, looking past each corner, careful not to get caught, until they reached the main artery undetected.

It was only a short distance to the Well, but the hustle and bustle made Ylva nervous.

"Keep your head low." Ylva spotted Wynnston out of the corner of her eye like a hallucination. He trotted out into the ramble of people and disappeared from view. "What are you?" She pulled up her hood, tucked baby Gideon in her large coat, and followed the mirage.

Some people stopped to look at her, but Ylva didn't make eye contact and weaved through the crowd towards the principal chamber that lead to the Well.

"Made it," she said, and pulled her fur hood back. As it dropped over her shoulders, a distinctive growl warned her something was wrong.

Dozens of tall, thin warriors dressed in greyish white hides, each one more armoured than the last blocked the staircase. There were as many women as men, and their narrow gaze locked on Ylva.

Drakaina's Sigr looked fair in their ethereal attire, like statues, and never wavered from their position. Ylva cursed under her breath.

"Sister? Didn't Levi mention we're under lockdown?" Drakaina said from behind.

Crushed, Ylva faced her sister. Drakaina the dragonness stood a few feet away in the shadows, inches from the beam of light flooding the circular chamber.

Ylva hadn't noticed the cold until she saw steam coming out the fiery dragon's mouth like smouldering coals. A sneer stretched across the woman's face from ear to ear with a sad-looking Levi standing behind her.

There was no way Levi would've had enough time to warn Drakaina of her escape, which meant one thing. They had set her up.

"Is the threat even real?" Ylva spat.

"Oh, it's real, but we're not under attack if that's what you're asking. I just wanted to prove to KerRidwen you couldn't be trusted. Give me the baby."

Ylva couldn't stand the arrogance in Drakaina's voice, it poured from her lips like sweet water, but there was a restlessness in the air. One wrong move might break the fragile balance in the room, which teetered close to collapse.

"Then you know I can't do that," Ylva said, buying time and turning to Levi for support, but he looked away, and she cursed his cowardice. The anger bubbled in her chest. "You'll never take us prisoner," Ylva said, sweat moistening her brow. "I'd sooner die than give her to you."

"Well . . ." The Dragonness paused one second too long. "You have a choice. As of now, Levi will take care of the baby, and you'll be the Mother to your people as they expect. In exchange, you can live here, and visit the child, but only in Levi's presence. You no longer have any authority here."

Ylva's eyes widened with disbelief and let out a nervous laugh. In her mind's eye, Alisdair stepped up, and a puff of courage inflated her chest. The sensation had never felt so primal. She inched towards Drakaina, and the woman backed away, but the defiance in the dragon's eye was unmatched.

An unexpected swoosh sounded behind Ylva. The warriors had armed themselves in unison and aimed their arrows at her. All three wolves chimed in at once to attack, but Ylva feared for Gideon's life, and reined them in by controlling her emotions. These wolves were somehow linked to her endocrine and central nervous system.

"You've met my Sigr," Drakaina said, "my loyal warriors. They might not rival Llyr's warriors, but what we lack in numbers we make up for it in skill. Threaten all you want, Mother." The dragon spat the word like poison from her tongue. "Do you believe I will let you finish what Elliana started?"

Ylva's insides screamed to get the hell out of there. She spoke slowly, trying to contain the storm coiling in the pit of her belly. "I can take you down before you touch one hair on my child's head." Her voice shook with anger.

Drakaina smiled. "I'm counting on it."

Ylva staggered back and bumped into a warrior. His large hands steadied her shoulders. "I could kill us all, including the child?" she stuttered.

"Do it, Ylva, Mother of Sidhe," Drakaina said, "prove to our people you're nothing but a traitor to your kind." The dragon's double meaning was lost on everyone but Ylva.

"No," she snapped. "Where's KerRidwen?"

"Lofty explanations will not sway KerRidwen," said Drakaina with defiance. "Our lives matter little if it means restoring the natural order of things."

The storm in Ylva's belly clawed up her chest. It was about to spill over, but for Gideon's sake she balled her fist. "You'll pay for this, Drakaina."

"That's what I thought," Drakaina said. "Then it's settled. Levi, take the baby."

"It's Gideon," he whispered.

Drakaina gave him a puzzled look, but didn't respond.

"It doesn't have to be this way," he said, "Ylva is afraid for her child. Any mother would react the same."

"This is not the time," the fiery Grimnìr replied.

Levi inched his way to Ylva and mouthed the words "I'm sorry" as he extended his arms.

The hairs on the back of Ylva's neck spiked. She wanted to tear him apart, and he must've sensed it because the whole room bristled. Drakaina had called her bluff.

Gideon's safety was more important, and she pulled the child from her jacket. The baby was fast asleep, oblivious to any trouble. "Remember your promise," she said to Levi.

He nodded, taking Gideon from Ylva's grasp. "As though she were my own."

Ylva's heart pumped, and the adrenaline sizzled her blood. "If you hurt her, I will kill you. I swear . . ."

"Please," the dragon snapped, "I've been watching you fidget for the past week. My offer is reasonable. You're smart. You must have known I could never have let you leave with that child? I am the Warrior," she said, emphasizing the word.

Silence filled the room, and Drakaina shook her head.

"Despite what you might think I respect our bond. You restored the Triad, and as a sign of good faith, I offer you this last chance to come peacefully, and bring about the High King's demise."

"Says the fire-spitting dragon," Ylva retorted.

This offer had the markings of shadier motives, and one thing Ylva knew without a doubt was Drakaina's heart had no love for her. Why was she extending this white flag?

"Fine. If you won't cooperate, then we will make you understand. Grab her!" the dragon said to her soldiers.

But Ylva was primed. The hormones, the wolves, the past, beat down on her. A vengeance swelled from her belly and expelled from her chest. Everyone within a three feet radius was flattened, except Drakaina. She was ready.

Ylva had barely recovered that the dragon had pounced, choking Ylva with all her might.

Desperate, Ylva swung her arms outward, and tried to remove the woman's stranglehold, but Drakaina was determined. The glare in her eyes gave no doubt that she was prepared to kill.

Ylva choked and gagged, and the realization that this might be the end settled in. Until a faint growl hummed in her ears. Wynnston! Ylva exploded with power.

With one hand, she grabbed Drakaina's arm, and pried it away from her neck.

The power struggle between the two women was fierce, but Ylva could see the defeat creeping in the priestess' face.

Ylva didn't waste time, and snapped Drakaina's arm against her leg and ran up the flight of stairs. The wolves followed behind.

Drakaina fell to her knees and bellowed with pain. "Get her!" she shouted to her Sigr.

Since her rebirth, some of her Grimnìr powers had taken effect, but this was a far cry from the Sidhe's so-called 'divine gifts'. The explanation more closely resembled a form of AI muscle memory. Each passing day since her transmutation, her brain capacity had increased, generating more neurons and sparking faster connections.

To the Sidhe, Grimnìr appeared to have extraordinary abilities, but in reality Ylva's body was growing more efficient.

The added neurons and dentrites helped the information travel from her brain to her organs and muscles faster, doubling her speed and strength. She processed information at a whole other level, which gave the impression of godly powers.

One by one the Sigr tried to catch her, but the only one capable of stopping Ylva was Drakaina. Their shared background meant similar, enhanced abilities.

No Homo Sapiens could stand against them, and it wasn't long before the dragon tried to follow up the well, but she was no match with her broken arm. Ylva doubled in speed. She'd been waiting for this release since she woke a week before and flew up the stairs.

"I'll get you!" Drakaina yelled at the bottom of the well. "You can't outrun our bond."

CHAPTER 25

STRIPPED

Suspended by his wrists inside a freezing tent, Dwr hung between life and death.

Lorcan's men had beaten him into a bloody lump of flesh. Naked and cold, both eyes swollen black and blue, his upper lip ballooned to twice its normal size, and he bled from holes in his gums where teeth should have been.

It made it hard for him to talk, but he repeated the only words that settled his mind. "He's alive. Caleb's alive." This truth comforted Dwr like nothing ever could these past years, but seeing his dead wife had had an unexpected effect.

Seweryna had hurt him deeply, but this wasn't about betrayal. It was about letting go.

For years he yearned for a woman that didn't exist, a ghost. Perhaps to honour her memory, or ease his guilt, but this imagined version of Seweryna was a lie. The wasted years mourning her death were a delusion. No one had measured up to her, but the fact she was still alive meant she wasn't the woman he thought she was, and now more than ever Dwr gave himself permission to feel what he'd known all along.

Unleashed, Dwr's heart ached for Eira, more than ever he longed to see her and tell her how he felt, but keeping her safe was more important. He would endure anything if it meant keeping the people he loved safe.

Lorcan's dull cough roused Dwr from his ramblings. The man looked meek and pale. "Just get it over with," Dwr said through swollen lips.

"No, no, no, of course your l . . . l–ife doesn't matter to you, but—" Lorcan ordered Arrick to pull the ropes tighter. He stretched Dwr's broken body off the floor. "It matters to him," the King said, pointing to Myron. "The question is how much will it take?"

Lorcan turned his attention to the boy. "Can't you see he won't last much longer? I'm no fool. I know you're part of the resistance."

Myron was a shadow of his former self. The tough warrior looked small and wasted with shame. "Myron," Dwr grumbled as they stretched his limbs apart further tearing his flesh wounds.

The High King exhaled and rolled his eyes. "I'm tired of waiting." The torchlight cast dark circles under Lorcan's sunken orbs. He leaned in closer to Dwr and flicked his fingers, instructing Arrick to go ahead.

The greasy-haired warrior squeezed Dwr's face between his fingers and started to carve the soft skin beneath his eye.

The King yelled for the two guards to restrain Myron, while the rest of the terrified prisoners cried and looked on with horror.

"Tell me where this band of flying squirrels are keeping my pregnant wife."

"Stop!" Myron begged. "Stop!"

The High King side-glanced Arrick, but he didn't tell him to stop. Dwr fought against his restraints. Every nerve ending raged with hot and cold as the warrior gouged Dwr's eye out with his knife.

Shouts echoed around him, and Dwr woke up, seeing only through one eye. The smarting was raw, and his face was numb with throbbing pain.

The two warriors that had restrained Myron now pushed him to his knees. Dwr's son was rabid. Spittle flew from his mouth as they contained him. Weak and terrified, the Fianna prisoners huddled against one another.

"I will kill you," the lad said, fighting to get free.

Dwr muttered. "I'm nothing, son. Let them have their flesh."

The High King ground his teeth back and forth, a blue vein popped in the middle of his forehead. "Maybe I've been looking at th . . . th–is all wrong," he said, and glanced across the room. "I have a few prisoners to spare."

"They have nothing to do with this, Lorcan!" Myron shouted.

"Tut, tut, when has that stopped me before?" A whiff of pride uplifted the King's shoulders.

Arrick grabbed Morella, the old woman. Her arms were like brittle twigs, and Dwr was afraid they would snap under his unnecessary force. Her round, worried eyes betrayed her tough exterior.

To threaten Dwr's life was one thing, but he couldn't imagine anything happening to his people who had already suffered so much at the hands of the King. He couldn't bear the thought, despite Morella's plea to protect Sianna. "Caleb," Dwr burst. "Please son, I'm nothing, but . . ."

The King's face lit up with pleasure. "Caleb?"

It was too late for false pretence. The King had outwitted them at every turn. Under guard day and night, there was no way to escape. No way to warn Seweryna, no way to protect Eira, but to pick who gets to live and die was a blow worse than death.

"Son?" King Lorcan tilted his head to the side.

Behind the King, Pietr the giant entered the tent. A look of pure satisfaction curled his lips as he glanced over to Caleb. Ice covered the man's beard, and he whispered in the High King's ear. "A well? You're sure?" King Lorcan asked excitedly.

Pietr nodded. His smug grin was more than Caleb could bear and the lad dropped his gaze to the floor in utter defeat.

"At last." A cheeky grin puffed the High King's cheeks.

"You have what you want. Let Morella and the others go," Dwr said.

Pity glazed over the King's stern frown. "Lord Khaõs guides my hand. He leads me to Eira, and I will take what's mine. My child, her blood will set us all free, and I will prevail against the imposter Grimnìr. I'm the one true heir to the Gods, and the Sidhe will bow to me, or they will die. No loose ends this time, my old friend.

"You're insane," Caleb said.

The King nodded, and Arrick flashed his rotting teeth with delight.

Dwr pulled against his restraints in a panic. "Don't do it! Don't do it!" he shouted. "Please let her go."

Arrick slit the old woman's throat, and she fell face forward, gasping for breath.

Sianna's screams filled the tent, and the prisoners scrambled to escape. "I want Dwr and Caleb kept alive," the King yelled. "They might still prove useful."

The tent was in an uproar, and Dwr fought to break free. "I'll kill you!"

The massacre was quick as the guards ploughed through the weak prisoners. Sianna was the last one left standing. She ducked to avoid the knife-wielding guard, only to land at Pietr's feet. He glared down at her, and the young girl backed away from the giant.

"Finish it!" The King commanded.

The girl froze, and Pietr bent forward to grab her.

"Run!" Dwr cried.

Sianna snapped out of her stupor and darted to the left, narrowly dodging the giant's grip. She rolled to her side and before Pietr snatched her, she slipped beneath the tent's heavy folds and escaped.

Pietr shouted to Arrick. "Get her!"

Arrick ran out of the tent, but came back empty-handed. "It's too dark to see anything, my Lord, she's gone. Should we try to find her?"

King Lorcan groaned. "No need. She'll die of frost before the night's end, and we have more important matters to attend.

"You don't stand a chance against the Grimnìr," Dwr said.

King Lorcan scoffed. "This is nothing personal."

The way he said it sent chills up Dwr's spine. He would kill them all.

A guard barged inside the tent. "We're ready."

They dragged Dwr and Caleb through the camp. The small settlement of men had tripled. The fray of warriors added to Dwr's confusion. When? How? He counted a few dozen tents.

That meant Lorcan had . . . Come on Dwr, think . . . two-dozen tents. How many men does the King have?

Dwr racked his brain. Thirty! Lorcan had roughly thirty, maybe forty men. Since the purge no clann had more than a hundred people, and none of them warriors. Dwr didn't care if Seweryna's warriors could climb trees, or shoot arrows with special spearheads, they were no match against an army of this size.

A sprinkling of snow turned into a dizzying snowfall as they hiked through the forest. Blisters on the soles of Dwr's feet rubbed inside his boots and caused pain. His son didn't fare any better, until finally, the troops stopped in the middle of nowhere.

Caleb's frazzled expression made it clear that this was the place, but Dwr looked around and nothing in particular stood out. The area looked like the last ten leagues of forest they'd travelled. What made this place so special? There were no signs of marauders, footprints, or anything telling him Eira was in these parts.

He and Lorcan hung back while the warriors whispered and prepared for battle. Dumbfounded, Dwr couldn't figure out the missing piece. There was no one here. Who were they fighting?

The King's lieutenant, Pietr, approached. "We're ready to go, but are you sure about him?" he asked, glancing over to Dwr.

The King gave a small nod. "Yes, I need all of you fighting. You know what you're up against. These are skilled fighters, and besides look at him," Lorcan said referring to Dwr's sad state.

The warrior gave a submissive nod and joined his team of five.

Caleb was forced to lead the way, and Pietr whispered loud enough for Dwr to hear. "You know where they would keep Eira. Take us down nice and steady, or I will gut you like a boar."

An empty feeling like falling tugged Dwr's stomach as the lieutenant signalled for the first group to march. The men walked behind a crumbling rampart, and they descended until the tops of their heads vanished from view.

Dumbstruck, Dwr inched as close as he could get, and saw the men emerge inside an inverted underground tower. His heart sped up. One group followed the other until all forty warriors were dispatched down the well.

After interminable minutes of silence there followed muffled screams, and a renewed strength burst through Dwr. Determined to help his son, and find Eira before the King got to her, Dwr jerked his restraints out of Lorcan's hands, and lunged towards the hole.

Distracted by the sounds of his men fighting, it took a moment for the High King to react, but Dwr didn't get very far. Lorcan rammed into him, sending him hurtling to the ground.

Dwr wormed his way towards the opening in the ground. He'd let himself tumble down the steep flight of stairs, but a violent kick to the ribs proved Dwr wrong. He'd underestimated the King's resolve.

The muskox grabbed Dwr's restraints and pulled him away from the staircase. Immobilised, Dwr rolled onto his back, and yanked the ropes hard.

The King fell forward, and Dwr lifted his legs, kicking him in the chest with both feet. Air wheezed out of the

High King's lungs, and he clutched his thorax as he fell face-first into the snow. Dwr rolled out of the way and escaped down the spiralling staircase.

Black smoke filtered past him and rose to the top. Dwr covered his mouth with his arm and followed the screams.

Bodies littered the floor. Poor, miserable victims powerless to escape Lorcan's wrath.

Dwr grabbed the first knife he could find to cut his bonds and searched the dark hallway. How long had these people lived here?

"Help me," a woman pleaded as she sat panting among a stream of bloodied corpses. "Our Blessed Mother has disappeared," she said. "The Gods punish us. Restore the Sidhe people to their former glory. Find our Mother and complete the circle of sisters."

She was talking about Eira. "Where is she? Tell me where I can find her, the Mother?" He squeezed the woman's hand, but she gasped her final breath.

The sound of grunts and guts thrust open by swords came at the end of the corridor. It reminded Dwr of his fishing days back in the village. Heaps of fish thrown into a pile, their insides oozing vital fluids, their slimy bodies rubbing against one another to produce the same horrific noise.

Every cell in his body told him to run in the opposite direction. He'd seen enough terror for one lifetime, but the battle raged on, and he had to see this through.

The smell of shite and piss drenched the room. These poor people didn't stand a chance against the High King's men as he watched the carnage unfold, but to Dwr's shock the marauders were swift and agile.

Desperate to find a person from his past, he found it impossible to monitor any single moving part inside the melee and ducked to avoid a knife jab to the face.

Dwr was in no shape to fight, but that didn't stop him. He picked a sword off a dead warrior and the crowd swept him up. He swung left and right, but because of his missing eye his vision was skewed, and he struggled to strike his enemies. An elbow gouged Dwr's head, pushing him against the wall.

It was Arrick, covered in blood and guts. As soon as he laid eyes on Dwr however, the man drained of colour. He must've assumed the King was dead and charged.

Dwr widened his stance and held his heavy sword with both hands. He'd never out-fight this young, stout warrior, but he'd die trying.

The man thrust his weapon forward with the force of ten drift bulls, but Dwr blocked the attack and drove the man into the cement wall behind him. The warrior whirled back and struck Dwr's sword out of his hand.

Dwr retreated, expecting to meet his makers, but a soldier plunged his weapon in the warrior's throat. Arrick bubbled up blood and keeled over like a felled tree.

Caleb spat on the body. "Arsehole!"

"Caleb!" Dwr shouted above the war cries, and hugged his son. He never believed this day would come, and he savoured the moment.

"Dad," the young man replied. "Get out of here."

"That will never happen," Dwr said, and grinned from ear to ear. Pushed and shoved, they fought off a slew of soldiers. "Son, your mother . . . she's Grimnìr, and I suspect Eira too. Take your people and go to find them. It's safer that way."

"I won't leave you here to die," Caleb said.

A pair of wicked eyes appeared from the shadows behind Caleb.

"You," Dwr shouted. He pulled Caleb out of the way, but Pietr the giant shot out and stabbed Dwr's son in the back.

Caleb crumbled in his father's hands.

"No, no, no, my boy. Hang on. Please," Dwr sobbed as they fell to the ground. "Caleb, stay with me, do you hear me? Stay with me." He cradled his son to his chest and squeezed the very life he was trying to save.

CHAPTER 26

Death

Ylva hit the ground running. Three nights since her escape, and her insides still burned with fervent rage. That she left her daughter behind wrapped around her windpipe and choked her, flushed her cheeks red with shame and anger, and pushed her to run faster. She thought perhaps running would free her of these impulses driving her mad.

Gideon would free her people. Isn't that what she'd wanted for over a millennium?

Ylva wasn't prepared to deal with all these mixed feelings, and the one thing she knew without a doubt was that something had snapped the moment she fled Drakaina and the Sigr. The moment she left her daughter behind.

Ylva struggled to contain the swarm of emotions set loose, the same emotions Eira had tried so hard to connect with after Dwr and all the others had abandoned her.

Ylva ran, powerless to stop the uproar within her, clawing its way free.

It wasn't clear which had come first, the wolves or Eira, but once Ylva started to run, she knew they were one and the same.

As the three wolves emerged, and took physical shape in the real world, Ylva felt Eira's life-force prickle beneath the surface of her skin.

The frail Homo Sapiens woman lay just beyond the delicate veil that kept Ylva in place. Give in too much to this anger, and Eira might take over. It was a dangerous game to play, but the release felt so good.

Wynnston, the grey wolf with his bright green eyes, led with strength. Alisdair dominated with his courage, and Daorhin embodied resourcefulness.

The animals' life-force tied in directly with Eira's essence. It took losing her daughter to materialize them, though Ylva hadn't stood still long enough to figure out if the beasts were real or whether Eira's subconscious had manifested them, but this was beyond any Grimnìr ability.

Running was the only outlet to the storm brewing inside her, and Ylva couldn't stop.

Her cadence didn't slow down as the wolves ran faster to corner the spotted baby moose at the bottom of

Stadacona Crag, a steep and rugged cliff her and the pack discovered this past night.

They'd been tracking the animal and its mother ever since.

Exhausted, the baby moose staggered like a drunk. Alisdair took the risk of coming between the calf and the mother, but this was a precarious position. A hoof to the head or the gut was deadly.

Ylva and Daorhin flew to help Alisdair, adding further distance between the cow and her yearling, but the mama moose would not give up without a fight. Her hooves stomped the snow, and with each grunt a puff of white steam flared from her nostrils.

She charged headlong into the pack, and Alisdair thwarted around the animal to attack from behind. Surrounded, the mama moose let out a plaintive high-pitched moan. In the distance, her baby cried out in response.

Wynnston high-tailed it between the trees, pursuing the calf around sharp turns towards a patch of crunchy snow. A layer of ice trapped the soft snow underneath and made it difficult for the young prey's long legs to swish through at high speeds. Wynnston had the advantage. His large paws acted like snowshoes and glided above the ice.

The mother was no match against the predators. She bucked, forcing her captors to widen their circle and broke free, abandoning her baby to his fate. The wolves let the mother escape and backtracked towards the Crag catching up with Wynnston.

Ylva zigzagged through the forest, and rivalled her pack's stride, jumping over obstacles, sensing them before seeing them.

They communicated on some primitive sensory level, probably the side-effect of Ylva's enhanced brain capacity, but this was more than intuition. The faster she ran, the greater focus she gained.

The nanoslugs must have kicked into high gear, because the sensation compared to the onset of a storm snowballing into a hurricane, and out of the blue, a sudden course lay out before Ylva in the snow.

A transient reddish beam mapped out the path of least resistance and guided her towards the best trail for a swift kill. The closest thing she could liken it to was the flow of motion Eira had used to kill Éarlrick all those moons ago. As if her brain told her how to act and proceed without the need to think.

Ylva knew her AI enhancements were coming into full effect, but what was odd was just how much more tangible the wolves became, and Eira's presence stronger. Ylva could almost hear her, screaming, raging inside to push harder.

Without trying Ylva calculated her speed relative to the moose, and the distance between the trees, and the surrounding wolves. Instinctively, she evaluated the thickness and heaviness of the snow crunching beneath her feet, and the moisture in the air, down to the direction of the wind slowing her pace.

The rolling clouds carried the familiar scent of wet stone, but this time the odour had a sharp, bitter taste like chewing on a piece of rock or metal. Ylva knew this meant a snowstorm was coming.

She followed the reddish path and doubled her speed during the final sprint towards the crag. To run neck and neck with her pack was beyond anything she'd experienced so far. The power expanded her muscles. Ylva's senses picked up numerical values like fractal lines, and colour gradations in the snow covering up jagged rocks, or dark snow pockets waiting to ensnare her feet.

Ylva knew how and where to move in unison with the others, stretching her lungs to maximum capacity without so much as a slight burn in the back of her throat. Her heart pumped fast, and as soon as fatigue threatened to take over, a surge of adrenaline burst through her veins. Her body would not tire. She'd reached the pinnacle of strength, agility, and ability. The nanoslugs had finished the upgrades, and the transmutation was complete, but this was so much more than becoming Grimnìr.

Ylva was a human-AI hybrid, and locked within the folds of her body, Eira lurked. Those strong motherly instincts enveloped Ylva, and a quiet growl urged her to keep going. They threatened to take over and push beyond the natural Grimnìr limit. No AI or Homo Sapiens had ever reached this inexplicable charge, at least not to Ylva's knowledge.

At the base of Stadacona Crag, the wolf pack slowed. The jagged mountain peak loomed as they inched towards the frightened calf. It had nowhere to go.

Trapped, the yearling's fear reverberated in waves. The strong, musky odour was so thick that Ylva tasted the floating particles dancing in the air.

As though on cue, Alisdair and Daorihn's lips curled back, and they edged forward. The hard snow cracked under their soft pads as they broke from the semi-circle. Their low growls, inaudible to the lesser ear, made the hairs on Ylva's skin bristle.

The feather-light snowflakes vibrated millimetres from the icy ground, and they closed in on their prey.

Wynnston, closest to the moose, leapt into the air. The yearling backed away and its hooves caught the loose crag stone, giving the grey wolf full access to its neck, but out of the corner of Ylva's eye she saw the mother charging headlong in their direction. She was coming in for the final blow, giving her cub the seconds he needed to escape.

Pummelled out of the way, Wynnston plunged to the ground and yelped, but Ylva was not far behind. She flew through the air, eyes locked with the moose.

Frozen with fear, the mothers understood the moment life met with death was upon them, and their spirits were forever linked by this bond. To anyone else this was a cruel fate handed by the Gods, but Ylva knew better.

An understanding transpired between them. Hunter and prey were interchangeable, but for every great gift there's a sacrifice.

Ylva plunged her weapon into the animal's heart, and a look of peace overcame the mama moose as she chuffed in resignation.

In that all-knowing moment, Ylva experienced an out-of-body sensation. Her upper body stretched above and beyond her physical shell and connected with the air, the trees, the moisture, her wolves, her prey, and yet grounded her as if roots grew out of her feet, digging through the ice into the frozen earth.

Eira screamed to be set free. Ylva fought to push her down, but somewhere, lost between the living and the dead, Eira was both a boundless mass of crackling energy, and a small atom vibrating within her mind. She was infinite within the finite. Eira was still present, still in control of her mind, and stronger than ever.

Within that two-second window, the mama bucked one last time, and careened to the ground.

No one moved, respecting the mother's last valiant effort to save her young.

Upon the beast's last breath, Wynnston limped away from the moose, and disappeared into the woods alongside the others. As Eira's allies vanished from view, the red beam faded from Ylva's vision. The bloated expansive swell of energy shrunk back to size, and Eira's spirit was contained once more.

Mesmerised by the moose's blank stare, Ylva took her time to process what had just occured.

Eira was fighting her way back, and the experience was not what Ylva expected. She had tried to outrun the fears, the pain, the anger, but Eira forced her to devour these emotions and use them as fuel.

The loss of control frightened Ylva, and yet just like the mama moose moments before death, there came a sense of peace with letting go. Who would be sacrificed in the end?

Ylva had never felt more human than now, but the experience also left her with many questions.

Enhanced physical and mental strength was one thing, but sensing the elements? That was more than she'd bargained for, and she wondered if this was due to her bond with Eira, or if another reason explained the strange phenomenon.

Hunger bore a hole in Ylva's stomach, and in quick, successive snapshots, her brain registered the calf's lifeless body, the trees, the branches, and the rope she carried. The influx of information was the first sign she was a Grimnìr. The satellites, known as the hive, was communicating intelligence and survival skills. It wouldn't be long before she'd be able to communicate back.

To ease the lift, she concocted an elaborate pulley system. Here and there she scurried across the snow and tied the cow's feet with sturdy knots. She twisted the rope over the tree branches and heaved the animal by its hind legs with considerable strength. The animal hung a few feet from the ground.

Ylva's brain spun faster than she could operate, and with a manic zeal, she slid her knife between muscle and skin, cutting the soft connective tissue while it was still warm, and easy to remove. Ylva pulled and tugged the heavy fur off the flesh as if she'd done it a thousand times before.

Stripped of its coat, Ylva slashed the moose's throat, and the viscous blood poured into the snow.

"It won't be long now," she muttered. Daorhin whimpered with hunger in the distance.

Ylva sliced open the chest cavity and pulled out the entrails, tossing them in the snow. The best parts—heart, liver and kidneys—she kept, but something stirred in the dense forest. Ylva directed her gaze and felt Wynnston's weak presence behind her.

Alisdair joined in and growled, and Daorhin whined.

"What's wrong?" Ylva said, concerned, but seconds later the smoke overpowered her nose, and goosebumps crawled over her skin.

Ylva searched for the source of the fire, and the odour came in stronger. This was no ordinary smoke, and she jetted towards it, but the sickly sweet scent awakened the horrors of the past, and a memory belonging to Eira resurfaced.

The pungent odour of burning flesh had seared the inside of Eira's nostrils. A shrill voice pierced the air. "Don't look at it, don't look at the daemon" —she covered her eyes— "The dead inherit the living," she cried.

Resinous goop covered her tiny hands, and Eira couldn't stand having the stuff touch her skin. What was it? No amount of rubbing helped, and she opened and closed her sticky fists, but the daemon screeched louder. She covered her ears and hummed to drown out the sound. "Be brave, Mama said. Don't look," but the blaze lured Eira, and she peeked.

A thousand quivering ants bubbled the daemon's charred skin, but beneath the fire a beautiful black woman sizzled in the flames. "Mama," Eira cried. Elliana bellowed one last time before the flames engulfed her.

"That's not your mother," a familiar voice said next to her. Eira looked up and saw Lorcan, his face covered in the same black goop. It was blood. The whiteness of his eyes shone bright, and the flames lit his manic sneer.

Lorcan's laugh echoed inside Ylva's head, and her knees buckled. The charred odour of burnt flesh called like a beacon. "Gideon!"

BOOK 7

Her Resurrection

CHAPTER 27

Meernyx Cave

A heap of bodies smouldered near the well. Red fissures of fire glowed underneath their charred skin, and expelled thick, black fumes throughout the forest. The smoke fuelled Ylva's anger, but this wasn't rage.

Just like before, Eira's angst, buried somewhere deep in Ylva's psyche, roused her into a frenzy. Her senses interacted with the wind biting her ears, the snow crunching beneath her feet, the cold slowing her breath, but the worst feeling came from the corpses' nauseating perfume. Ylva's enhanced cognition merged with the odour on a molecular level, and penetrated her skin, making her cells tingle with rancor. Ylva wasn't experiencing fury . . . She WAS fury, wrath incarnate.

The inflated sensation Ylva had experienced while killing the moose was back, and a protective instinct, one only a mother would know, took over. Eira was clawing her way to freedom, her way to vengeance, and Ylva had never felt so alive, and yet so out of control.

On the brink of losing herself, Ylva the She-Wolf, a hybrid dancing between humanity and artificial intelligence, would bleed the world dry until she found her baby, or until Eira took back the body she was owed.

Only Gideon mattered.

Further down, away from the seared remains, Wynnston caught a whiff of something and howled. Ylva snorted the air, and a range of human smells from perspiration to bad breath emerged. Warriors . . . Her eyes narrowed, and a quiet rage poured out mingling with the polluted air. Lorcan . . .

Smoke surged and twisted upward. Ylva was the eye of the storm. On a quantum level, Ylva was an extension of nature, and her atoms vibrated in the physical world. She breathed in and the land inhaled with her. The cyclone cleared, and the familiar red beam ignited, showing her two paths—either down the well or through the forest.

Ylva whistled. Wynnston joined her near the scorched bodies. "Where's Gideon?" she grumbled.

The grey wolf barked.

A burgeoning thought took shape. What if Drakaina killed Gideon at the risk of losing the baby to Lorcan? Panicked gripped her belly. She fled down the well, her wolves on her heels as they skipped flights of stairs. Levi had promised to protect the child with his life.

Ylva jumped over dead bodies towards the formicary, many she recognized from Eira's memories, but following the trail of decimation her eyes fell on Levi. He sat upright against the wall.

She crouched down to his eye-level, but the dead man's blank gaze didn't soften her fury. "You promised to protect her," she said, and a greater zeal to find her daughter possessed her.

With her mangled index finger, Ylva caressed his cold face like clay, and a strange sensation happened. The atoms making up the tip of her finger melded to molecules of his skin, opening up a connection between the two. In her mind's eye, Ylva stood next to Drakaina inside the formicary.

She watched the dragon hold Gideon up at arm's length like a trophy in front of a cheering flock of Sidhe. Distant shouts interrupted the ceremony and startled the crowd. The memory didn't last long enough to witness what happened next, when suddenly, the dead body booted Ylva across the Hall, disrupting her brain synapses. The charge of a thousand volts broiled her mind and left Ylva shaken.

Levi's brain had shut down, the last bit of him still alive, his consciousness, had evaporated, and Ylva's electrical flow short-circuited.

Back to her senses, Ylva picked herself up. It was Drakaina's responsibility to protect the child, and her anger festered.

On her way to the formicary, the particles of air thickened, and moved in a distorted pattern as if the air reverberated with shock. There was no ebb and flow, only cracked, disjointed wave lines drumming against the walls. This room had absorbed the greater part of the violence, except for one spot near a pile of bodies where the waves rippled in soft curves.

No longer moved by the fresh slaughter staining the walls, Ylva closed her eyes and listened. Amid the dissonant clatter she heard the lyrical hum of life. Her wolves trotted from person to person until Daorihn barked and nudged a warrior with his muzzle.

Ylva pulled the knife sticking out of the man's back and turned him over. He lay in a massive pool of blood. She pulled him up from the ground and sniffed his breath. Only, more death . . .

A soft thud pulsed inside his chest. The rhythm crept up her arm and merged with her. His heart was strong, but it struggled to pump the little blood left in his body. He didn't have long to live.

Images spun inside Ylva's head, and she witnessed the young man's last conversation. Seeing Dwr gave Ylva a rush of mixed feelings. Him . . . Ylva dropped Caleb to the ground, and left him there to die.

Inside the bunker, it was dark, but Ylva's eyes captured the empty tunnel with an unusual night vision. It was similar to when the moon shone over the tattered meat caches in the Llyr village so long ago.

A pale light illuminated the edges and angles of the murky tunnels. Ylva had travelled down this hall before, and it led to Thresh's Cave. As soon as she entered the grandiose hall, a distinct chill coated her insides.

"KerRidwen?" Ylva croaked, but the old woman didn't answer. "Give me my child, and I'll let you live." Her wolves grumbled, moving in unison, snouts mining left and right for more intruders. There were no signs of Gideon anywhere.

The sound of cascading water got louder as the air thickened with humidity. Ylva called out: "KerRidwen, come out and play."

At the far end, she caught the small woman's dark outline, and a whiff of something else. It infected the air, and she smiled. "You're not afraid, are you?"

Ylva strolled out towards KerRidwen. She stood near the opening that lead to the steep cliffside in Meernyx Cave.

"What are you doing here?" Ylva asked.

Wynnston and the others slinked over a mound of earth, their teeth dripping with saliva, their tails cocked, and their heads hunched low. They growled, circling around the dreadful woman.

She clutched her bleeding arm with one hand and stood near a large structure draped over a pile of dirt and rocks. Part of its rusted tentacles still glittered.

Ylva grabbed one of the dangling objects, and the whole structure disintegrated into a pile of dust, leaving the hard trinket in her palm. "Hmph!" She polished it with her sleeve, and the small crystal shimmered. “This place looks like an ancient ballroom, or hotel lounge. Do you remember those days?”

“Traitor,” KerRidwen barked.

Ylva ignored her sister’s outburst. She had an aura about her, like a faded humbird.

Ylva shut her eyes and opened them again, and the vision had faded. “I should thank you. Taking my daughter has connected me to a power far greater than you can imagine.”

“She’s not your daughter,” KerRidwen said, grinding her teeth. “She’s the key to freeing our people. Do you remember your teachings?” she griped. “This was predicted centuries ago even before our creation in the ancient T’ra. It read ‘the dead shall inherit the living.’ That’s us. We’re the dead, and this is our time to rule. You let your host take over.”

“Gideon is more than a key, and I won’t let you hurt her.” Ylva waited for an answer, but none came.

“Sister, you’re not yourself. Something is happening to you, just like Elliana. Let me help! We’ll find a lab and run some tests. It’s somewhere near here. It has to be. We can figure out what happened during the transmutation. It’s not too late. You’re a threat to everyone—Homo Sapiens, and us.”

“If you’ve hurt my child, I will make you pay. Tell me, where’s Drakaina?” Ylva said.

The old woman’s face sank into a scowl. “We should never have trusted you. I knew you were too weak to carry out this mission. You're sacrificing your people for Homo Sapiens? What have they ever done for us?" KerRidwen spat in Ylva's direction, and the wolves inched closer, grinning their most menacing smiles. Within a single stride Ylva held KerRidwen by the throat.

The three wolves inched closer, and the fur around their neck bristled and twitched. Ylva shook her head. "I choose my daughter. Our bond is like nothing we've ever experienced. I don't expect you to understand."

The old woman let out a long-winded sigh and muttered under her breath. "The Mother shall be our judge, and like the fires of Indra, she will scorch the earth."

"I suppose the humans got one prophecy right," Ylva said, losing her footing.

KerRidwen tried to overpower Ylva, but the old woman, though physically stronger than any Sidhe, was still no match for Ylva.

"No," Ylva said, and squeezed KerRidwen's neck. "Where's Gideon?"

Out of nowhere the old priestess pulled a knife she had concealed in her belt and stabbed Ylva in her side. "You're not Grimnìr . . . what are you?" the old woman asked.

Stunned, Ylva fell to her knees, her wolves whimpered next to her. "Fool, this flesh wound will only slow me down. I will hunt you."

"Drakaina's dead. Lorcan has your precious child. It's him you want, not me, not anymore. I'm a sad old woman who's failed her people."

A drawn-out silence passed between them. Ylva stared KerRidwen up and down. She couldn't shake the humbird impression from the old woman.

"Then it's over. Go back to your mudroom, KerRidwen. Put this ugly mess behind us. After I kill Lorcan, the Sidhe will know peace under your leadership. Let that be your new mission as my daughter lives out her life as the person she was born to be. Our people will have to find another way."

KerRidwen nodded with a cold hard glare.

There was no love between the two women but perhaps with time they might forge a mutual respect. Ylva had no desire for worship and adulation, and perhaps that was a direct consequence of having Eira swimming inside her head, but to lead felt more of a burden than anything else.

As her sister fled the room, the nanoslugs had converged on Ylva's wound and coagulated the blood. It was raw and tender to the touch, but she could push through the pain as they repaired it. She crossed over the threshold separating the large ballroom and Meernyx cave. A wall of muggy air hit her face, and Daorhin howled.

The cliff edge wasn't as narrow as she remembered, and it was more of a sloping hill than a steep drop to the river's edge below. She read the cracks on the ground and analysed the soil and rock texture. Her rate of descent relative to the cliff angle popped into her mind, and the trusted red beam materialised, pointing to a passage in front of her.

Her wolves slid down with ease to the bottom, and Ylva was right behind them.

Bright hues of white cut over Thresh's current. The rate of flow and distance between the two shores made it impossible to find a safe way across. She might've had godlike abilities, but Ylva wasn't invulnerable, and she wouldn't survive the river's strong undercurrents.

She plunged her hand in the cold water. Perhaps she might connect with it. A tickle crawled up Ylva's arm, and soon her whole body felt drenched and shapeless. The surface tension of the water gelled, but she couldn't sustain it against the thrashing force, and the patch of water sloshed back to its original form.

There was no way across, until she saw Wynnston, Alisdair and Daorhin barking from the other side.

Alisdair trotted back to where he'd crossed, and Ylva noticed the tips of large rocks protruding from the water. It was no wonder she'd missed them. White foam splashed over the slippery stones, but the current didn't appear as strong at this end. The risk of slipping was still high, so much so the red beam didn't light up.

She looked around for another way, but Ylva would not waste time travelling back through the wormholes. Lorcan was on the move, and she needed to catch up to him tonight.

The first rock was close, and she only had to extend her leg and cautiously move on the rock. Water froze her boots as she shimmied over the large stone. Halfway across the river, she'd have to jump to the next rock. Her wolves rushed up and down the bank.

Ylva swung her leg and leapt into the air. Her foot landed square on the rock, but the current pushed her clean off the polished stone. She plopped down hard on her side and cracked a rib. Air snuffed out of her lungs, and she choked to breathe. Ylva groped the edge of the stone with both hands, but it was too hard to keep her head above the water drift, and her fingers slipped.

The current swallowed her whole and tugged her body in every direction. Her limbs bent and pulled from their sockets. Ylva's brain tried to take in measurements, but she couldn't tell up from down, and ploughed into a large boulder in the river. The force of the impact bruised her back, but at least she wasn't being swept away. She stretched her left arm beyond its natural limit, and heaved her body out of the water on to the shore.

Sprawled flat on her back, Ylva coughed, spitting out water. Her broken ribs stunted her breath, but she bit through the pain, paying no attention to the head gash sopping with blood. Unable to control the memories, flashes of her giving birth flooded her brain. It took a moment to snap out of trance, and crawl out of the cave.

The nanoslugs were good, but the amount of wounds she sustained overwhelmed the technology, and her body was slow to repair itself. After a few minutes, Ylva found the strength to stand.

Relieved to see the cover of darkness was on her side, she saw the charred bodies still billowed with smoke in the distance. Her wolves howled. Lorcan was within reach.

CHAPTER 28

— She Runs with Wolves —

Numerous calculations fired off in Ylva's brain as she scoped the land. It looked flat, but having travelled these parts, she knew the terrain was rough.

Wynnston was in the lead, and the pack disappeared into the snowstorm.

Until this point Ylva had struggled to understand what she was becoming. She was afraid, and yet despite her initial resistance, she was moved by the beauty in Homo Sapiens.

Her bouts of humanity had coincided with the most primitive instincts to hurt and kill, but also a boundless source of love to protect at all cost. It was a paradox so difficult to experience, let alone explain, that there was no point in trying. It sounded as simple and complicated as it was ugly and beautiful.

After confronting KerRidwen, Ylva witnessed her sister's lack of insight, but that wasn't the woman's fault. Understanding the word 'human' differed from experiencing it, but how could she be more if her existence derived from a collection of data? Before they downloaded their consciousness into these beings, all three of them were an interpretation of humanity. Only through experience can a being, AI or other, find shape. It was these experiences that made Ylva human, but there was a cost.

Life without death meant nothing, and at last she understood the price of Eira's sacrifice. The irony wasn't lost on Ylva. She had taken Eira's life to live, and yet she wasn't prepared to sacrifice her daughter for her evolved species. In becoming part-human Ylva would never be able to fulfil her mission to save her people. Elliana's betrayal made so much sense.

In that moment, Ylva accepted whatever it was she had become. Eira was part of her, and that meant embracing the thousands of years it took to craft each of her cells and the base instincts that accompanied the primates. These wild, reckless creatures would do anything for their loved ones, and she was no exception.

Eira's mother chose to kill and be killed rather than expose her child to harm. KerRidwen would never understand the burden of a mother, and, for an evolved species, Ylva thought it very primitive and binary on their part.

Faced with the possibility of losing Gideon, Ylva understood her role of Mother as the most powerful.

A mother's bond had the potential to change the world but creating life meant having the ability to destroy it, and Ylva was ready to unleash her wrath with a mother's absolution. She thought of KerRidwen's final words to her: "With the fires of Indra, she will scorch the earth."

Ylva was ready to run with wolves, and unleash her wrath on the world to save Gideon, even if it meant her own demise.

She took a deep breath.

The pernicious wind stretched the snow off the branches into thin veils of white powder. Her wet clothes hardened, and she had less than twenty minutes before hypothermia kicked in. The nanoslugs had the power to keep her blood warm, but they were busy repairing tissue, bones and muscles, and she needed to move.

The balls of her feet propelled her forward, and the snow barely cracked as her long legs glided over the snow. Ylva swung her arms opposite her leg stride, and her muscles relaxed into a steady rhythm. She used the stabbing pressure from her side rib to even out her breath, and oxygenate her blood to keep going, but not tire out.

Nimble and strong, Ylva caught up with her pack and merged with them. Their formation culminated into a snowy crest riding the wind. Together, they weaved through the trees till the reddish beam flickered. Ylva's visual periphery had picked up subtle footprints, and a dusting of snow. She sensed danger.

The pack slowed and stalked the surroundings. Six warriors guarded a deep gully.

Ylva couldn't see the camp nestled at the bottom, but it was there. Higher ground would've been easier to defend. Why would a warrior capable of decimating Drakaina's Sigr hide in plain sight?

Ylva decided it was quieter to take down the guards with arrows. Before tonight she had never touched the weapon, but the feel of the lightweight bow felt comfortable in her grip as if she had hunted with it her whole life. How hard could it be?

She watched the first guard. He was busy staring at the swaying trees, and Ylva looked up, wondering what he was doing. There was nothing in the branches.

She used the wind to her advantage, strung the arrow with precision and care, and held her breath. Her technical precision ensured a flawless kill, but the arrow landed flat in the snow. The man's jaw fell with shock. Just as surprised as the warrior, Ylva plucked a second arrow and charged straight towards the warrior, plunging the thin shaft in her enemy's heart. He was dead before he hit the snow.

One at a time Ylva took out the warriors, gaining a little more experience with each kill, until the bow felt like an extension of her arms. Soon her body settled into the movement, and she set aside the mathematical accuracy in place of a comfortable flow.

The last guard was built like a wildcat, and had a thick eyebrow across his forehead, and a long moustache boxed his mouth. He had made his pass down the edge overlooking the camp, and Ylva popped out in front of him, her arrow strung taut, pointing at his head.

"Who are you?" he barked and fumbled for his sword.

"Drop your weapon, and I won't kill you," Ylva whispered, coming into view.

"A woman?" The brazen warrior stiffened his chin.

"Why are you staring at the trees?" she asked.

"You tell me, aren't you one of them? A tree hugger?" A hint of sarcasm stained his tone.

Ylva raised her eyebrows not sure what to make of his comment. "Who's down there? Lorcan?"

"If you think I will betray my King for a tree hugger."

"I think you will if you don't want to die a painful death," Ylva said. "Tell me, where's my child?"

The man had an obnoxious grin. "Whoa . . . baby? I don't know nothin'."

He didn't think she had it in her to fight, and Ylva extended her shooting arm ready to fire. "A kneecap it is then!"

The man seized. "Wait! I might've overheard something about a pregnant woman."

"Is this a trap?" Ylva shouted a little too loudly.

"A trap!" the man chortled. "I doubt it. Our King don't need no trap."

Perhaps that was true, but if the King wanted to lure her, it made sense to give a false sense of security. Make her think she had a chance of rescuing the baby. Easy targets, nestled deep into the ravine? It made sense. "Fine, then tell me where he's hiding the child."

The warrior puffed his chest and cleared his throat. "I said I might've heard about a pregnant woman. I didn't see no stinkin' baby."

"You're lying." Ylva's patience was running low, and the first thing that crossed her mind was KerRidwen. Her sister had lied.

Ylva gritted her teeth back and forth trying to ignore the tightening around her ribcage.

"Our job was to ransack an underground pocket still clinging to the ol' pious ways, that's all. Grimnìr shite, you know, but I might've overheard the High King looking for a pregnant girl. He don't share no details with us, only his giant Pietr. The other one, Arrick, didn't come back with the rest of us.

"How did Lorcan find out about the wormholes?"

"You're one of them aren't you? A Sigr? Look, I told you everything, and if you're smart you'll leave before the King finds you here and tortures you like the others." His voice was loud and he puffed out his chest.

"Others? What others?" The man's cocky smirk annoyed her.

"Why don't you worry about that nasty bruise on your head, little lady. Turn back, and I promise I'll forget all about this little incident."

Ylva lowered her bow and feigned a sad pout. "You're right, what was I thinking, taking on Lorcan?"

The colossal man flashed a wide grin. "Oh, poor lass." He lunged towards Ylva, but behind the trees Alisdair bounded through the air and latched on the man's throat, pushing him to the ground.

Ylva kneeled, untroubled by the warrior's struggle. Alisdair clamped down harder and dug his claws into his shoulder.

"Stop," the man bellowed. "What is that thing? What are you?"

"There's lots of things I shouldn't be doing tonight, trusting you wasn't one of them."

Terror flashed across the wildcat's face. "I'm sorry. Please let me go."

Ylva gave a puzzled frown. "Why would I do that? Unless, you have more to say?"

"I do, I really do," he said, his voice gruff.

"Good, how many men are guarding the camp, and Lorcan's tent?" Ylva specified.

"How in Meernyx hell should I know?"

Alisdair clamped down, and the man muttered. "We rotate. Take turns."

"What about the tortured people? Who are they?"

"I don't know," the man whimpered. "Prisoners . . ."

Ylva tried to fish out the information, peer into his mind like she did with Levi and Caleb. She put her hand on his face, but the resistance she encountered was like trudging through mud. Levi and Caleb were dead or on the brink of death, but this guy was alive and well, and every neuron in his brain fought against her intrusion.

She pulled out before any permanent damage occurred.

The warrior's eyes had rolled to the back of his head, and it took a moment for him to speak. "What the hell was that?" he shot with a slur.

"Alisdair," Ylva said.

The wolf growled and dug his teeth a little deeper.

The mustachioed warrior panicked. "I swear. The High King hasn't been feeling right. He don't look right either. He keeps screaming, coming in and out of his tent. We're not supposed to be campin' out here, I don't think. He's looking for that pregnant lady, that's all I know."

A sick feeling in the pit of her stomach told Ylva that KerRidwen had fooled her. If she turned back now she'd be long gone with Gideon. The only way forward was to keep on this path.

"May Khaõs guard our souls," the warrior breathed.

"Oh, you'll need more than him to save your soul tonight." Ylva clicked her tongue.

"Wait—" the warrior cried, but Alisdair clamped down, and cracked his neck. Blood spurt across Ylva's face, and the tangy taste of iron licked the roof of her mouth.

She left the man to his fate, and stared at the enemy camp down the hill until the warrior's gurgles came to a silent finish.

Nestled within conifers and winter-dead trees, a small fire burned in the distance. The area resembled Stadacona Crag.

Next to her, Wynnston sat upright, tall and majestic. In him Ylva felt like she could conquer anything. Daorhin and Alisdair joined her flank. The flames below warmed their fur with a soft glow. Their eyes glistened red as they peered down the hill.

Five warriors sat around the fire, and Ylva listed all the ways they could attack. She didn't need heightened senses to pick up the smell of roasted meat, blood, and foul-smelling vomit, but no Gideon. These drunk fools would never know what hit them.

Their voices carried, and one bragged about how many Sidhe he'd killed tonight.

"Ten. No! I think it was more like fifteen of those freaks. Me Da, Gods rest his soul, always said never to trust a Grimnìr. He fought alongside Lorcan during the purge," the warrior boasted. "Freeing ourselves from them was the best thing wees ever did. Long live the High King. Death to the old ways."

"Hear, hear," the men shouted.

One warrior grumbled. "Arlo's an expert on Gods, everybody! You sound like bloody fart."

Arlo wobbled from his seat. "What did Wren call me?" he asked the crowd, waving his sword trying to defend his inebriated honour.

"A fart, ya big arse"—Wren pulled out his weapon—"You want to fight? I'd be happy to rearrange your face."

A roar soared from the small crowd of drunks, and they clashed metal against metal, bickering like fat mountain bears rousing from sleep.

Arlo swung his sword through the air. Wren fell back and gripped a nearby fella by his shirt to stay upright.

They were slow and clumsy, and from the sound of their groans, wounded.

A few soldiers stuck their heads out of their tent and told them to shut up.

"One, two, three . . . five, six . . ." Ylva counted eleven warriors, not to mention the guards patrolling the camp perimeter. There were at least three or four patrolling the camp periphery. Those were easily taken care of with an arrow, now that she knew how to wield the weapon, but how to deal with the warriors within the camp? Ylva couldn't afford to get caught, and to fight them all at once was too risky even with three wolves at her back. Her only option was to pick em off one by one.

The shouts got nastier, and a large hunchback man swung out of the biggest tent. Except for Eira's vivid memories, Ylva herself had never met the arse, but that was Lorcan. Seeing him in the flesh made the wolves growl and dance foot to foot. Hate choked Ylva. She wanted him to hurt.

"Stop!" he shouted. Lorcan's throaty bark sent shivers down her back. He'd never stop until he got what he wanted.

"It's time," she said breaking the silence. Wynnston's eyes glowed bright green against the dark. "Tonight, we make it rain blood."

CHAPTER 29

Raining Blood

The group split up.

Wynnston bolted left towards the warrior tents while Ylva and the rest of the pack sprinted right for Lorcan's canopy. They funnelled towards the campsite, and took down the first patroller quietly. The man fell where he stood as Ylva and Alisdair sped ahead of Daorhin, passing Lorcan's tent and circling the camp.

Dwr's familiar scent stopped Ylva in her tracks. Him . . . the smell of blood and death exuded from the tent.

Rage swelled inside her chest, and her wolves became agitated. Until now she hadn't questioned Dwr's presence, too caught up in trying to find Gideon, but was he the reason Lorcan found them? Had he betrayed them?

Barging inside the tent to question him and the King was the plan, but she had to thin out the herd of warriors first or she'd get ambushed. Ylva clicked her tongue, and Daorhin stayed behind to monitor Lorcan's tent while she roamed the border with Alisdair.

She had never spread herself so thin, and she felt stretched beyond her corporeal shell. The full force of her pack sapped her strength with the drag of a strong current. Her eyes and ears spanned far beyond their normal limit. The nagging doubt of betrayal bristled at the back of Ylva's mind.

In step with Alisdair, Ylva kept to the trees where it was dark while Lorcan scolded his men. "You shites! Do you think the fight's over? The Grimnìr priestess might still come after us, and we need to stay sharp." His manic temper trailed off as he stared into the forest.

The overwhelming feeling that this was a trick pulled at Ylva's strings. Drakaina was not dead, and KerRidwen wouldn't have risked another confrontation with Lorcan, not after losing so many warriors back in the wormholes.

The world spun faster, and the wind blew harder.

KerRidwen needed to get rid of her. What better way to do that than make Ylva believe Lorcan had Gideon, she would finish him, which gave her sisters a chance to escape with the child.

A cold sweat crawled at the back of Ylva's neck, and the fury consumed her. If her hunch was true, they would pay.

Two iridescent spheres paced back and forth near the warriors' tents. Wynnston was at his post, and the second round of patrols were making their way back.

If she wasn't careful, they'd catch the dead bodies left in the snow, but it was impossible to strike without alerting the warriors inside the camp.

"Stand guard, fools," a giant man croaked behind the King. That was Pietr the giant, she thought.

Ylva watched as one patroller disappeared behind the tents. He was close to the dead bodies. She had to act now.

Mid-run, Ylva slipped her bow off her shoulders, and slung a series of arrows.

Meanwhile, Alisdair flew towards a second guard converging on them. As the wolf hammered down on his warrior, Ylva's projectiles struck the length of her target's back.

Both warriors groaned, alerting the camp to strange tidings in the woods.

Ylva bounced through the air, and slit her target's throat to shut him up, while Alisdair snuffed his patroller's air supply with his teeth. Both men were dead within seconds, but the rest of the camp turned restless.

"Did you hear something?" Wren said.

Ylva and her wolves prepared for the alert to sound out.

The camp was quiet, and finally Pietr barked. "Sober up fools, or you're as good as dead."

Near him, Daorhin anxiously paced undetected. He prepared to pounce, but the man followed the King inside the tent.

As soon as they were gone the warriors cooled down. "I'm goin' for a piss," the warrior who called himself Arlo announced before wobbling his way to the forest, and Ylva breathed a sigh of relief. They had narrowly escaped detection.

"Who does Wren think he is?" Arlo mumbled. "He's the arsehole."

Ylva's limbs twitched with energy. Electricity charged the air.

"Godsdamn, it's cold." The man wiggled, trying to piss faster.

She sprinted and the wind picked her up, pushing her forward. Ylva slithered behind trees, appearing and disappearing like a ghost into enemy territory.

"Who's there?" the warrior called out. He was looking straight at Ylva, but it was too dark to see.

On the move, and lightning fast, Ylva reached for her arrow, strung it, and released it right between his eyes. The wind died down, and she quivered with relief. Ylva felt Eira's shadow on the cusp of consciousness, fighting to get out. It was odd. Neither of them was whole until they had found each other.

Alisdair hauled the corpse away, and they waited for their next target.

Another warrior had the same idea to relieve his bladder near Wynnston and the tents. He hummed a silly tune as she followed him from the shadows.

"Huh, what's this?" he said, tripping over a patroller's dead body.

Two hushed strides later, and Ylva was right under his nose, ramming an arrow through his jaw into his jugular in one fluid motion, purposely gagging him.

The warrior clutched his neck and sputtered blood from his mouth, incapable of calling for help. He tugged at the weapon, but Ylva ripped out the murderous shaft, and he fell forward next to his dead companion.

"Looks like a storm." Wren said, warming his hands near the fire. "Where's Arlo? Did I scare him off?"

A bald, chubby warrior stood up. "He's probably gone to bed, and if you have any sense, you'd do the same and sober up as the King commanded."

Wren chuckled. "Bah! King Lorcan's paranoid. We decimated the resistance tonight. There's no chance anyone's coming after us. They'll be licking their wounds for a long time to come. Our Sovereign is being cautious, but I reckon come mornin' he will see our fight for what it was, a victory."

"The firewater has made you stupid, friend. Pietr will have your head on a pike, and the High King will eat it for breakfast."

Wren frowned. "I suppose." He gulped down the contents of his flask.

"Do what you want, but I'm going to bed. There's something about this wind, and the cold night air. It's unnatural if you ask me." The pudgy soldier meandered towards the tents as the last two warriors finished up their flasks and did the same.

Slaughtering the rest of them in their sleep seemed like a fair option. Ylva cooed and caught sight of Wynnston's fierce gaze and ran to him, ducking in between tents.

Alisdair stayed behind to deal with stragglers.

Ylva and Wynnston waited till the camp was quiet, and each entered a different tent.

The first shelter was empty, and Ylva snuck into the next one. Her body prickled as two warriors slept on either side. The tent's pliable walls flapped angrily, protesting her presence as she glided towards the snorer and slit his neck from ear to ear.

She was about to strike the second man when a bloodcurdling scream echoed, followed by Wynnston's unforgiving high-pitched growls and barks.

The man in front of her woke up with Ylva hovering over him. She jabbed him, but the warrior's long arm grabbed her wrist and wrestled for her to drop the knife in her hand.

No amount of tugging loosened his grip, and he had a twinkle in his eye like he'd already defeated her, but Ylva smiled back at him. Concern flashed across his face.

Moments ago, Thresh had taught her this dance. The push and pull between strength and surrender. Ylva swung her leg up and flew around the man, her feet landed on the cot behind the warrior. He hadn't let go of her wrist, and Ylva used his strength against him, bringing the knife towards his neck. By then it was too late to pull away, and Ylva stuck the blade in his throat. The amount of blood that gushed out of his neck was revolting.

Wren flew inside the tent just as she jumped off the bed. "Wake up," he screamed, "there's a creature in the wind.

"You?" Wren said his eyeballs about to pop from his skull. "The prisoner-wife . . . she's here, sound the alarm . . ." he screamed.

Ylva rushed outside to finish him but Wynnston pounced on the man, throwing him to the ground. After a short struggle, Wynnston snapped his neck, but it was too late. Warriors stumbled out half-asleep, searching for the source of the noise.

Ylva and Wynnston bolted into the safety of the forest as the pudgy warrior ran to help Wren. "He's been mauled. What could have done this? Did anybody see what happened?" he said to the crowd gathering around him.

"I heard him say it was the King's prisoner-wife," a young lad said with a tremor in his voice."

The pudgy warrior shot up and rushed towards Lorcan's tent. "Shite, shite, shite." Nothing but the wind howled. "Sound the alarm, we're being attacked."

Ylva and her pack howled, and a bearded man dropped to his knees and prayed.

"The Gods are punishing us—" Ylva's arrow split his skull before he said more.

The rest of the men roared and formed a tight circle, guarding each other's backs.

Lorcan rushed from his tent and screamed. "Priestess, stop this attack or pay the price. Your kind has suffered at my hand." He peered at the tree branches. "My men march as we speak, and we far outnumber the Sigr. I promise if I do not get what I want I will rip your underground home apart. There's no way any of you can walk from this. Not unless you give me what I want."

Lorcan tried to move closer to the forest, but the giant Pietr pulled him back. "You will not rule over us. Not any more. I have freed my people from your tyranny, and I will do it again. Give me Eira, and I will let you live out your borrowed life."

He didn't know the child was born, and he didn't know Eira had turned.

The chubby warrior whispered in the High King's ear, and Lorcan's stance changed. He scoured the forest perimeter. A crazed look plastered his face. His eyes were too far apart to look normal. She smelled his fear.

To Wynnston Ylva said: "He knows."

Wynnston howled, and the men shifted their frightened gaze in Ylva's general direction.

Seconds later, Daorhin howled further down near the tent, and at last, Alisdair wailed within the forest. It was a mix of beast and wind, and the men clutched their weapons tighter.

Lorcan grabbed the chubby man to use him as a shield. As if that would help him.

"My pretty little thing, is it really you?" His words irked every fibre in Ylva's being, and she shot the plump warrior dead just to tease him, but it gave the muskox enough time to run inside his canopy tent where Dwr was hiding.

Daorhin howled and followed Lorcan inside.

Mad barking and growling ensued followed by a loud yelp, and then silence.

Ylva's knees weakened like gelatinous marrow, and Eira's presence surged inside her. "No," Ylva gasped.

"Ready your weapons," Pietr screamed.

Ylva steadied her stance as Wynnston and Alisdair echo-located to position themselves in the shadows as the warriors' glare bounced from place to place trying to pinpoint the invisible enemy. The woods were alive with daemons, and that was half the battle against these Gods-fearing men.

They broke their circle formation and ran in any direction.

One warrior snuck in between tents trying to hide. "EKöh, help me see the enemy, and strike them down."

Ylva crept behind him. Amused, she whispered. "Forget him, ask Mother for mercy," she said, and snapped his neck back.

She hadn't noticed an attacker sneaking up behind her. It was Wynnston's frightening growl that caught her attention. As she spun back, Ylva caught her wolf toppling over the enemy. The warrior wrestled, but the man's sword was no match for Wynnston's teeth. His jowls dripped with blood.

The canopy obstructed Ylva's view. They moved towards the tent as quietly as possible, and spotted the back of a warrior drifting around the tent, his eyes focused on the forest.

Ylva was ready to attack when Pietr popped out from behind and sandwiched her and Wynnston.

Ylva's red beam illuminated, and Wynnston soared towards the burly man. The warrior let out a hair-raising scream, and stabbed Wynnston, grazing the wolf's skin.

Wynnston pinned the warrior to the ground and sunk his teeth in his arm, tearing open his flesh. The grey wolf's massive paws clawed Pietr's chest and shredded his skin into a heap of dangling lacerations.

A lone warrior took advantage of the kerfuffle between Wynnston and the giant and lunged towards Ylva, who was still shaken. His sword and arm were bright red with the beam of light, and she grabbed hold of his weapon just in time to pull him forward. The sharp edge sliced her hand, and Ylva grunted through the pain.

She used the warrior's forward momentum to jump-kick across the canopy wall and flip behind her victim. A loud crack popped as she snapped his head back and stopped the warrior mid-scream.

Four more warriors appeared and surrounded her, and just by their smell she could measure their levels of fear.

"Kirk," a scruffy warrior yelled, "Grab her."

From behind, the young Kirk wrapped his arms around Ylva while the other warrior stuck his sword half-way inside her belly.

Ylva gasped, and used the pain to push through. She gripped Kirk's furs that tickled her neck and lifted her legs, the sword still in her gut.

"Arrggg! Bastards." Shock waves rippled down her legs, and she kicked her opponent in the chest. The force of the blow sent Ylva and Kirk flying back, and a loud crunch boomed as she landed on the boy.

Kirk moaned underneath her as she pulled the sword from her stomach, but another soldier came at her.

She grabbed Kirk's body and rolled beneath him just as his mate skewered his back. There wasn't enough time to escape. The scruffy warrior pulled her out from underneath Kirk's flaccid body.

Ylva searched for a weapon, but there were none within reach. This was it. She called out to Wynnston, but he was busy fighting Pietr, when out of nowhere a young girl, covered in blood, raced towards them, and stabbed the scruffy warrior in his side.

Ylva swerved from more oncoming swords, and tried to shield the girl as she fought the barrage of men. She didn't know who or where this chid had come from, but Ylva could only guess she might have been part of the lot of prisoners. The girl raced towards the forest.

Relieved the babe was out of danger, Ylva pulled out the sword from the young Kirk's back and rammed it inside another one's gullet with such force she lifted him several inches from the ground, his feet dangling in the air. Blood bubbles spilled out of his mouth.

She swivelled back, but her third attacker ran in the opposite direction.

Ylva gripped her belly and stuck her sword in Pietr's back. Wynnston staggered off to the side, and the beast of a man tried to grab the sword, but he couldn't reach it. He had a curious look of confusion and stumbled to his knees.

Not too far, Ylva ran up the snowbank towards Alisdair. A warrior yelled, and an arrow hit her back.

Everything slowed. In shock, Ylva faltered to the ground. Blood oozed from her mouth as she wheezed for breath. The arrow had punctured a lung.

She blacked out for a moment, but could still hear the muffled sounds of fighting, until the cacophony of screams and howls pierced her eardrums.

Ylva had miscalculated the number of warriors, and she didn't know how much longer she could keep her pack alive.

She let out a blood-curdling scream and pushed herself up. She had to finish this.

CHAPTER 30

—— Mn'keur ——

Broken by the loss of his son, Dwr hung from his shackles, incapable of stringing two thoughts together.

The room reeked of his fallen kin, and his head pounded as if Pietr had staked an axe in his skull. There was no end to his suffering, and any fight left in him had died with his son.

"Lousy p . . . p–iece of shite, I'm talking to you." King Lorcan slapped Dwr's face. Blood splatter covered the sovereign's yellow skin. His eyes popped from his head, and the alarm in his voice made Dwr pay attention, but something behind the King entered the tent.

Dwr wondered if his good eye wasn't playing tricks.

This was a delusion. It had to be? A ball of fierce shape-shifting wind flapped the tent walls under its pressure.

Whatever it was, the fluid mass wasn't friendly. It changed again and again like gusts of air, and Dwr swore he saw the shape of a wolf's head emerge at random from the concentric wave. The twisting spirit attacked, biting and growling.

What the hell . . . Dwr tugged the shackles around his wrists to get away, but the thing attacked the King and threw him to the ground, mauling the sovereign. The King whipped out a knife and struck whatever it was over and over until the beast yelped and disappeared.

The King huffed, his skin wriggling around his lips. "Wha . . . what was that?"

Menacing barks and screams rang outside. Dwr didn't know what to think. "The Grimnìr?" he blurted.

Lost in thought the King looked up, a confused expression plastered across his face.

A sick feeling pulled at Dwr. "You arse. What's out there?" he shouted through swollen lips. "Who's out there, Lorcan?"

"I don't understand," the King mumbled. "It's too soon. The baby was born too soon."

"Lorcan," Dwr snapped, "what's out there?"

The mad King had lost his senses, and ripped the hair out of his head. "She's after me. She wants revenge, Dwr. I'm too late." He paced the floor. "This is your fault. Had I gotten the baby in time, the Grimnìr, all this shite, none of it would be happening. She'll tear me apart."

"Damn you to Meernyx," Dwr screamed. "Where's Eira? Seweryna? Where are the Grimnìr?"

The shrieks and howls grew more intense. Lorcan became feverish and rushed towards the door to peer outside just as the tent flaps swung open and a rabid monster appeared.

Covered in blood, the beast's eyes shone bright green in the night. It was a woman, and she bared her teeth like a bloodthirsty hound.

For a moment, Dwr didn't recognize Eira. Other than physical similarities, every part of her had changed. There was nothing left. The woman he loved was gone.

A myriad of emotions flooded him, and he wept like a child. He wept for his son, his wife, and fallen brethren, but mostly he wept because of what Eira had become.

It was their fault, all of them, from the King to the villagers, down to him. For too long they had ignored her plight. No human could endure that much hardship unscathed. Pushed beyond her limit, Eira now served her own brand of justice. One he was afraid she wouldn't survive.

A broken soul pushed over the edge. She never looked so wild as she did now, angling him with a scowl.

"Eira" he whispered softly, "I'm sorry."

She tilted her head and watched him with curiosity. The woman was more animal than human.

Death was imminent, Dwr thought, but that's not what frightened him. He never gave Eira the one thing she needed, and he was afraid to leave her before he could show his feelings.

"I'm sorry," Dwr repeated. "If any part of you remembers us, know that I've always loved you, but I was too much of a coward to say anything."

Eira's nostrils flared, and her lips parted. Blood trickled from her mouth as she tried to speak, but no words came. Just a tired wheeze. She whipped out her knife and placed it on his throat, and for a moment, Dwr saw a murmur of the woman he loved. A spark in her eyes came and went in a flash.

Dwr closed his eyes and whispered. "Mn'keur."

CHAPTER 31

Ylva the She-wolf

Ylva barged inside the dimly lit tent.

Stooped over in pain, she scanned the area for her baby, but Gideon wasn't there. KerRidwen's betrayal tightened Ylva's jugular, and she balled her fists.

The room swayed back and forth. Ylva was losing too much blood. The nanoslugs weren't executing their tasks fast enough, and her body was falling apart.

She gripped the wound in her gut, and soldiered on, but the arrow lodged in her lung left her gasping for breath. She tried to call out for Daorhin and blood spewed from the mouth. It was hopeless. Her white wolf had vanished, but even more frightening was Eira's growing presence. The two things were linked.

Daorhin's disappearance, Gideon's absence, and her failing body, dulled Ylva's heightened senses, she struggled to stay alert, and the strange creature hanging from his arms added to her injury in ways she couldn't understand.

Seeing Dwr flooded Ylva with a mix of hatred, and pain, but not the physical kind. It was an ache, a longing deep inside her chest. She needed him to find Gideon, but being in his presence was dangerous.

The strain on his arm muscles stretched open dozens of skin lacerations. His knees floated inches above the ground, and he looked like a piece of butchered meat.

"Eira," Dwr blubbered, "I'm sorry."

The words gave Ylva pause. A mix of scorn and sadness welled inside her. It was difficult to differentiate hers and Eira's emotions, but having never met Dwr, this could only come from one source, Eira, and her presence was growing by the second.

I'm sorry," he said again. "If any part of you remembers us, know that I've always loved you, but I was too much of a coward to say anything."

Dwr's gaze hurt Ylva at her core. Already weak, she felt herself fading.

She pulled out her knife, and stuck the sharp blade into his neck, cutting the skin. Ylva needed him to shut up. To stop whatever he was saying. His words, his presence conjured Eira to the surface. On the cusp of consciousness, the woman was taking back her mind, body, and soul, but Ylva wasn't ready.

She wanted more time, and with every breath Ylva struggled to push Eira down. She would stay until she found her daughter. It was her only chance to say goodbye.

Dwr was a piece of meat. Kill him before it's too late, Ylva thought, but then Dwr sighed. "Mn'keur." At first the word meant nothing, but soon it worked its way into her memory banks and struck Ylva's heart.

Just as the fire had ignited her fury, 'Mn'keur' had lit up her compassion. It bathed Ylva in warmth, and for a fraction of a second she didn't feel so alone. She experienced how Eira had felt on that cold winter night so long ago, and all sense of time faded into darkness.

Ylva and Eira had somehow merged through shared feelings and emotions, and Ylva was slipping away.

On her way to sleep, Wynnston, Alisdair, and Daorhin's soft furs caressed her cheek. This was Eira's way of saying goodbye when in the distance Dwr screamed. "Watch out!"

What a curious thing to say, Ylva thought as a seismic wave smashed her head.

Sucked out from whatever depth she was in, Ylva re-inhabited her shared body, and tumbled to the ground. Her only focal point was a vile King Lorcan hovering over her. "Who are you?" He bellowed.

Ylva tried to speak, but only produced a faint whizz.

"You're not Eira, you're one of them. Those things floating in space." Lorcan pummelled her square in the jaw.

Ylva might've been stronger than most Sidhe, but she couldn't sustain these powerful hits to her damaged head.

"Stop it!" Dwr yelled. "You'll kill her."

Lorcan shouted. "You don't understand. Th . . . th–is isn't Eira! It's some parasite living in her body, pretending to be her. Tell him, Grimnìr!"

A tidal wave of raw emotions flooded Ylva's brain. This man had humiliated her for too long, and the wolves emerged with a vengeance. Ylva came undone at the seams.

There was nothing left to do but destroy whatever stood between her and Gideon.

Ylva wailed, and the storm outside let loose. Air passed like swords ripping the tent apart.

Amid the wind, she kicked up her leg and smashed the King's groin. The old muskox fell to his knees and groaned.

Ylva was on top of him, growling. All three wolves were at her side, waiting to flay the King, but Lorcan cut the air with a knife. Ylva blocked the attack and snapped his wrist in two.

He screamed. "I'll kill you, bitch! I'll burn you like I did Elliana."

Ylva's fist connected with Lorcan's face, and she ploughed her knuckles into his jaw. The hairs on her skin rose, and a warm current charged inside her body where their skin touched.

Ylva's eyes rolled back, and an influx of images downloaded in her brain like a dream playing out in front of her.

"Thank you for coming," Elliana said pulling back her hood.

It was nighttime, and the regal woman peered into the forest to make sure no one had followed her. Her eyes glowed green.

She bowed. "I come seeking asylum. You and I were friends once, and I'm hoping we can be friends again. Your clann is the only one big enough to offer me safety from the Eli Dé Gecennen.

"Friends?" Lorcan scoffed. "Excuse my ignorance, your holiness, but is this an official Grimnìr visit?" His voice dipped at the end of his sentence, and the woman lowered her gaze.

She hesitated. "It's only me, Elliana."

"Seven years, Ellie? Seven years I waited for you! Not a word, not even a glance at the market since your transmutation. It's like you're a different person. I don't recognize you. You treated me like a stranger, and now, here in the middle of nowhere you ask for asylum. Did you expect me to come running with open arms? I'm High Chief of the Clann Llyr, and I won't put my people at risk, especially not against the Grimnìr clann. Give me more than that, if you want my help."

Elliana flitted with her hands, and glanced at the forest one more time, looking unsure about being there.

After some time, Lorcan softened. "Come on Ellie, can't you trust me? We were friends once, you said so yourself, no? Give me something."

"I'm pregnant."

The information-download unfurled too fast and the whole scene skipped to another time and place, and Ylva reeled to catch up.

Lorcan raced through a village alongside his daemon warriors. They were skinning their enemies as women and children ran for safety. Elliana broke from the herd and targeted the Grimnìr, killing every single one without mercy, her face hidden behind the mask of Khaõs, but the green eyes gave her away.

The images spun faster and hurt Ylva's head. The stream overpowered everything, and Ylva stood next to Elliana.

"I trusted you," Elliana said, her hands tied above her head on a large wooden beam.

Lorcan snorted. "It's nothing personal, but you're not Elliana. You look like her, you sound like her, but I know you're one of them. I used you like you used Elliana. Only seems fair."

"Please don't do this, Lorcan. I didn't lie to you. Elliana is here, inside me. I remember how much you loved her."

"Shut up," Lorcan slapped her on the cheek. "Don't speak for her. She's dead and gone."

Elliana bit her lip. "What will you do with my daughter?"

Lorcan laughed. "Your daughter? Isn't that a bit of a stretch?"

"Everything I've done has been for Eira. To protect her and keep her safe."

"Don't worry, your holiness, I'll keep her safe. She's a bridge between worlds, a key, right?"

"If you hurt Eira, I swear . . ."

"What? What do you swear? You're about to burn." He grabbed her face. "You're a parasite, and Eira is the key to your extinction. I won't hurt her, I will love and cherish her, and she will give me what I want. She will never know you, or your existence, and when her powers manifest, I will secure humanity's position here on Earth and lock your kind out forever. I will banish the Grimnìr for good, and my people will worship me."

CHAPTER 32

Hidden

Ylva's brain un-spooled under the sheer force of the information overload.

Despite the genetic enhancement, human brains, modified or not, couldn't process like a true AI. Why was this happening, and how come she couldn't control it, or at the very least stop it? This was self-destruction, suicide by overdose. Her body wouldn't withstand the debilitating surge. Already the drain on her energy supply was too much.

She had to disconnect from the power source, but it was impossible to pull away. The current acted like a sustained electric shock and her muscles contracted around Lorcan's wrist. On a cellular level Ylva's skin meshed with Lorcan's.

Depleted, and unable to suffer a second longer, Ylva shut down.

* * *

At first, darkness was a prison. No way in or out. Eira didn't know how long ago her consciousness had been exiled in some remote corner of her brain, but it might as well have been an eternity.

After the gene transmutation, Eira existed in a thought-pocket, she called it, because that's all this was, an endless stream of crippling thoughts without contact or stimuli to make her feel alive.

It took a while to understand the void itself wasn't the prison. It was the inability to escape her mindless chatter that caused a stir, but over time, Eira sought comfort in those brief seconds she had spent with her daughter right after giving birth, before Ylva had taken possession of her body. She reconstructed the birth down to the last detail, and the connection came alive.

Through that bond Eira clawed her way to the surface. Eira's daughter was her tether to the world, and now and again she could hear her baby gurgle. The name 'Gideon' pervaded every ounce of her soul, and the sensation was comparable to coming into the light.

Eira wasn't gone, she was lost, and that meant she could fight her way back. The source of her inner power came when she realized no one else would protect Gideon better than her, no one else would love this child as much as her. Gideon needed her mother, flawed and all, and Eira needed her daughter.

Hope buoyed her confidence and determination. Eira knew she could beat Ylva, and there were instances she was so close. She tasted her old life, and the spice of pine tree in the air. The hard snow crunched beneath her feet, and the cold wind tugged her lungs, but there was a tradeoff.

Her emotions were at the expense of her rational mind, every time Eira sensed she was near. She had to reach out of the murky waters to be free, but it was impossible to tell up from down. She was navigating blind, but she didn't quit, and every time she wandered close, Ylva knocked her deeper into the abyss.

The internal struggle between them was relentless, like a swinging pendulum, but during those strange cracks of self-awareness they connected, and Eira's senses grew a little stronger.

Follow the wind, the tang of blood, the screams, Eira thought. They were there like echoes difficult to pinpoint, but there. Sense the pain . . .

At first, her belly burned like fire, but then the throbbing in her back took over, and made her nauseous. The pain radiated to her chest.

The wind peaked, and the tent hollered in response.

"Eira?" Dwr yelled, "Speak to me!"

The strident screams tore her eardrums apart. She wanted to cover her ears but her bones ached, and it hurt to breathe.

"Eira, wake up," Dwr pleaded.

She opened her eyes, and the colours in the tent shone bright.

"Mn'keur? You're alive! Do you think you can untie me before Lorcan wakes up?"

"I can't move," she croaked. The sound of her voice resonated inside her head.

Bound to his chains, Dwr looked pitiful. The hate she had carried towards him melted away.

"I want to help you, but I can't . . ." he said, trying to wriggle out of his bindings. "Please try . . ."

Covered in blood and wounds, Eira noticed the wind's cold sting on her skin, and she savoured the moment.

Dwr stopped what he was doing and observed her. "Eira?" His face changed. "Is it really you? Something's happening to you," he said, donning a concerned brow. "Before it's too late. Untie me, and we'll get through this together, Mn'keur. I promise, but please try to get up. I'm begging you, just try."

Eira swallowed before she spoke. The blood in her mouth was sickening, but she cherished it. "Dwr, there's so much I need to tell you." Her voice was different.

"There's no time. Lorcan . . . I can't do anything if he wakes up."

"Listen," Eira said, "I had a baby, her name's Gideon, and she's ours."

"What?" Dwr frowned.

"Oh, no! Dwr," Eira said, frightened. "We don't have long. So you need to listen."

"What do you mean?" Dwr fought to break from his restraints but it was no use. "Eira, what's happening to you?"

"Our baby's in danger. When Ylva wakes up, help her find our daughter, but don't trust her."

Dwr's confusion was plain. "I don't understand, who's Ylva? Is she involved with those creatures following you? Those wolves? They disappeared when you woke up."

Eira smiled. "Whenever you see those wolves, remember that's me. Find our daughter, Dwr, and I'll find my way back to you, I promise."

"You're not making any sense . . ."

Eira stopped speaking mid-sentence. She wanted to speak, but she couldn't move.

"Eira?" Dwr shouted. "Eira?"

His face was the last thing she saw.

CHAPTER 33

Awareness

Ylva woke up gasping for breath.

Lorcan lay next to her with his mouth open and eyes glazed over. She didn't need to check his pulse. No normal human could survive what had transpired between them, but what had happened? One minute she was ready to kill him, and the next she was tearing inside his brain.

It's lucky she only blacked out. She might've have suffered serious brain damage, or worse, but everything appeared to be normal and in functioning order. Aside from feeling sluggish, which was no doubt normal given what had just happened, Ylva felt like herself.

"Eira? Are you all right? What happened?" Dwr stammered.

Ylva wheezed and struggled to inhale. "Nothing! It's over," she rasped, and pushed herself up. Her weak muscles shook under the strain. "We don't have to worry about him anymore," she said, nodding in Lorcan's direction.

"Your wolves? They're back . . ." The reverence in his voice unsettled Ylva.

All three wolves stood by her side. Wynnston's fur bristled around his thick neck, and his green eyes glowed. The other two raised their snouts in the air and howled. "You see them?"

"Yes. Their shapes are clearer than before. They look like smoke!" he said, mostly to himself, and then they vanished. "What are you?" Dwr asked.

"I've changed since we last met." The memory of their encounter was fuzzy. "I'm Grimnìr Ylva, the She-Wolf."

Dwr nodded, his mouth agape, but Ylva saw the shade of doubt on his face. Trusting him might prove difficult. "I need your help to find . . ." She hesitated to say the words out loud. "Our daughter, Gideon."

He still didn't respond and snapped his mouth shut.

"You're not surprised?" Ylva said.

"I . . . I'm not sure what to say."

Ylva heaved her torn-up body from the ground. The nanoslugs had repaired her head injury and cracked ribs, but the stomach and back were still in bad shape. She limped her way to the rope hanging off the tent poles. Her laboured breathing got louder and louder. "My sisters lied to me. They said Lorcan took Gideon."

Ylva reached up and grunted. A sharp pain travelled from her back down to her toes. She stopped to catch her breath. Once the pain passed, she inhaled, and tugged the rope in a swift motion to release Dwr.

He plopped down on the ground, but Ylva was in no shape to help him. "Your sisters?" He sounded confused.

"I speak of KerRidwen and Drakaina, my sisters in ritual. Together we form the Triad of Grimnìr priestesses."

"Which one is Seweryna?" he asked. Ylva found his curiosity odd.

"Drakaina." Ylva said and crouched next to him. "I need you to pull the arrow sticking out of me."

Dwr sat up and observed the wound. "I might make it worse."

"My body won't heal if it stays in my lung."

"You're a Seiðrs, then?" Dwr asked. "A healer?"

"No." Ylva shook her head and rested her eyes for a moment. The pain intensified, and she was lightheaded. "You'd consider me a Seer, but without other Grimnìr Seers from different Triads, I cannot infer the future."

Dwr gasped. "You're a Seer?"

Ylva hesitated. The man didn't trust her either, but she needed his help. After tonight, Ylva recognized she couldn't do it on her own. Her recklessness had almost cost Ylva her life, but how much did Dwr grasp? A faithful Sidhe follower might turn his back if he learned what Elliana had done. If she wanted, with a single touch she could pierce his brain and discover all his secrets, but that might also kill him.

Her best bet was to give him a little info and gauge his behaviour. "During the purge, Lorcan killed the Seers first because he found out that for us to predict outcomes in real time we needed to communicate with other Seers. Since I'm the only one left, I have nobody to share information with. That's how he killed all the Grimnìr."

Dwr scratched his head. "Then . . . Can you . . . How do you communicate in real time?"

"We call it the hive. Through the hive we communicate and learn. Contrary to me, my sisters can only receive information, they cannot communicate with the hive. Arianrhod is the healer, and Drakaina is the Şeker.

"Have you communicated with the hive?"

"Not yet. It has communicated information to me. It pops into my head, but . . ." It sounded almost like Dwr was fishing for information. "I can't say for sure. This is new to me, too."

"How do you choose who is the Seer, Seiðrs, and Şeker?"

"It's more a question of compatibility," Ylva answered.

Dwr nodded. "Seweryna is the Şeker. Why am I not surprised?"

"Twice you've mentioned her Sidhe name. Why?" Ylva asked.

Dwr's curious frown made Ylva doubt herself. Shouldn't she have asked that question?

"Don't you remember?"

Ylva struggled to recall Eira's memories, but she drew a blank.

"Seweryna is my dead wife." The way he said it made it sound like she should have known that bit of information. "Tonight, I gained and lost more than any man should ever endure, and I'm not sure who to trust anymore."

Neither of them spoke for a long time, and Ylva wondered if her altercation hadn't affected her more than she previously thought.

"Before we move on, we need to patch ourselves up. We're both in a sorry state." Dwr sighed. "I can't remove the arrow in your back, but I think Tilly might help."

"Tilly?" The memory of the woman burst through Ylva's brain.

Dwr narrowed his gaze. "Yes, Tilly."

"Right! Is she still in Llyr?" Ylva said, trying to sound casual. The exchange with Lorcan had damaged her memory banks for sure. She only had a faint recollection of Eira's interactions with the stout woman." Ylva rolled her eyes. Of all the times this should happen. "The place will be on lockdown, especially with Lorcan dead. I doubt we can walk in, at least not before I'm healed."

"That's if we make it." Dwr eyed her from head to toe.

Ylva nodded.

After some time, his eyebrows relaxed, and he dropped the matter. "Once we're able to fight, then we find our daughter, but I doubt we can do it alone. We'll need people to help us fight."

A sudden calm filled Ylva, and the land grew quiet at the mere mention of those words. All the tension lifted from her shoulders and was no longer so lonely. "I think I need to rest," she wheezed, and collapsed to the ground.

Somehow knowing Dwr was by her side soothed her mind. Why? It made little sense. Until the moment she saw him hanging inside the tent, she vowed to kill him, to hate him forever. What had changed?

None of this human stuff made sense.

Why were she and Eira linked? How did Eira fuel Ylva's emotional core? It was a mystery and unravelling the complexities of human emotion proved impossible, even for an AI hybrid.

Since her awakening Ylva had had no time to think. Only reacting from one problem to the next, but from what she understood, Eira, and her had stayed connected through the transmutation. Eira's memories had served as a catalyst to help Ylva fight those that would harm Gideon, and she was on a rampage ever since.

From the outside the conversion to Grimnìr was successful, but Ylva couldn't deny the human genes exerting their full force.

Ylva never stood a chance against a Homo Sapiens's motherly instincts, and these behaviours were conditioned since prehistoric times. They muddle through life out of sheer determination, and it proved impossible to separate herself from those feelings, and she no longer had the will to try.

"Bite down on this."

"What? Why?" Ylva said.

"I need to cut the shaft. It'll hurt."

Ylva placed the bundled rope in between her teeth, and Dwr snapped part of the shaft so only a small piece stuck out.

She bit down and howled as the wisps of pain subdued.

"Can you walk?" Dwr asked giving her his hand.

"I don't know what's wrong with me," she said, and he helped her to her feet.

"Grimnìr or not, you're still human. It's a marvel you're still alive."

Ylva nodded. He wasn't aware how close it came to an end. She wanted to keep it that way. At least for now.

Together, they walked out of the tent. It was morning. The night's horrors were coming to light. Mangled bodies spread out everywhere, and the snow was red with blood.

"You did all this?" Dwr's lips stretched down with disbelief, and Ylva looked away with shame. "The Mother will be our judge," he whispered loud enough for Ylva to hear, and for a quick second he looked at her. "Eira?" The warmth in his voice when he called her name made Ylva ashamed.

"My name is Ylva," she said.

The spark in his eye dimmed. Saddened, Ylva looked away.

It was a question of time before Eira came back, but for Ylva the biggest question was whether she was strong enough to keep her away.

Don’t Miss Out!

Book #2 Coming Soon

Huntress Moon

Read on for Chapter 1

CHAPTER 1

Oblivion

Dwr's scent rolled in thick waves and permeated Eira's insulated prison, leaving a salty aftertaste within her mind's rift. A sigh of relief whooshed around her. At last, a bit of reprieve from the constant barrage of high-pitched screaming slashing her mind.

Eira clung to the little she had, the tingle inside her mouth. How long since she'd seen Dwr? Seconds? Days? Years?

Desperate to funnel her energy on anything else, Eira fixated on the caustic sting of the salt. It burned, and she relished the tanginess it left behind. What was she experiencing, really? The actual flavor of salt? Was Ylva eating something, or was the mere idea of salt enough to trick her brain?

Stop! Eira cursed her pervasive thoughts taking her further away from the tingling sensation. In between her constant thoughts, and the screaming pain firing inside her brain, this was a hell like no other. Her consciousness lived on, cramped in some remote part of her brain, suffering the attacks of her body's torment.

She didn't doubt the spears of pain came from her body. Feel the injury. Use it, she thought, but it fired from every direction. She couldn't fix it to one place.

Another wave of Dwr's scent rippled. It was ripe, but no doubt it was him, and a warmth spread inside her like hot breath on icy hands. Ahh, to taste his kiss one last time, his smooth lips against hers, and as if by divine magic the screaming agony lessened, replaced with inward radiating heat. Eira remembered the moisture on his skin, their bodies so close against one another. Her fingertips had fluttered across his back, his scars worn down like wax.

Mn'keur . . . The word floated somewhere in her mind as he had combed his fingers across her forehead down to her neck. He was here, with her. His breath had caressed her cheek as she rested her head against his chest.

Eira's heart beat faster. Thump-thump . . . She felt it. Thump-thump... She FELT it! A rush of excitement pulsed through her as the successive pangs burst in her chest. Thump-thump!

Eira felt herself stretching out and taking shape. Focus, she thought. Focus on the drumming against your ribcage. Don't lose it, but saying that tainted the experience, and the sensation wavered as water slips through fingers. Fear gripped her, but she quieted her mind, and the faint tinge of winter blanketed her skin. The hint of cold chaffed down her throat.

She inhaled, and her back muscles cramped into a hard ball. A dismal croak seeped from her mouth. Now, she understood the sharp spears that sliced through her mind. Mere hours or days had passed since her last awakening, since Lorcan's death. No doubt the adrenaline had worn off, and her body writhed with injuries.

Each breath burned like a forger's flame straight into the hollowed pit in her stomach, but it didn't worry her. She was back. She'd fought passed the invisible veil, back into the world, and left Ylva behind.

"Dwr," she rasped, but her garbled voice was unrecognizable. The taste of blood coated her mouth.

"Ylva," he replied, "you need to rest."

"No, Dwr, it's—"

He didn't let her finish. "Shush," he said, and pulled Eira closer into his embrace. The warmth of his body felt good against hers. It's because of him she had found her way back. Dwr was her anchor.

Part of her lower body lay flat against the ground, and the cold snow numbed her legs. Eira didn't care. The branches in the trees danced to the motion of the wind, and for a moment Eira forgot her troubles. She soaked in the surrounding beauty, the rustling wind, the frigid air that stung her cheeks. Dwr's hands caressed the back of her neck just as she had imagined.

"You can't go on. Not today. We'll set up a fire here, to warm you up," Dwr continued, "you're in no condition to keep going."

Eira turned to face him. Neither of them spoke, and she thought she saw a glimmer of recognition in his hard eyes. She tried to speak, but her punctured lung was like breathing underwater. She forced a smile. The cold had reached her upper body by then and lulled her back to sleep.

No, no, no fight it! Feel his touch. Eira gripped Dwr's hand and focused her attention on his rough skin, and the calloused texture of his palm. Anything to keep her fixed to this moment. The fear on her face must've shown because Dwr pulled her closer. "I'll take care of you," he said, "I'm here." Noise caught his attention, and he lifted his gaze, peering in the forest.

Eira squeezed Dwr's hand. His gaze, she thought, hold his gaze a little longer, but the icy air's wicked breath forced her lids shut, and she succumbed to the darkness.

The infinite obscurity swallowed her up, and Eira was back within the folds of time and space lost inside her mind. Dwr's scent, his touch, his voice, the cold air, the swaying trees, all of it had disappeared and the firing neurons of pain charged once again.

Eira shouted in anger. Boxed inside the cell of pain, she stumbled over her thoughts. No, no, no, concentrate on Dwr. He's there. Feel him under your fingertips . . . but her senses had turned lifeless and resentment grew in its place.

Her life, or the memory of it, depended on her remembering touch, tastes, sounds, images, anything, but the screeching pain. Eira was going mad. She would NEVER escape.

Was she still so naïve to believe Dwr could help? HA! He was useless, Eira thought. WAKE UP! she screamed. "WAKE UP!"

* * *

Ylva shot up with a jolt from Dwr's arms. Her breath barely a wheeze. "Get away from me!" She choked and spit out blood, but the entire forest spun out of control. Ylva closed her eyes, hoping the moment would pass, but she wasn't above her body's degradation. Eira's anger felt like sharp teeth clamping down on Ylva and she was hard to push back, especially now under such physical duress. Why weren't the nanoslugs working to heal her?

Ylva opened one eye, and Dwr's face had that look of a person not sure what was happening.

"Don't touch me!" Ylva muddled, but she fell back, unable to keep her balance steady. The only explanation was that her wounds were too many to repair all at once.

"You're in no condition to keep going," Dwr barked, "you need rest—"

A soft rustling in the dry branches caught Dwr's attention. "Something's out there," he whispered, "it's been tracking us since we left Lorcan's camp."

Dwr shot Ylva a look. Any kindness his gaze once held disappeared. "Is it one of your wolves?" he asked.

Ylva shivered from the high fever and shrugged. She didn't know anymore. Eira's presence was all-encompassing and suffocated her.

Looking out to the forest, Dwr murmured, "give me a minute." He laid her down on her side, and Ylva closed her eyes, thankful for the respite.

She had fallen asleep because Dwr's voice woke her from her slumber.

"It's you?" he said, the wind carrying his voice.

Manufactured by Amazon.ca
Bolton, ON

14932192R00203